WHY AMERICA
NEEDS SOCIALISM

The Argument from Martin Luther King,

Helen Keller, Albert Einstein,

and Other Great Thinkers

◇◇◇◇◇◇◇◇◇◇◇◇◇◇◇◇◇◇

G.S. Griffin

New York, NY

Printed in the United States of America.
10 9 8 7 6 5 4 3 2 1

Ig Publishing
Box 2547
New York, NY 10163

www.igpub.com

ISBN: 978-1-632461-01-8 (paperback)

For Jeff,
friend on the Right

"I find I'm a good deal more of a socialist than I thought . . ."

—Walt Whitman

Horace Traubel, *With Walt Whitman in Camden*, vol. 2, p. 4

CONTENTS

INTRODUCTION

CONSIDER THE WORDS THAT A SHORT African American minister with a black mustache penned while sitting in a Selma, Alabama, jail cell in 1965, having just been arrested during a voting rights demonstration: "If we are to achieve a real equality, the US will have to adopt a modified form of socialism."[1]

The minister, Dr. Martin Luther King, Jr., was not just a brilliant orator and champion of civil rights. He was also anti-war, anti-capitalism, and pro-socialism. He saw capitalism as exploitive by nature, an economic structure that bred poverty, injustice, and death. Dr. King studied Karl Marx's works, wrote of Marxism in essays like "How Should a Christian View Communism?" and "My Pilgrimage to Nonviolence," and was inspired by socialists like Mahatma Gandhi and W.E.B. du Bois.

When I discovered that Dr. King was a socialist, I wondered if it was possible to build a case for socialism in America today based on his writings and those of other famous radical historical figures. This book is the answer to that question. In these pages, you will find many well-known thinkers, writers, and artists, from around the world, who believed that socialism could help end poverty, exploitation, authoritarianism, war, and even some forms of bigotry (even if some of the individuals herein were quite bigoted and otherwise seriously flawed). I think it's safe to say you're in for a few surprises.

In order to determine who to include, I had to first figure out who was known well enough to be featured. Would the average reader immediately recognize the names George Bernard Shaw, Sinclair Lewis, Dorothy Day, Paul Robeson, Pete Seeger, Ella Baker, Elizabeth Gurley Flynn, or Dalton Trumbo? It's rather subjective. So, I focused on those whom most people would probably know, especially readers who were not already socialists.

Second, while this too is subjective and there are a few exceptions in the text, it was important to exclude figures mainly known for their radicalism. This isn't a book featuring Karl Marx, let alone less commonly known radicals like Friedrich Engels, Rosa Luxemburg, Emma Goldman, Fred Hampton, Bobby Seale, Huey Newton, Eugene Debs, Bertrand Russell, or Jean-Paul Sartre. This likewise excluded modern anti-capitalist figures like Barbara Ehrenreich, Noam Chomsky, Gloria Steinem, Cornel West, Alexandria Ocasio-Cortez, and Bernie Sanders.

I also sought to avoid interpretation, lifting up the voices of those who flatly stated the flaws of capitalism or benefits of socialism, rather than arguing whether Herman Melville's *Moby Dick* and *Bartleby, the Scrivener* are critiques of capitalism. Also, those who were very private about their views and thus did not write or speak much on the subject, or merely had some socialist or anti-capitalist sympathies, were also largely excluded—people like Ernest Hemingway, Charlie Chaplin, Nina Simone, Susan B. Anthony, and Cesar Chavez.

Finally, someone could have been left out in error. This of course haunts me, particularly where the women of history are concerned. The book is male-centric, which may be a testament to how patriarchal societies held countless women back from great renown and accomplishment. It may also be that anti-capitalist views were more likely to hurt the success of women than that of men, causing the former to be less recognized for their radicalism. The same is likely true for radicals of color as well.

The people in this book did not all perfectly agree on what socialism should be, nor how it should come about (they weren't all specifically thinking of America when voicing the necessity of socialism, either). Some are in fact better called communists or anarchists, and I try to differentiate between these philosophies and socialism while at the same time finding common ground. My view is simply that all the thinkers included in this book in their own unique ways envisioned a better, socialistic world, and that the modern case for socialism in America can be justified and supported using their beliefs. Ultimately, they are here to help us, to serve as reasoning, free-thinking guides—as they always have, now just in a new way.

PART ONE

CAPITALISM

One

HUMAN NATURE

IN 1950, ALBERT EINSTEIN PENNED AN essay entitled "Why Socialism?"[1] In it, he wrote, "I am convinced that there is only *one* way to eliminate these grave [capitalistic] evils, namely through the establishment of a socialist economy."

Importantly, Einstein addressed the common criticism that socialism is incompatible with human nature, that greed, individualism, and competitiveness are the dominant traits of our species, thus explaining why capitalism exists and why socialism cannot succeed. In this thinking, anything venturing into the realm of cooperation, generosity, and solidarity simply isn't feasible. Indeed, Einstein wrote that we have "a biological constitution which we must consider fixed and unalterable, including the natural urges which are characteristic of the human species."

It is true we humans evolved to be capable of some very dark things. For example, our nature grew to include the ability to kill and steal, fueled by selfishness, in order to survive. Those entirely incapable of such things were less likely to survive and reproduce, and their genes disappeared with them, per natural selection. Many readers of faith believe that higher powers created humanity to be sinful by nature. Thus, it makes sense to many that capitalism is natural, and the way things must remain.

Capitalism is an economic system characterized by the private ownership of business and industry, where earning a profit by selling a good or service is each owner's basic and necessary goal. Under this system, private firms compete to seize a larger and larger share of a given market, to scale and meet (and, in the modern world of advertising, create) the demands of the greatest possible number of consumers, the ultimate success being to control the market at the expense of other businesses. The *capitalist*, the owner, can take an even greater piece of the market with each competitor that goes under, which leads to more consumers, and thus more profits. Profits not only enrich the capitalist (and company shareholders) personally, they also allow the business to expand into markets in other neighborhoods, cities, or countries. Profits also provide opportunities for investment in new technologies that reduce the cost of production, the number of hours needed to create each commodity, and the number of workers the capitalist needs to create each commodity, leading to even more profits.

While this cycle is not without some positive effects for ordinary people, the individual pursuits of capitalists in competitive environments often work against the social good, wreaking havoc on human beings, the planet, and national and global economic stability, as we will see. All this sounds like a predictable outcome of the human nature described above.

However, this is not the end of the story. Einstein reminded us that each person "acquires a cultural constitution which he adopts from society" that "is subject to change." After an individual is born, countless factors impact how he or she will think and act. Influences on human nature include geography, resources and wealth, class structure, economic systems, political organization, religion, traditional or commonly held ideas and values, education and literacy, scientific progress, family dynamics, individual observation and experience, and so on, all varying within complex societies. Human nature, our desires and traits, can be dramatically modified, because our biological blueprint is only one influence, and it doesn't have the final say. It is largely the individuals and society that came before you and surround you that determine your values and behaviors. Social reformer Elizabeth Blackwell, the first woman in the United States to receive a medical degree, wrote that "pauperism and vice, drunkenness and crime, mammon worship and frivolity, dishonesty and corruption, are all bred by ourselves. They are largely produced by the conditions of society into which children are born, and by which they are molded."[2] One might add greed, selfishness, and competitiveness to this list. Different societies and environments produce rather different people. Suffice it to say, this is basic anthropology.

It simply cannot be said that improving our nature is impossible—we have been doing this for thousands of years, changing and growing in ways large and small. Step back and consider the wide variance in human nature between societies, and reflect upon how far many have come over time. It then grows clear that, as Oscar Wilde wrote, "the only thing that one really knows about human nature is that it changes."[3]

Think of how societies have changed in just the last century, and are still changing, regarding sexism, racism, homophobia, and so on. The victims of course often think differently than the oppressors—within cultures there is diversity of thought—but the point is widespread cultural practices, and the popular views behind them, are not static. One can study any society, observe its common values and behaviors, and then easily examine another society in a different time or place where people had radically different "natures." For example, consider the current age of consent laws in the United States. We'd like to think they are a result of our biology, that it's in our nature to protect children. Yet just over a century ago, the age of consent for sex was—though it varied by state—approximately ten years old (and in Delaware it was seven.)[4] Back then, older men taking child brides wasn't an issue for most people. Today, our views are the opposite, and the age of consent is higher. If human nature cannot change, which view toward consent best reflects human nature? Further, is it a natural urge to kill people who are different? The ancient Israelites, for example, killed gay people, but in ancient Greece, homosexuality was more accepted and mainstream. Varying views on cannibalism, human sacrifice, infanticide, incest, polygamy, and much else spring to mind, too. One begins to suspect such differences are cultural, and not that some societies follow a singular, unconquerable biological nature, while others do not.

Would anyone then disagree with Einstein that the way we think and act are "very variable and susceptible to change"? He knew that while our biology affects who we are, human nature is "largely formed by the environment in which a man happens to find himself during his development, by the structure of the society in which he grows up, by the tradition of that society, and by its appraisal of particular types of behavior." Whatever evolutionary drives and biological urges we possess can largely be conquered by culture, or at least controlled to a degree that makes certain behaviors far less frequent. If human beings can move past common acceptance of so many horrible things, from racism to child brides, are we really to assume we cannot move past *less* egregious attitudes, behaviors, and practices? Like those related to what our tax dollars should be used for, or who should own workplaces and vote on public policy?

One could easily blame American slavery, and many other terrors, on the selfishness, greed, and competitiveness of human nature. If true, human nature was clearly overcome, and a more decent society established. Yet we are to believe that other things blamed on human nature, such as resistance to the socialistic sharing of power and wealth, somehow cannot be overcome. Not only is it possible, but Einstein saw it as the true purpose of socialism: to keep growing, to keep bettering ourselves. Likewise, Mahatma Gandhi disbelieved in the supposed "essential selfishness of human nature" because man can "rise superior to the passions that he owns in common with the brute and, therefore, superior to selfishness and violence . . . Our socialism or communism should, therefore, be based on nonviolence and on harmonious co-operation . . ."[5]

Many cultures reveal that resistance to sharing wealth and power can be conquered or lessened. As we will see, great progress on that front has been made in many advanced democracies, including our own. Most significantly, however, people in "primitive" societies, past and present, are often utterly baffled when they encounter foreigners espousing individualistic ideas, confused as to why they shouldn't help each other on tests or tasks, nor give to others who have less so things are equal.[6] It's a whole different mindset; it's the culture they were born into and perpetuated. Einstein pointed out that less technologically advanced societies had different forms of organization, which affected people's attitudes and behaviors. Rather than seeming natural, competition, individualism, and greed can seem silly to cooperative-based societies. Let's not forget that before the agricultural and urban revolution of 10,000 to 5,000 BC, human beings lived in small groups where labor was cooperative, land was commonly owned (if at all), resources were distributed equally or according to need, and political structures were more decentralized and democratic.[7] Even gender relations were more egalitarian compared to later times.[8] The era is sometimes called that of "primitive communism," about which Nelson Mandela wrote:

> The land and forests in which [people] hunted and picked up wild fruits, the rivers in which they fished, belonged to the whole community and not to any particular individual property and was shared equally by all . . . There were no classes. There were no rich or poor, no exploitation of man by man, and all were equal before the law. The affairs of the village were discussed publicly in a village council and all members of that community could attend the meetings and take part fully in the discussions.[9]

This does not mean that everyone lived in perfect utopias. There were still crimes like theft, murder, rape, wars with other tribes, and other problems. But it does mean that for nearly 200,000 years—most of human existence—people survived on cooperative economics and a more classless society, where the life, wealth, and work of the ruler or leader (or body of leaders) was not significantly different than any other member of the group. Survival necessitated sharing and everyone working together, more or less as equals.

The point is not to go back, to forsake modern society and its technology. The point is to look back (or look around, at secluded, traditional indigenous peoples today) and observe a different human nature and the functioning societies in which it existed. If we do, it grows clear that a competitive nature doesn't produce a competitive society—it's the reverse. Being born into a society that stresses, say, solidarity and pacifism, will breed a child of a different nature than one born into a culture that emphasizes individualism and war. (There is in fact no scientific evidence that making war against other groups is inherent to our biology.)[10] Therefore, we see that when human societies were based on cooperation, individual self-interest did not destroy their social, economic, or political organization.

This should not be surprising, as biologists have determined many evolutionary reasons for cooperative, selfless, protective behavior.[11] Here we turn back to the biological blueprint for a moment, because these are included in those "natural urges" Einstein mentioned. The ability to fight, kill, cheat, or steal served a survival purpose, but so did more positive traits. We are a social species, after all. Caring for others earned repayment in one's own time of need, helped attract mates through generosity signaling, and other advantages to survival and reproduction, like the ability to find more food and hold a better defense against predators when working together.[12] This isn't exactly the selfishness capitalism's advocates speak of, where everyone just looks out for him or herself; it's rather helping yourself by helping all, a good foundation for a socialist society. Studies indicate that modern adults are not instinctively selfish—our first impulse is typically to cooperate and care for others.[13] It's rewarding in various senses, including neurochemically.[14] Experiments with infants show that they demonstrate a rudimentary understanding of empathy for those who are hurting and fairness for those who have less than others, and possess a keen interest in seeing kindness rewarded and meanness punished.[15]

It would perhaps be remarkable if this wasn't the case, because it is true with other species. Not only do many creatures experience the same emotions humans do, they also punish cheating, dislike betrayal, favor equality, reconcile after fighting, offer gifts of gratitude, comfort others, care for the young of others, form friendships, cooperate and share, and help or save others with no benefit for doing so—and not just when interacting with their own species.[16] Humans are the same way, even under a system like capitalism. Our biological constitution cannot be altered, but it is not all bad.[17] There is much good within us as well, and that good can be amplified by culture.

However great or small our natural capacity for competition, greed, and individualism, these traits don't chain the human race to capitalism. Class societies have only been around for several thousand years, and embryonic capitalism only appeared in the feudal world of the fourteenth and fifteenth centuries (and before the Industrial Revolution, most people were still not wage laborers, employees of capitalists). It's just as easy to argue that capitalism is the aberration from human nature. After all, our anti-capitalist history is far longer than our capitalist history—and the countless souls who believed over the millennia that their social, economic, and political systems were the way things would always be due to human nature were simply wrong. As Mandela wrote, "Just as primitive communal society was replaced by slave society, and just as slave society was replaced by feudalism, and feudalism by capitalism, so will capitalism be replaced by socialism."[18]

Capitalism was certainly a better system for ordinary people and societies than feudalism, as acknowledged by Marx himself and other prominent socialists, but that doesn't mean an even better system isn't possible or desirable. It's like how a constitutional monarchy is better than an absolute monarchy, but a representative democracy is better still. Human nature is no impediment to radical change and progress. George Orwell said that "the claim that 'human nature,' or 'inexorable laws' of this and that, make Socialism impossible" is a misguided "projection of the past into the future . . . By the same argument one could have demonstrated the impossibility of aeroplanes in 1900, or of motor cars in 1850."[19]

Now that we know society largely determines human nature, rather than the reverse, there is only one logical question to ask: what kind of society should we create?

Two

EXPLOITATION

IN 1952, DR. MARTIN LUTHER KING wrote to Coretta Scott, explaining his political and economic philosophy. "I am much more socialistic in my economic theory than capitalistic," he said in the letter to his future wife. "Today capitalism has out-lived its usefulness. It has brought about a system that takes necessities from the masses to give luxuries to the classes."[1] King was talking about how capitalism transfers wealth away from the workers at the bottom of society to the owners, the capitalists, at the top. Later in his life, King would speak of the "tragic exploitation" of people around the globe, which he believed justified "a more humane and just economic order."[2]

Dr. King understood that workers create wealth, as it is workers who construct the good or provide the service to be sold by the capitalist. It is the capitalist who needs workers, to make a product or perform a service at a pace and on a scale he cannot do himself. This is true of both heirs to billion-dollar businesses and creative, driven geniuses who start from nothing—Steve Jobs would not have gotten very far without his workers. "Capital is perfectly helpless without labour," as Gandhi phrased it.[3] Let's consider this in some detail. Say a woman starts a business by herself. At that stage, she is a worker creating her own wealth, selling something to others and exploiting no one when she decides how much profit she will keep for herself as income, and how much she will invest back into the business. Should this woman take on an equal partner, and they together decide how to run the business and what equitable earnings to subtract from the profits, exploitation is still a non-issue. But when the founding woman assumes a managerial position by hiring people, these employees will not democratically decide earnings or business goals. Instead, it is the owner who will retain total decision-making control, as well as taking a larger income out of the profit pool than she will award to individual employees. In *Principles of Political Economy*, John Stuart Mill, famous economist and philosopher (who said his ideals put him "under the general designation of Socialists"),[4] described the system this way: "a capitalist as chief, and workpeople without a voice in the management," who had to "work at the bidding and for the profit of another."[5]

As we can see, the system of exploitation has begun. The workers create the commodity or carry out the service, but the capitalist reaps more of the wealth created by their hands than they do. The capitalist, while perhaps still working hard overseeing, strategizing, investing, and so forth, is no longer doing the basic tasks necessary to directly generate wealth. The owner no longer cooks in the back of a fast food joint, or operates the machines sewing the clothing. Nor must she do an architectural technician's drafting or a computer programmer's coding. Instead, she decides what to do with the profits created by others. And by taking more of the wealth created by others as personal income, she steadily builds for herself a much better life than her workers will experience. She'll also likely keep her worker's wages down to protect profits, as a means of earning herself a higher income and expanding her business. The workers in turn will not get an equitable portion of the money they have made for the company. Their lives may see little improvement unless they strike to convince the capitalist that more of the profits should go to those who generate the profits. Later, the owner will hire more people, and they too will be exploited, with most of the wealth they create ("the fruits of their collective labor") being appropriated by her, "not by force," as Einstein noted, "but on the whole in faithful compliance with legally established rules." The owner may eventually even hire someone to run the business for her and never work another day. Helen Keller, who argued the labor of the poorly paid made others rich and comfortable, declared that

> the foundation of society is laid upon a basis of individualism, conquest and exploitation, with a total disregard of the good of the whole . . . Crushed, stupefied by terrible poverty, the workers yet demand that they shall have some of the beauty, some of the comforts, some of the luxuries which they have produced.[6]

The writer Jack London looked back with regret at his own exploitation of others, taking a disproportionate slice of the profits from his small enterprise when his employee worked just as hard as he did.[7] George Orwell likewise called capitalism "the right to exploit" other human beings.[8] It's about unrewarded value. Nelson Mandela said realizing this very fact drew him to socialism.[9]

For the capitalist, the sale of each good or service must cover three things: the cost of production (replacing the raw materials and supplies, maintaining the technology and facilities, etc.), the cost of labor (worker compensation), and profit that the owner uses as he sees fit—to expand the business, create more commodities, build new factories or stores, hire more workers, invest in new technologies, raise wages, or give himself a larger paycheck. Thus, in the capitalist system, workers are not paid the full value of what they produce. If they were, there would be no such thing as profit. At least, no profit for the capitalist; it would instead belong to the workers. Under capitalism, workers create the wealth, but they control none of it and only receive a portion of its value. Einstein wrote that

> The owner of the means of production is in a position to purchase the labor power of the worker. By using the means of production, the worker produces new goods which become the property of the capitalist. The essential point about this process is the relation between what the worker produces and what he is paid, both measured in terms of real value.

> . . . What the worker receives is determined not by the real value of the goods he produces, but by his minimum needs and by the capitalists' requirements for labor power in relation to the number of workers competing for jobs. It is important to understand that even in theory the payment of the worker is not determined by the value of his product.

The ability of the capitalist to pay workers whatever she can get away with—which is even less when the number of workers competing for jobs is higher—is only possible because capitalism is authoritarian, with each business structured like a dictatorship or an oligarchy. The capitalist (or capitalists) holds all decision-making power. Capitalism is rule by the few, who grow rich off the labor of the many. That is, after all, how ruling minorities, concentrations of power, tend to function. Mark Twain asked, "Who are the oppressors? The few: the king, the capitalist and a handful of other overseers and superintendents. Who are the oppressed? The many: the nations of the earth; the valuable personages; the workers; they that make the bread that the soft-handed and idle eat."[10]

As businesses grow larger, exploitation worsens. On average, today's American CEOs are earning some 300 times the pay of their workers (in 1965, it was a 20:1 ratio).[11] In 2014, the CEO of Walmart, the world's largest employer, took home $26 million, 1,133 times the median Walmart employee salary of $22,500. At CVS, the wage gap was 1,192:1, with the company's CEO raking in $32 million and the typical employee making $27,000. The CEO of Chipotle took home $29 million, 1,522 times the $19,000 that his workers typically made per year.[12] And that's just salaries—there is also the value of company shares that come with ownership. The Walton family, which founded Walmart and owns half its shares, is worth $140 billion (the company earns some $14 billion in profit, its net income after expenses and taxes, each year).[13] Nike makes over $4 billion in profit a year, and its founder is worth $25 billion.[14] Microsoft earns around $25 billion; Bill Gates is worth $90 billion.[15] In a few decades or even years, a capitalist's wealth can explode. Are the workers who made this wealth increase possible also growing tens of thousands or hundreds of thousands of times richer? Of course not.

Capitalists also find it profitable to outsource work to poor Third World nations in order to pay workers in these places even less and avoid job safety and environmental regulations. Workers in places like Bangladesh earn $140 dollars a month, or $1,700 a year, to churn out cheap clothing for Walmart, H&M, and the Gap in abysmal and dangerous working conditions.[16] Yes, the cost of living is cheaper in many of these countries, but that isn't the point. The point has to do with the value of each individual's work. Is the value of the capitalist's daily work really 1,000 times greater than an employee's? Or, in the case of exploited foreign labor, 17,000 times greater? Is all this not like supposing the work of the king a thousand times more valuable than the work of the serf, whose very labors keep the king's belly full? Or the work of the slaveowner being tens of thousands of times more valuable than that of the slave? Harriet Beecher Stowe, in *Uncle Tom's Cabin*, wrote that "capitalists" and slave owners alike were "appropriating" the lower class, "body and bone, soul and spirit, to their use and convenience." The rich man believed "there can be no high civilization without enslavement of the masses, either nominal or real. There must, he says, be a lower class, given up to physical toil and confined to an animal nature; and a higher one thereby acquires leisure and wealth . . ."[17]

Exploitation doesn't just exist in hot factories, grimy diners, and corporate farms. It is also found where workers are highly paid and workplaces safe, comfortable, and enjoyable. The median worker pay at Discovery Communications is $80,000, for example, yet their CEO awarded himself $156 million in 2014, a 1,951 multiple, the highest of any company.

While it is true that many business owners work very hard, adding value to their companies in a variety of ways, without their workers, the efforts of the owner are essentially meaningless. Capitalist apologists may insist that without the capitalist there would be no jobs for the workers, and thus they should be grateful for employment and devoted to the current system. But, as we will see, capitalist-structured firms are neither necessary nor superior to the alternatives. The boss needs workers; workers do not need the boss.

•

While it might seem paradoxical, companies that give their employees raises as profits rise are often *widening* the chasm between the value workers create and the value they receive. For example, if profits rise 25 percent but wages only increase 10 percent, workers are receiving a *decreased* proportion of the total wealth created. Thus, exploitation can worsen even when workers earn better wages. From 1978 to 2016, corporate profits boomed and CEO pay rose 800 to 940 percent, while worker pay rose just 11 percent.[18] Productivity rose 72.2 percent during this period—why did wages not rise accordingly?[19] Inequality is at historic levels today in the United States due to more and more wealth being taken by capitalist owners at the top. In 2012, corporate profits comprised its largest share of the national income since 1950, but employees had nearly their smallest portion of the national income since 1966.[20] Between 1989 and 2006, the top 10 percent in the United States appropriated 91 percent of the income growth; the top 1 percent took 59 percent. Between 2009 and 2012, 95 percent of income gains went to the top 1 percent.[21] And that's just income. If we look at overall wealth, from 1989 to 2018 the top 1 percent became $21 trillion richer, while the bottom 50 percent became $900 billion poorer, due to increasing debt and other factors.[22] That's virtually no advancement for the masses, huge gains for the rich who rely on the masses. Helen Keller said that there is no true "freedom as long as you are doomed to dig and sweat to earn a miserable living while the masters enjoy the fruit of your toil."[23]

Even corporations where the executive joins the "one-dollar salary" club are exploitive by nature, as the workers still have no power over the direction of the company, how profits are used, what they earn, working conditions, and so forth. These companies remain structured like dictatorships, with one person or a small group holding all authority (and usually not giving up their shares with their incomes). Workers are not paid the full value of what they produce, nor do they have control over that value.

After a half century of capitalism running amok, the bottom 80 percent now own 16 percent of America's wealth, while the share of the top 1 percent is approaching 50 percent.[24] The poorest 50 percent own just 2.5 percent of the country's wealth, and the top 1 percent has as much money as the bottom 95 percent.[25] This is not exclusively an American phenomenon. Globally, 82 percent of the wealth created in 2017 went to the world's richest 1 percent, who own 46 percent of the world's wealth overall (the top 10 percent has 86 percent). Eight people had the same wealth as the poorest half of humanity—3.6 billion people.[26] The money the world's billionaires made in 2017 alone would have been enough to end extreme poverty worldwide seven times over.[27] But under capitalism, wealth is not distributed to meet human needs, it's concentrated in the hands of the powerful few. As Dr. King said, "The trouble is that we live in a failed system. Capitalism does not permit an even flow of economic resources. With this system, a small privileged few are rich beyond conscience and almost all others are doomed to be poor at some level . . ."[28] Privately, capitalists will admit that they grow wealthy at the expense of labor, as leaked 2005 and 2006 internal strategy documents from Citigroup revealed.[29]

To conclude this chapter, it might be valuable to note that even those who weren't socialists were still able to recognize the true nature of the capitalist-worker relationship. Take, for example, economist Adam Smith, who wrote *The Wealth of Nations* in 1776, a work that later influenced Karl Marx. Rather than being the conservative bible that some consider it, the work plainly shows that Smith favored higher taxes on the rich, low profits, strong wages for labor, equal land distribution, and other practices that could create more social equality and free workers from powerful business owners.[30] Smith wrote that in pre-capitalist societies, "the whole produce of labour belong[s] to the labourer. He has neither landlord nor master to share with . . ." He also believed it was through labor that "all the wealth of the world was originally purchased" and that wealth is "precisely equal to the quantity of labour" that created it. Yet, Smith added that, "the value which the workmen add" is divided into "parts" like "their wages [and] profits for their employer . . ." In this way, one person takes advantage of the hard work of many: "The landlord demands a share of almost all the produce which the labourer can either raise or collect . . . [The landlord] would have no interest to employ him, unless he was to share in the produce of his labour . . . This share consists his profit."[31] Smith also described the fundamental clash between workers and owners, the poor and the rich: "The interests of the two parties are by no means the same. The workmen desire to get as much as possible, the masters to give as little as possible." Writing of proprietors, he declared "all for ourselves and nothing for other people" to be the "vile maxim of the masters of mankind."[32]

Abraham Lincoln was no socialist either. However, he had many socialist friends, appointed a socialist as his assistant secretary of war and another as his ambassador to Spain, and even exchanged cordial letters with Karl Marx, who despised slavery, during the American Civil War.[33] Lincoln declared in his 1861 State of the Union Address that

Labor is prior to and independent of capital. Capital is only the fruit of labor, and could never have existed if labor had not first existed. Labor is the superior of capital, and deserves much the higher consideration. Capital has its rights, which are as worthy of protection as any other rights. Nor is it denied that there is, and probably always will be, a relation between labor and capital producing mutual benefits. The error is in assuming that the whole labor of community exists within that relation. A few men own capital, and that few avoid labor themselves, and with their capital hire or buy another few to labor for them . . .[34]

Ultimately, defenders of capitalism often insist that authoritarianism and exploitation are justified because the capitalist started the business from nothing, working tirelessly. First, we shouldn't forget that many come to ownership through birth luck, inheriting a family business whose living labor and "dead labor" alike allow for lives as "idle capitalists," as the poet Ralph Waldo Emerson put it.[35] But initiative and great effort don't always justify what's created, as one would say to any new slaveowner or king. One must weigh the hard work of people to launch their own companies against how it affects everyone else. Many famous historical figures decided it was most ethical to favor the needs and desires of the many over those of the few, or the one. George Orwell and Oscar Wilde denounced capitalists as slaveowners and thieves.[36] Franz Kafka, anarchist sympathizer and author of *The Metamorphosis*, said that under capitalism "everything is in chains" because "the luxury of the rich is paid for by the misery of the poor."[37] Upton Sinclair laughed at those who called themselves individualists while being used by their bosses to make millions.[38]

We should listen to what these voices from history can tell us about our present condition.

Three

THE PROFIT MOTIVE:
AND PRESENT ECONOMIES

THE PURSUIT OF PROFIT UNDER CAPITALISM produces serious dangers to human economies and the availability of work. In this chapter, we will examine automation, outsourcing, monopolization, and economic crises.

Let us first consider the use of technology under capitalism. Capitalists invest in technology that makes their systems more automated, allowing them to reduce the size of their workforces. While technology costs money to create, purchase, install, and maintain, it can save huge sums compared to human labor, as it's more efficient. The Ford Motor Company, for example, needs only one-third of the human workers it needed in the 1970s to maintain the same production levels.[1] In 2017, the Japanese insurance company Fukoku Mutual Life Insurance replaced dozens of employees with artificial intelligence, anticipating a 30 percent increase in productivity.[2]

Technology also enables a company to sell its product for a lower price, undercutting the competition and seizing a larger share of the market—or, with a lower cost of production, a greater proportion of the original sale price can simply go to the capitalist. More product and more sales at lower production costs mean greater profits. The owners benefit immensely, massively increasing their wealth, but many workers are sent packing (and those that remain are in no way guaranteed a higher wage). In "The Soul of Man Under Socialism," Oscar Wilde wrote that

> Up to the present, man has been, to a certain extent, the slave of machinery, and there is something tragic in the fact that as soon as man had invented a machine to do his work he began to starve. This, however, is, of course, the result of our property system and our system of competition. One man owns a machine which does the work of five hundred men. Five hundred men are, in consequence, thrown out of employment, and, having no work to do, become hungry and take to thieving. The one man secures the produce of the machine and keeps it, and has five hundred times as much as he should . . .[3]

New technology and broader divisions of labor also make specialized labor obsolete. When a task that originally required training or higher education can be accomplished by "low-skill" labor, a capitalist has no need for workers with advanced qualifications and expectations of a high salary. As a result, competition among workers for that low-skill, low-wage task is broadened, driving wages down further. If a human task can be totally replaced by a machine, the job opportunity vanishes entirely.

Einstein, as well as Orwell and Wilde, noted that instead of layoffs and hardship, automation could easily mean lives of leisure for workers.[4] Advances in technology and productivity, and thus profits, should theoretically allow for higher wages and shorter workweeks. The authoritarian structure of capitalism doesn't encourage that, however. Instead, workers are simply fired. Productivity has skyrocketed in the US since the 1970s, while wages have hardly budged. And while human beings are working fewer hours today than in years past, particularly in Europe, four in ten Americans work over fifty hours a week, sometimes seventy or eighty, and full-time employees average forty-seven hours per week.[5] We must recognize that while technology works toward the expansion of leisure time, the structure of capitalism works against it.

The competitive frenzy to invest in new technology and get rid of workers, increasing productive output, profits, and the wealth gap, can also pose a threat to the economic system as a whole. A worker who is fired, or whose hours and wages are slashed, cannot fuel the economy as much as he or she could previously. And this is done at the precise same time productivity increases. Productive output grows as worker purchasing power shrinks. Jack London marveled at this, writing that because productive output takes off while workers suffer, it is fair to say the capitalist class has "criminally and selfishly mismanaged."[6] As we will see, consumers being unable to afford the goods and services industry can produce not only slows down the economy, it can send it crashing.

Supporters of capitalism will insist that the advent of new technology often creates new high-skill, high-wage jobs, which is true. New technologies, from computer programs to hypersonic airliners, require trained personnel to build, upgrade, and operate. However, the people who can take advantage of these technologies are not usually the ones displaced by them. Instead, the losers (usually older folks) find their once-valuable skills irrelevant and their jobs eliminated. Firms often do not wish to spend the money to retrain workers, and new jobs may be in faraway cities, requiring obsolete workers to move even if they are lucky enough to receive new training.[7] And even the winners are not safe for long, as the cycle continues: firms divide labor, turn high-skill work into low-skill work, and fully automate tasks.[8] Eventually, everyone's job will become obsolete.

Now, it is also true that new technology can create low-skill employment. Apps allow people to be personal drivers and delivery workers, and companies that spring up around new technologies will need receptionists and janitors, and so forth. The point, however, is that capitalists will always do what is most profitable, which means that while new jobs will be necessary, old jobs—and eventually those new jobs, too—will be wiped out, to the detriment of workers who helped build the company and helped advance it to the very stage where it could create or purchase the new technology. People who devoted their entire lives to a business are shown the door, all in the name of the capitalist's profits.

While the growth of new jobs can at times outpace the loss of jobs due to automation—especially as the economy shifts from manufacturing to service-based—this does not mean there will always be enough jobs for everyone.[9] (Even during economic boom times, there are not always enough jobs for every worker, whether they be low or highly skilled). At some point in the future, most labor will be abolished by automation. As Franz Kafka said, those with "economically inadequate skills will soon be replaced by frictionless thinking machines."[10]

Machines can already operate a warehouse, pick and inspect fruit, build cars, and lay bricks. Google and Uber are perfecting driverless cars, Amazon is working out drone delivery systems, and restaurants are installing tablets at tables or counters that take orders and payments. Amazon Go is a cashier-less grocery store. Robots are also becoming more prevalent throughout different industries: China is building a weaponized police robot (Anbot); Toshiba is using a temporary robot employee (ChihiraAico) in a Japanese department store; Nanyang Technical University is perfecting a robot secretary (Nadine); and MIT is asking PR2 to bake meals. Even sex robots are in development, competition for flesh-and-blood sex workers.

High-skilled work is also not free of risk. Who wouldn't want a robotic lawyer with advanced knowledge of every legal case ever argued, able to easily out-think a human attorney? That's already underway, with AI programs like Case Cruncher Alpha and LISA in Britain. Radiologists and journalists are likewise threatened by technology able to do parts of their jobs faster, cheaper, and with fewer errors. In China, they are creating an AI news anchor at the Xinhua News Agency.

In the United States alone, economists estimate that 47 percent of jobs are at high risk of automation over the next few decades (including service, sales, office and administrative, production, and transportation jobs), 19 percent are at medium risk, with only one-third considered low risk (including education, media, legal, healthcare, business management, and engineering jobs).[11] Forty-five percent of human work could be automated with *today's* technology, work that makes up $2 trillion in annual worker pay.[12] Within a matter of years, machines will do one-quarter to one-third of this work.[13] The number of factory robots in manufacturing centers like Detroit, Toledo, Grand Rapids, Louisville, and Nashville tripled between 2010 and 2015.[14]

Automation could threaten developing nations even more than advanced ones, with two-thirds of all jobs at risk of being taken over by robots.[15] Experts predict full automation of all human jobs will be possible within 125 years, with AI superior to any given task long before that, just forty-five years from now.[16] As a result, capitalist owners will increasingly be able to do away with human labor, maximizing efficiency and profits. "Today, machinery merely helps a few to ride on the backs of millions," Gandhi said. "The impetus behind it all is not the philanthropy to save labor, but greed."[17] This was partly why he wanted to "end capitalism."[18]

While there may always be demand for some types of human labor in future societies—teachers, preachers, or caretakers, for instance—the vast majority of people will have nothing. With no consumer base, no one with wages to spend, the market system will collapse. We will then need new mechanisms, a new social organization, to replace capitalism so as to avoid widespread joblessness, poverty, and starvation. Jack London, writing of machines, stated: "Let us control them. Let us profit by their efficiency and cheapness. Let us run them for ourselves. That, gentlemen, is socialism."[19] Physicist Stephen Hawking was once asked about this topic, replying:

> If machines produce everything we need, the outcome will depend on how things are distributed. Everyone can enjoy a life of luxurious leisure if the machine-produced wealth is shared, or most people can end up miserably poor if the machine-owners successfully lobby against wealth redistribution. So far, the trend seems to be toward the second option, with technology driving ever-increasing inequality.[20]

In addition to automation, outsourcing is another trend of capitalism that is eliminating work in the United States and beyond. Many companies outsource their workforces to places like India, China, and Mexico for cheap labor and to sidestep regulations that hurt the bottom line. The conditions in these workplaces are often horrific. In some cases, workers must *live at the factory*, packed into dormitories like sardines. They work long hours at exhausting speeds, and can be exposed to deadly chemicals, machines, and even buildings. Companies like Apple have to deal with suicide scandals, as some workers in China cannot tolerate the grueling conditions under which they labor.[21] In

Bangladesh, where building safety regulations are minimal, over 100 workers burned to death in a factory fire in 2012, and over 1,100 workers died the following year when their manufacturing center collapsed—just typical costs of doing business for giant clothing sellers like Walmart and J.C. Penny's.[22] In South Korea, seventy-six employees died at Samsung from exposure to toxins used to make commodities for the market, while hundreds contracted leukemia, lupus, lymphoma, multiple sclerosis, and other diseases.[23] Dr. King said we must "look across the seas and see individual capitalists of the West investing huge sums of money in Asia, Africa and South America, only to take the profits out with no concern for the social betterment of the countries, and say, 'This is not just.'"[24]

Keeping labor costs down is central to profit maximization, and is the driving force behind the loss of American jobs and the brutal abuse and exploitation of foreign workers. Helen Keller wrote, "A dollar that is not being used to make a slave of some human being is not fulfilling its purpose in the capitalistic scheme. That dollar must be invested in South America, Mexico, China, or the Philippines."[25] In the 2000s, the largest US corporations, employing a fifth of American workers, reduced their American-based workforce by three million jobs while increasing outsourced jobs by 2.5 million.[26] The nation as a whole sent three million jobs to China alone between 2001 and 2013.[27] Some fourteen million people currently work for American corporations overseas—higher than the typical number of unemployed Americans.[28] Most at risk are manufacturing jobs, as well as call center, tech, and human resources jobs. Bob Dylan sang in "Union Sundown" that

> Well, you know, lots of people complainin' that there is no work
> I say, "Why you say that for

When nothin' you got is US–made?"
They don't make nothin' here no more
You know, capitalism is above the law
It say, "It don't count 'less it sells"
When it costs too much to build it at home
You just build it cheaper someplace else

Another self-destructive tendency of capitalism is the march toward monopolization. Historically, industries become concentrated in fewer and fewer hands as larger firms take over or crush smaller firms to increase their share of a given market. The unregulated pursuit of profit destroys competition itself; in other words, competition eliminates competition.[29] Orwell wrote that "the trouble with competitions is that somebody wins them . . . Free capitalism necessarily leads to monopoly."[30] Einstein added that "private capital tends to become concentrated in few hands, partly because of competition among the capitalists, and partly because technological development and the increasing division of labor encourage the formation of larger units of production at the expense of smaller ones."

The dangers of monopolization are many: prices can rise, innovation and quality can decline, choices can grow more limited, and workers can't find higher wages for the same positions at competitors because there are none. In the past, the government has passed legislation like the Sherman Anti-Trust Act to ban monopolies and block mergers, but these regulations are not nearly strict enough. And, corporations influence the government to destroy their competition, from easing anti-trust laws to erecting barriers that inhibit new businesses from getting off the ground.[31] Many small business owners learn of monopolization's effects the hard way, like those whose enterprises are stomped out by the arrival of a Walmart. American presidents of all stripes have long complained about the increasing concentration of business power.[32] Woodrow Wilson—no anti-capitalist—lamented that "small groups of men wield a power and control over the wealth and the business operations of the country."[33] William Howard Taft said, "If the abuses of monopolization and discrimination can not be restrained; if the concentration of power made possible by such abuses continues and increases, and it is made manifest that under the system of individualism and private property the tyranny and oppression of an oligarchy of wealth can not be avoided, then Socialism will triumph."[34]

Since the 1990s, two-thirds of business sectors in the US have concentrated, with mergers accelerating.[35] Today, six percent of US companies make 50 percent of this country's profits.[36] The market shares held by the two biggest companies in some sectors is 50 to 80 percent.[37] Recently, the top five auto manufacturers reached a 60 percent global market share; the top five oil companies 40 percent; the top five steel companies 50 percent.[38] Six banks now control 74 percent of the banking resources in the United States.[39] There are but four major airlines in this country, down from ten in 2000, which control 83 percent of air traffic.[40] Six companies—Disney, Comcast, CBS, AT&T, Viacom, and 21st Century Fox—control nearly everything we read, listen to, and watch.[41] (This list was further consolidated in 2019 when Disney purchased 21st Century Fox.) More than half a century ago, Aldous Huxley, anarchist and author of *Brave New World*, offered a prescient take on the capitalist consolidation of the modern business world:

In competition with the Big Man, [the Little Man] loses his money and finally his very existence as an independent producer; the Big Man has gobbled him up. As the Little Men disappear, more and more economic power comes to be wielded by fewer and fewer people ... To parody the words of Winston Churchill, never have so many been manipulated so much by so few.[42]

The threat of being pushed out of the market and destroyed in a frantically competitive environment creates the urgent need to continually increase profits at all costs. If your company isn't growing while your competitors are, you're committing corporate suicide. You're increasing your risk of falling behind, losing market share, and eventually going out of business or being forced to sell. One of John Steinbeck's characters in *The Grapes of Wrath*, speaking of a bank but pointing out a universal trend of capitalism, says that "the monster has to have profits all the time. It can't wait. It'll die . . . When the monster stops growing, it dies. It can't stay one size."[43] It's not merely that some capitalists are greedy; it's that *all* capitalists operate within a system where survival requires or encourages certain mindsets and behaviors, with harmful effects.

Finally, there's economic crises—recessions and depressions. Einstein wrote that "the profit motive, in conjunction with competition among capitalists, is responsible for an instability in the accumulation and utilization of capital which leads to increasingly severe depressions." What did he mean by this? "Instability in the accumulation and utilization of capital" refers to the fact that where money ends up and who can use it has a major impact on the economic system. The engine of the economy is consumption—the masses, the consumers, making purchases. But capitalism distributes most income toward the top of society. Wealth that's going to capitalists is not going to the working class, who comprise the huge majority of consumers. As more and more wealth shifts to the owning class, while wages are kept low, the natural result is greater production capacity but not enough consumption to keep up.[44] Workers become too poor to buy everything capitalists could theoretically sell—commodities created by the workers' own hands.

The result of underconsumption is economic contraction, something Marx recognized and many mainstream economists acknowledge today.[45] "Since unemployed and poorly paid workers do not provide a profitable market," Einstein wrote, "the production of consumers' goods is restricted, and great hardship is the consequence." Even business titans occasionally recognize the danger of too great a decline in the masses' share of the national income, and too large a wealth gap between consumers and owners. Staunch capitalist Henry Ford, for instance, understood that the economy needed a working class with strong purchasing power to afford the cars he was mass producing, and thus he offered his workers an astounding five dollars a day and encouraged other businesses to follow suit.[46] He wrote that

[t]he owner, the employees, and the buying public are all one and the same, and unless an industry can so manage itself as to keep wages high and prices low it destroys itself, for otherwise it limits the number of its customers. One's own employees ought to be one's own best customers . . . We increased the buying power of our own people, and they increased the buying power of other people, and so on and on. It is this thought of enlarging buying power by paying high wages and selling at low prices that is behind the prosperity of this country.[47]

This idea, that if purchasing power fails to rise with profits and productive capacity the economy will repeatedly suffer, explains an array of findings. Like when the International Monetary Fund—no leftist commune—confirmed that lower inequality is strongly correlated with faster and more stable economic growth, and, conversely, that increased inequality hurts growth.[48] Or when the Congressional Research Service looked at sixty-five years of data and concluded that tax cuts for the wealthiest Americans have no impact on economic growth.[49] Simply giving more money to the wealthy does not fuel economic growth, as some tirelessly insist—it will actually do the opposite if the wealth gap grows too large. In reality, growth is fueled by the masses, by making *all* people strong consumers, not just the elite few.

The booms and busts of the economy, times of prosperity (for some at least) followed by times of unemployment, falling wages, foreclosure, homelessness, and hunger, are built into the capitalist system. Since industrial capitalism arose some 200 years ago, the advanced capitalist nations of the world have been regularly devastated by economic crises. The United States saw depressions in the 1810s, 1820s, and 1830s, just as it did in the 1980s, 1990s, and 2000s. Currently, economists are warning that the next recession is rapidly approaching, right on time—about a decade since the last.[50] The increasing interconnectivity between national economies means countries pull each other into crises like a collapsing house of cards. Globalization ensures global meltdowns. "Capitalism cannot reform itself," W.E.B. du Bois, author of *The Souls of Black Folk*, wrote when applying to join the Communist Party. "It is doomed to self-destruction."[51]

Conservatives often argue that economic downturns are caused by government meddling in the free market, such as the swelling of the monetary supply and the regulation of banks. This can have harmful effects at times (at other times, it's extremely valuable). For example, the

Federal Reserve may order too much money to be printed, exacerbating inflation (price increases), or raise interest rates too high for bank-to-bank borrowing, which can mean less lending, or lending at higher costs, to individuals or businesses. Yet State interference is not the root cause of economic crises. In fact, crashes are regular and predictable because they are an effect of an established economic system that pre-dates such forms of government regulation. For instance, throughout US history, the dollar supply was capped, first linked to the gold and silver standards, and set at $347 million from 1879 until 1960.[52] Only after 1960 did the money supply take off. Likewise, interest rates for bank-to-bank borrowing were only regulated starting in 1913, when the Federal Reserve was founded.

The Federal Reserve is sometimes criticized for helping create the "Inverted Yield Curve"—when short-term bonds (money you loan a financial institution, company, local government, or the US Treasury) have higher interest rates than long-term ones, a situation that has occurred before the last seven recessions. However, this is primarily the result of actors in a free market. Investors who think a recession is coming buy more long-term bonds, for greater safety. This increased demand leads to lower interest rates on long-term bonds, while neglected short-term ones start offering better interest rates, eventually becoming the highest.[53] The Federal Reserve can at times be faulted for making investors think there's a recession approaching or for enacting policies that contribute to the shift to long-term bonds, but the yield inversion can occur without it (and the institution and its regulatory power is far younger than capitalism's booms and busts.) In any case, this change is more a signal that a recession is coming than a cause.

The same cannot be said of other consumption changes, which are both standard warning signs and the very illnesses that will soon kill the economy: home sales declining because people cannot afford them; prices rising and cutting into workers' paychecks; increasing credit card debt and late payments on loans as pockets empty; falling consumer confidence either causing or caused by a stock market dip; sales taxes declining as sales do, and so on.[54]

How exactly does the "business cycle" work? Well, just the way one would expect, given the realities of market competition and supply and demand. In times where borrowing rates are low, raw materials cheap, new technology available, consumer spending up, and other factors, capitalists see a chance to increase their profits, expand their businesses and market shares, and destroy competitors. They stampede into investment, building new factories and stores, buying new land and technology, hiring more workers. Production takes off. The competition pulls everyone in; no business wants to fall behind. This is the boom time. Firms benefit from the spending of all other firms. Each firm can sell more to some and buy more from others, and profits rise. Many unskilled workers find employment. Skilled workers sometimes see a rise in wages. Consumers spend more money still, an upward spiral. The economy prospers.[55]

But all good things must come to an end. Massive competitive demand eventually creates shortages, and this raises the prices of raw materials, technology, land, available loans, employees, etc., which starts eroding profits. These increased costs raise the prices of goods and services, and consumers start buying less. During the boom time almost all the new wealth and prosperity went to the capitalists at the top of society. The consumer base benefited a little, but not enough to prevent what's about to occur. Industry could keep producing, but the hoarding of wealth inherent to the capitalist system, its top-heavy distribution, creates a consumer base unable to absorb price increases.

Capitalists stampede out of investment—they see the writing on the wall. Production is scaled back. Firms are hurt by the slowdown of all other firms. Workers are fired. Rising unemployment cripples consumption further, as people have less to spend. Winding down production, cutting pay or hours, and letting employees go all deepen the crisis, rather than pull the economy out of it. Workers are then forced to compete with millions of others for dismal jobs, forcing down wages further, hurting consumption further. Things spiral downward. Depression sets in.[56]

The result is a squandering of our productive capacity and human talent. During the recession beginning in 2008, 35 percent of our industrial capacity stood idle.[57] "Unlimited competition," Einstein explained, "leads to a huge waste of labor." Workers desperately need work, and much work needs to be done, but they will not find it, as wealthy owners sit on their money, refusing to increase investment in people and production, riding out the dark days in leisure—as the pockets of poorer folks empty. Again, this capitalist behavior is a requirement of participation in the system, a natural response to its realities and pressures. During the Great Depression, education reformer John Dewey condemned the "appalling existence of want in the midst of plenty, of millions of unemployed in the midst of idle billions of hoarded money and unused credit as well as factories and mills deteriorating for lack of use, of hunger while farmers are burning grain for fuel." But that was the result of our "crazy economic system."[58]

Eventually things will recover, returning to the conditions that allow the cycle to begin again. But not before millions of jobs are lost, hours and wages reduced, employer healthcare coverage slashed, homes forfeited, retirement savings wiped out, debt increased, poverty worsened. Government funding to education and other important services are cut as tax revenues decrease.[59] Smaller businesses go under or get swallowed up. Increasing monopolization also makes these crises worse, as when one or two giants fall, they alone can wreck havoc on the entire economy, as we saw with the big banks in 2008.

These issues are grave, but we are just getting started.

Four

THE PROFIT MOTIVE:
PEOPLE AND THE PLANET

THE ABUSES OF CAPITALISM THAT COME with the quest for profits—the so-called "profit motive"—harm and kill innocent people, working against positive social goals like employee and consumer safety, and a clean and habitable environment. "Output," Helen Keller wrote, "is considered of greater importance than the production of healthy, happy-hearted, free human beings."[1]

Consider that 50,000 to 95,000 Americans die annually from long-term exposure to workplace toxins, with about 5,000 more dying from acute causes like fires, falls, and accidents involving machinery.[2] Several million others are injured or sickened by their occupation.[3] Around the globe, 2.3 million die each year from workplace-related accidents or diseases, while an additional 160 million get sick on the job, and 317 million are injured.[4] The incidents can be as absurd as they are tragic, from Fuyao Glass workers in Ohio being injured when they weren't allowed to wear safety gloves while cutting glass to seventeen American workers dying from methylene chloride in paint strippers after refinishing bathtubs for Lowe's.[5]

This is not to say that every single workplace death or injury is due to capitalist negligence in the name of profit. Many accidents are entirely unforeseeable, while others are due to worker error. Some careers are drastically more dangerous than others (construction, mining and extraction, transportation, agriculture), and people still wish to pursue them. That said, we need to keep in mind that many workers have no choice but to take or keep jobs that are unsafe in order to make ends meet. For example, workers sixty-five and older are two and a half times more likely to die at work, and their numbers in the workforce have steadily increased in recent decades.[6] Many of these older employees have to keep working beyond retirement age because they don't have the money to stop.[7] Seniors who are hurt, sickened, or die in the workplace are victims of an economic system that requires them to have enough wealth to avoid such fates, yet prevents them from earning enough to comfortably retire. And it's not just older folks; many workers of all ages must take any job available, no matter how dangerous, to provide for themselves and their families.

It's not only unsafe occupations that threaten the health and livelihood of workers. Physicians have long concluded that any type of overwork can kill people prematurely.[8] High stress, long hours, not enough time off, lack of control, and other factors present in modern office life can lead to chronic diseases, to such a degree that the way businesses are run could accurately be labeled the fifth leading cause of death in the US, with an estimated 120,000 fatalities linked to it annually.[9] In countries like China, it's quite literally ten times worse.[10]

It's undeniable that much suffering and death in the workplace is due to the capitalist pursuit of profit. For example, in 2010, 137 Chinese workers churning out iPhones for Apple were poisoned by inhaling n-hexane, a chemical in gasoline used to clean the phone's touchscreens. N-hexane was favored over something safer, like alcohol, because it dries very quickly, which results in faster production.[11] In a similar vein, had Shercom Industries fixed a shredder that had injured a worker ten days earlier, eighteen-year-old Canadian Cade Sprackman might not have literally been torn to pieces. Canada's courts later determined that profits had been put before safety.[12] It was also the pursuit of profit, US courts ruled, that led to British Petroleum's (BP) Deepwater Horizon disaster that blew up eleven American workers and injured many more in 2010.[13] When David Callazo was ground to death in a hummus plant in Massachusetts in 2011, the company, Tribe, insisted that it didn't have the time or money to update the safety procedures that would have prevented the tragedy. The company had been cited for the danger five years earlier.[14] The list goes on, with countless workers "wrenched and distorted and twisted out of shape by toil and hardship and accident, and cast adrift by their masters like so many old horses," as Jack London wrote in *How I Became A Socialist*.

Employees can easily see when profits are the priority over their well-being. Fifty-eight percent of construction workers in the US believe that their employers favor productivity over their safety; 36 percent of workers feel the same across a wide range of other industries.[15] A solid majority of those who work in agriculture, fishing, hunting, and forestry likewise say that safety takes a back seat to production.[16] And even when they are hurt on the job, many workers do not report their injuries for fear of being fired.[17] (The same is true for reporting sexual harassment and other crimes in the workplace.)[18]

There also exists a 5 to 15 percent increase in workplace illnesses and injuries at businesses that are fighting to meet earnings expectations.[19] The pressure to make sales goals means cutting corners. And there is often little reason for companies not to take short cuts, as the Occupational Safety and Health Administration (OSHA), the government agency tasked with ensuring safe working conditions in the

United States, has a staff and budget far too small for the magnitude of its task, and the criminal cases it brings are almost never prosecuted by the Justice Department.[20] Further, OSHA can only impose relatively light fines, as far as large companies are concerned. The standard penalty for an initial serious workplace safety violation, $13,260, may hurt a small business, but isn't going to worry a multi-billion dollar corporation.[21] Even when violations and penalties for inaction add up to big sums, it's not much of a concern. After five years of worker injuries and deaths, BP received a $50 million fine in 2010; the company made $3.6 billion in profit in the first three months of that year alone.[22] With fines like that, it's no wonder so many firms become repeat offenders—it's just a small cost of doing business. Time spent on worker safety training or money invested in creating safer environments can't be spent on production and profits. Not all capitalists think that way, but the immense pressures of the competitive system to protect profits or risk falling behind make that mindset commonplace. "You can't operate a capitalistic system unless you are vulturistic," Malcolm X once said. "You show me a capitalist, I'll show you a bloodsucker. He cannot be anything but a bloodsucker if he's going to be a capitalist. He's got to get [blood] from somewhere other than himself."[23]

Upton Sinclair wrote in 1918 that "capitalism is predatory."[24] His statement is true to the point that even the deaths of employees outside of work can be profitable to capitalists. "Dead peasant insurance," or "corporate-owned life insurance," is when a company takes out a life insurance policy on an employee or former employee and receives payment upon his or her death. This was originally a way for companies to insure the lives of top executives, and to buffer against turmoil and collapse in the case of an executive death, but it was later extended to cover even the lowest-paid employees because it was profitable to do so. Today, this is a common practice in corporate America, with Walmart, Procter & Gamble, Bank of America, AT&T, and Citibank among the many firms engaging in it.[25]

Corporate owners compare worker deaths and insurance rewards against "expected mortality" estimates to increase the efficacy and profitability of the system. When former employee Filipe Tillman died of AIDS in 1992, the company he worked for, Camelot Music, collected $339,302 (his family received nothing). When nurse Peggy Stillwagoner died in a car wreck in 1994, her employer, Advantage Medical Services, collected $200,000. When William Smith, a convenience store clerk, was murdered at his job in 1991, his employer, National Convenience Stores, collected a quarter of a million dollars.[26] It is difficult to call our society civilized when corporations actively find ways to profit from worker deaths. Government regulations in 2006 required employers to get employee consent before taking out an insurance policy, as well as restricted the use to higher-paid employees. But this has still left a deplorable practice legal and in use.[27]

Even if you're not injured or killed, the conditions in some workplaces are nothing short of an affront to human dignity. In 2016, it was discovered that workers in poultry plants were being denied bathroom breaks so often they had to wear diapers. (Many started eating and drinking less to avoid humiliation.) Managers mocked them and threatened to fire them if they complained.[28] Workers and undercover journalists also report appalling conditions at Amazon warehouses in the United States, the United Kingdom, and other countries, where workers urinate in trashcans and bottles to avoid bathroom break penalties, with some collapsing from exhaustion from the breakneck pace and leaving in ambulances.[29] Amazon also has penalties for sick days (as does Walmart),[30] and wages are so low that some workers resort to camping near the warehouses.[31] This is while Amazon's CEO, Jeff Bezos, is the richest person in the world, worth over $150 billion.[32]

Walmart and Amazon have also patented surveillance systems to listen to employee conversations and track worker movements in real time to make sure everyone's moving at a fast clip.[33] At Tesla factories in California, energy drinks are distributed to combat exhaustion, Lyft is called instead of an ambulance in the event of employee injury or illness, and not even a raw sewage spill under workers' feet stops production.[34] Those are the kinds of businesses run by the "Profit Grabbers," so labeled by Woody Guthrie, folk singer and communist ("I never sing nor play one single word or note that is not for the help of the working classes to know more, feel better, rise up, and to own and control this world that they have built"; "Socialism is the only hope for any of us").[35]

Undocumented workers are at particular risk of workplace exploitation and misery. Illegal immigration has enormously benefited capitalism by offering up cheap, vulnerable labor. With their employers holding the power to turn them in to the government, undocumented workers suffer from miniscule pay, long hours, harsh working conditions, and an inability to organize and unionize to improve their positions. (On top of all this, fear of deportation means there is no accountability for the racism and sexual assault that the undocumented experience in the workplace.) Thus, capitalists actively seek out undocumented workers for hire, despite it being illegal.[36] The outcomes are devastating. In 2008, authorities discovered children as young as thirteen working in an Iowa meatpacking plant, with beaten and bruised adults working seventeen-hour days.[37] Undocumented workers at a Target in Texas were paid just $4.35 an hour, and were never compensated for overtime.[38] Also in Texas, fruit cutters worked seven-day weeks, and were only paid if consumers bought produce, an exchange that added up to less than the minimum wage for the workers.[39] Other examples abound.

This is not a new phenomenon, as throughout history, capitalism has benefited from all types of bigotry. Racism, xenophobia, sexism, and so on not only divided and weakened the working class—especially when capitalists intentionally pitted groups against each other to prevent solidarity and unionizing—but also justified horrendous, yet cost-saving, treatment of certain sectors of the workforce.[40] For example, if a woman was considered less than a man, or a black man less than a white man, the capitalist could pay less for the same work, in addition to other forms of abuse. As a result, many black social and artistic leaders of the twentieth century were anti-capitalists. Malcolm X believed that "you can't have capitalism without racism," adding that if you encountered people who "don't have this racism in their outlook, usually they're socialists or their political philosophy is socialism."[41] He said he was for socialism himself, if it could help black people, a point Dr. King, who saw the connection between racism and capitalism, agreed with.[42] Author James Baldwin believed that socialism would one day come to America, but not until the nation had first ended racism, which he said ensured cheap labor by playing the races against each other.[43] W.E.B. du Bois stated in 1908 that "the only party today which treats Negroes as men, North and South, are the Socialists." He added fifty years later that "It is clear today that the salvation of American Negroes lies in socialism."[44] Richard Wright, author of *Native Son* and *Black Boy*, and one-time member of the Communist Party, wrote in a 1934 poem:

I am black and I have seen black hands
Raised in fists of revolt, side by side with the white fists of

white workers,
And some day—and it is only this which sustains me—
Some day there shall be millions and millions of them,
On some red day in a burst of fists on a new horizon![45]

Langston Hughes wrote a similar verse in his 1938 poem "A New
Song":

Revolt! Arise!
The Black
And White World
Shall be one!
The Worker's World!
The past is done!
A new dream flames
Against the
Sun!

Having discussed how the capitalist pursuit of profit endangers the health
and well-being of workers, we should also recognize that the same is true
for consumers. Take the auto industry, for example. In the 1970s, after
it was discovered that defective fuel tanks in Ford Pintos could potentially explode in an accident, Ford calculated that it would be cheaper to
pay lawsuit settlements ($200,000 for each case) than to recall and repair
the cars ($137 million). As a result, Ford did not fix the problem, and
180 people died each year from explosions linked to the defective fuel
tanks.[46] Forty years later, in 2015, the Justice Department declared that
General Motors had intentionally misled the public about defective igni-
tion switches, which killed 124 people.[47] At the same time, Volkswagen

was found to have installed software in its vehicles that could detect and trick emissions tests.[48] In 2017, Takata was found to have lied about the safety of its airbags, which killed eleven people.[49]

It's not just the auto industry that prioritizes profits over the lives of its customers. A *60 Minutes* investigation in 2016 found mass fraud throughout the life insurance industry, as firms such as MetLife, Prudential, and John Hancock didn't pay death benefits to family members of deceased workers, who weren't even aware they were beneficiaries. Instead of honoring the consumers, who had paid for the policies to make sure their families would have money in case something happened to them, the companies cancelled the policies and kept the money. Millions of such policies were wrongfully and knowingly thrown out, saving the companies billions of dollars. Eventually, twenty-five insurance companies settled lawsuits and paid $7.5 billion in owed death benefits, while thirty-five more are still under investigation.[50]

While free market advocates often insist that companies can police themselves, and that the desire for profit will make sure they do right by workers and consumers—who might abandon them otherwise—that's simply not how the real world functions. In the capitalist system, doing wrong is often more profitable that doing the right thing. One can find this in any industry. Profit is why corporations sell addictive cigarettes, which kill more people than all illegal drugs combined.[51] It's also why those same companies covered up their research about cancer and other diseases caused by their products.[52] Profit is why the National Football League tried to bury findings on chronic traumatic encephalopathy, the debilitating brain injury that many of its players suffer from.[53] Profit is why many products, like those made by Apple, are designed to wear out faster, so consumers need to buy them again—so-called "planned obsolescence."[54] Profit is why so much of our food is packed with dangerously addictive levels of sugar, salt, and fat.[55] It's also why animals like pigs are injected with drugs to add muscle.[56] "What they wanted from a hog," wrote Upton Sinclair in his famous work about the meatpacking industry, *The Jungle*, "was all the profits that could be got out of him; and that was what they wanted from the workingman, and also that was what they wanted from the public. What the hog thought of it, and what he suffered, were not considered; and no more was it with labor, and no more with the purchaser of meat."[57]

The pursuit of profit is also why many people are denied health insurance, or are dropped from their coverage when they get sick. Coretta Scott King wrote that her husband believed "a kind of socialism has to be adopted" because "so many people were in ill health with no way for them to pay their medical expenses."[58] Before 2010, the year the Affordable Care Act ("Obamacare") took effect, nearly fifty million Americans were uninsured; in 2017, the number was still at thirty million. Somewhere between 22,000 and 45,000 died each year from lack of medical insurance in the years before Obamacare went into effect.[59] Obviously, it is the poor whose access to care is the most restricted.[60]

The uninsured must sacrifice visits to the doctor, prescription drugs, surgery, and other forms of treatment because they cannot afford them. Problems worsen or go undiscovered, and people die from treatable issues. The uninsured have a 40 percent higher mortality rate.[61] Children without insurance are 60 percent more likely to die after hospitalization than those with insurance.[62] The same is true for uninsured adults, as a result of delaying hospital visits or receiving substandard, discriminatory care due to insurance status.[63]

As more people gain insurance, deaths are reduced. Obamacare was modeled after a Republican-led program in Massachusetts, where every 830 adults who gained insurance translated to one fewer death.[64] There is also one fewer preventable death for every 300 people added to Medicaid, which was expanded under the Affordable Care Act.[65] There is simply no question that programs that help citizens get health insurance reduce the mortality rate and make people healthier.[66] Simply put, the ACA is saving tens of thousands of lives.[67]

It should not be surprising that lack of insurance is a death sentence, considering how much medical treatment costs without it, from hundreds of dollars a month to treat diabetes (plus $5,000 to $7,000 for an insulin pump) to over $100,000 for just the first year of treating brain cancer.[68] And what can you do when the cost of a pill you need goes from $13.50 to $750 overnight on the whim of a corporate executive, as was the case in 2015 with a drug called Daraprim, which treats a life-threatening parasitic infection.[69] Those who don't perish from medical costs can be ruined financially. In 2013, an estimated 645,000 bankruptcies were linked to massive medical bills.[70] (This is the most common cause of personal bankruptcy.)[71] In 2016, 20 percent of insured Americans were having difficulty paying their medical bills.[72] Forty-two percent of cancer patients spend every penny they have to stay alive.[73] An estimated sixty-three million Americans sacrifice needed care due to cost, and an estimated seventy million struggle to pay their bills.[74]

Before the Affordable Care Act, private insurance companies denied coverage to citizens with pre-existing medical conditions, or charged them and the elderly much higher rates. Overall, one-quarter to one-third of Americans have some form of pre-existing condition.[75] Covering someone who was already ill simply wasn't profitable for insurance companies. As a result, 650,000 people were denied health insurance from 2007 to 2009 by the top four firms alone.[76] That's one out of every seven applicants. From 2007 to 2010, one-third of Americans trying to purchase insurance were denied coverage or given weaker or more expensive coverage due to pre-existing conditions.[77]

The list of medical reasons for denial was long. One company had 400 diagnoses that could get you denied, including diabetes, heart disease, and pregnancy (an internal email from a medical management director at Amerigroup Corp. praised marketing reps for not signing up pregnant women; overall, insurers habitually overcharge women for healthcare).[78] Across the board there were over 1,000 conditions, from breast cancer to lymphoma, that could leave you uninsured.[79]

Even those who were not denied initially often lost their coverage when they grew ill. Wendell Potter, a retired Cigna senior executive, testified before Congress in 2009 that insurance companies saved vast amounts of money by dropping sick policyholders (who had faithfully made payments) using undisclosed pre-existing conditions, no matter how minor, as justification.[80] Employees earned high marks and were often given bonuses for dropping sick policyholders.[81] For example, the *Los Angeles Times* reported that from 2000 to 2006, Health Net Inc. avoided $35.5 million in medical costs by dropping about 1,600 policies, which meant a bonus for the senior analyst in charge of the task.[82] When consumers are dropped, they are left to cover the bill, which can sometimes reach six figures. Parvin Mottaghi of Los Angeles was stuck with a $100,000 bill when Blue Shield refused to cover her heart surgery, which it had previously approved.[83] Brittany Cloyd of Kentucky went to the emergency room in pain from what turned out to be ovarian cysts. Her insurance company, Anthem, sent her the $12,600 hospital bill because it decided her medical problem wasn't "severe enough" for an ER visit.[84] In California, Kathy Mutchler was handed a $71,000 bill because she didn't get prior approval for treatment from her insurer during a medical emergency.[85]

Potter further explained in his congressional testimony that a priority for insurance companies was to satisfy Wall Street investors, as quarterly reports that show coverage costs haven't been cut can harm stock prices.[86] He also shared what most of us already suspected: that benefit documents are intentionally incomprehensible so consumers won't realize how bad a deal they are getting. Potter quit after Cigna refused to cover a teenager with leukemia in need of a liver transplant. She died. Her name was Nataline. This is the "utter rottenness of private capitalism," to use Orwell's phrase.[87]

Countless other tactics put profits over people: insurers capping the amount they will pay on medical needs yearly or over the course of one's lifetime; unwarranted rate hikes; raising premiums so high as to intentionally force businesses to abandon healthcare for their workers; scheming with healthcare providers to jack up prices; marketing scams; defrauding the government, etc.[88] The very practice of higher prices for better insurance coverage is criminal—why should society be structured so that those with less money have worse healthcare? (Or those who work for certain employers get it but not others?) Don't the poor need and deserve healthcare of the same quality as the rich? Not according to capitalism, where goods and services are distributed by purchasing power, not need.

Insurance giants also often overrule the treatments determined by doctors to be best for their patients. After her doctor prescribed a medication to battle her inflammatory disease, eighteen-year-old Chanel Bunce of Seattle was told by her provider that the cost would not be covered because the treatment was experimental. Without the medication, Bunce died three weeks later. This is not an isolated incident. In surveys, the percentage of doctors who feel insurance companies inhibit them from providing the best care to patients is 90 percent or more.[89] "Karl Marx said it could not last forever—the brutality and stupidity of capitalism," poet and socialist Langston Hughes noted. "It can't. Nobody can oppress, and oppress and oppress, without the hands of the new world rising to strike them down."[90]

Some defenders of the free market claim that all Americans have access to healthcare through hospital emergency rooms. Yes, you can get emergency surgery or medicine without insurance at the ER, but you cannot get chemotherapy, or a growing tumor removed, nor preventative care and tests that detect illnesses and disorders early on, a key to saving lives. ER visits also leave people with massive bills. Ambulance rides alone cost thousands of dollars, sometimes nearing five figures. If you have insurance, your provider may cover part of it.[91] Unless we switch to a model where taxes cover insurance for all, we will struggle to preserve this necessary and moral US law that no one can be turned away from an emergency room because of lack of insurance. Capitalism cannot support the current system, as the US lost a quarter of its emergency rooms between 1990 and 2011 because many patients had no money and no insurance provider hospitals could bill.[92]

While the Affordable Care Act did help millions gain access to affordable healthcare via government subsidies, and protected people with pre-existing conditions from rejection and rescission, it also allowed capitalism to largely continue per usual. Indeed, the program helped funnel money into the hands of the abusive private powers, even requiring that citizens purchase their insurance. Insurance companies hiked their premium rates, reduced benefits, or even pulled out of the "exchange" if they lost money.[93] Businesses slashed worker hours and kept employee totals low to avoid having to provide insurance.[94] Republican states were allowed to opt out of Medicaid expansion, which many did, leaving a large swath of Americans not poor enough for Medicaid but too poor for subsidies on the exchange.[95] Naturally, insurance companies still sought ways to avoid paying for the medical needs of their customers, even at times ignoring the law completely.[96] To this day, tens of millions remain uninsured. Clearly, under the current system the desires of insurance companies and healthcare providers for profit are antithetical to the medical needs of human beings.

In addition to harming individuals, capitalists' pursuit of profits also poses a threat to the very survival of the human species.

Since just before the industrial age, humanity has destroyed about 35 percent of the world's forests.[97] Nearly 20 percent of the Amazon rainforest has been wiped out in the last fifty years alone.[98] Tens of millions of hectares, areas the size of small countries, are wiped out annually by the timber and logging industries.[99] Like we saw with the insurance industry, not even the law will stop some companies, as illegal logging, which comprises 8 to 10 percent of the industry, is a massive, $28 billion-a-year enterprise.[100] Gandhi warned that "industrialism" and "economic exploitation" could "strip the world bare like locusts," while Helen Keller said we must prevent "our machine age from wiping out all traces of the wilderness."[101]

Cutting down the forests is a threat to all life on the planet because photosynthetic organisms are what convert carbon dioxide (CO_2) and other gases in the atmosphere into oxygen. (The Amazon is an important supplier of the world's oxygen.)[102] While we destroy the forests, our industries run on fossil fuels, releasing CO_2, methane, and other greenhouse gases into the atmosphere, far more than what photosynthetic life can consume. Thirty gigatonnes of human-produced CO_2 now poison the atmosphere each year.[103] We are eliminating our sources of oxygen while creating new sources of CO_2 and other gases that are lethal to breathe at high levels.[104] This is the most perilous self-destructive trend of capitalism. Without regulations slowing deforestation and greenhouse gas emissions, we'd be even further along our suicidal path. But the restrictions that currently exist are not nearly enough. The fossil fuel industry fights viciously against regulations on emissions and clean energy initiatives.[105] To them, short-term profits are more important than the long-term survival of our species and the health of the planet.

Trapped in the atmosphere, greenhouse gases prevent the release of heat, warming the globe—to devastating effect. Geoscientists and climatologists are virtually unanimous that human industry has warmed the planet at an unnatural pace.[106] By one calculation, humans are changing the climate 170 times faster than natural forces.[107] (Even oil companies were forced to bury such findings when scientists they hired to investigate the matter confirmed that burning fossil fuels warms the planet.)[108] Climate science deniers rely on unethical scientists like Wei-Hock Soon, who was paid over $1 million by the fossil fuel industry to publicly discredit climate change.[109] Or they wave off concerns by pointing to the "carbon eating" technologies that governments and companies are developing, an encouraging sign but hardly a defense of free market capitalism, which is responsible for the mess in the first place.

The warming planet is experiencing worse droughts and heat waves. In the US, this is causing historic wildfires and growing populations of insects that thrive in the heat.[110] In countries that already experience dangerous droughts, the warming is directly responsible for hundreds of thousands of deaths due to hunger, as crops perish.[111] In the past few decades, we've seen a fifty-fold increase in the number of areas on Earth experiencing extreme heat. Within a century, many places will simply be uninhabitable. The Middle East has already recorded temperatures of over 160 degrees Fahrenheit. The high temperatures alone will be a death sentence for half the world if we warm the planet another ten degrees, which is possible on our present course. If the heat doesn't kill you, the lack of water and food will, as areas that grow bountiful crops today will be too hot to grow any in the future. Warming will also mean a global spread of malaria and other diseases carried by insects that reproduce faster in hotter temperatures, more fires burning down oxygen-producing forests (releasing carbon), increased ocean acidification (which can also lower oxygen levels), and more violent storms (monsoons, tsunamis, hurricanes, floods). Melting icecaps will raise sea levels (decimating coasts and affecting fresh water routes), release greenhouse gases and diseases trapped for millions of years in the arctic ice, and reflect less heat than they do today.[112] Plants will also absorb less carbon dioxide as warming increases.[113] At our current rate, the planet will warm 2.7 degrees Fahrenheit by 2040, putting coastlines permanently underwater, worsening droughts, food shortages, and fires, and destroying much of the coral reefs.[114]

Meanwhile, several corporations have publicly described how more disasters, more sick people, and so on may prove quite profitable. According to data collected by CDP, a British company that asks firms to report their environmental impact, many businesses see potential benefits in global warming. Wells Fargo wrote that, "[p]reparation for and response to climate-change induced natural disasters result in greater construction, conservation and other business activities," which the bank can finance. Home Depot stated that higher temperatures could increase sales, as people will need more air conditioners. And tech behemoth Google reported that conditions related to climate change could push more people to use their Google Earth maps, which "could have a positive impact on our brands."[115] For capitalism, the end of the world is still good for the bottom line.

In addition, thanks to capitalism, our "cities are gasping in polluted air and enduring contaminated water," as Dr. King put it.[116] Pollution, whether in air, water, or soil, is devastating to the lungs, heart, and arteries, especially in children and the elderly. The organ failure and cancer it causes slashes lifespans by years; by the end of the century two billion people could be breathing unsafe air.[117] A 2012 report commissioned by twenty nations revealed that pollution was killing nearly 4.5 million people a year worldwide.[118] In 2015, seven to nine million people worldwide died due to (mostly air) pollution—one in six deaths.[119] This is more than war, malnutrition, AIDS, and malaria combined.[120] The same year, 155,000 Americans died due to pollution-related causes.[121] In addition, a huge increase in ozone smog is expected for the US and the rest of the world.[122] Breathing in air with more CO_2 decreases human cognitive ability.[123] One study found that every increase in pollution of 5 micrograms per cubic meter was equivalent to a loss of over a year of education.[124] Cities around the globe are already so polluted that outdoor exercise does more harm to your body than good.[125] Some, like Beijing, are shrouded in smog: a warning of what humanity could potentially do to the entire planet.

"Earth," Gandhi said, "provides enough [for] every man's need but not for every man's greed."[126] This highlights an important dichotomy. The interests of the fossil fuel industry and companies that profit from environmental destruction fundamentally conflict with the desires of ordinary people for a healthy environment and a habitable planet. As we have seen, free market capitalism is defined by such clashes of interests, and it's the powerful who too often win.

Five

POVERTY

A LARGE NUMBER OF PEOPLE IN America fall into what Jack London called the "social pit" of poverty.[1] While the government might officially report that the poor are limited to the 15 percent or so who live below the "poverty level" (the threshold of which for a single person is an annual income of just $12,000), in reality, 48 percent of Americans live in or near poverty.[2] This is not a surprising statistic when you realize that over 40 percent of US workers make under $15 an hour, and 50 percent of all jobs in the country pay $31,000 annually or less.[3] Though it varies slightly by state, $31,000 after taxes is typically less than $2,000 in take-home pay a month. (If you make minimum wage, you'll earn just over $1,100 a month working full-time.)

The social pit gets deeper still, as there also exists a population of 1.5 million families (three million children) that live on just two dollars a day—Third World poverty levels—due to unemployment, underemployment, lack of knowledge concerning welfare programs, etc.[4] Persons with disabilities also have it bad, as an obscure section of the Fair Labor Standards Act allows employers to circumvent minimum wage protections in their case. As a result, many earn under $1 per hour.[5] As mentioned earlier, undocumented immigrants are likewise often paid less than minimum wage. In public and private prisons, inmates are sometimes forced to work for corporations for pennies an hour or nothing at all, often in unsafe, horrific conditions, facing solitary confinement and other retribution if they refuse to participate.[6]

Overall, today's wages are dramatically lower than what they should be, weakening in value as living costs have gone up. According to the Center for Economic and Policy Research (CEPR), if you adjusted for inflation, the median hourly pay would have to be $18.50 an hour today to match what it was in 1979. Further, the minimum wage would be $10.52 if it was properly adjusted for inflation, and about $22 if it had kept pace with economic productivity. The CEPR used this same criteria to determine that in 2010, only 24.6 percent of American jobs were "good jobs," defined as employment that pays at least $18.50 per hour—or $37,000 per year—plus options for healthcare and retirement planning (this was down from 27.4 percent in 1979).[7]

Unsurprisingly, poverty worsens if wages fail to keep up with the rising costs of living. While wages have risen slightly since the 1970s, the cost of college has increased over 1,100 percent, medical costs by 601 percent, and food prices by 244 percent. Electricity bills have outpaced inflation; water bills tripled from 2001 to 2013, and the number of people spending half their income on housing rose by 46 percent.[8] Adjusting for inflation, median home costs doubled from 1970 to 2000, with rent skyrocketing as well.[9] While the cost of living varies by state—the burden on the poor and minimum wage earners is far greater on the more expensive coasts—the median cost of just a single-bedroom apartment in the US eliminates half of that $2,000 a month take-home pay so many people earn, and nearly everything a minimum wage worker earns.[10] And as *Forbes* reported in 2015, rent costs are still rising rapidly, about twice as fast as wages since 2000, noting the median cost of rent in cities like Charlotte ($1,235), Denver ($1,827), Los Angeles ($2,460), and New York ($2,331).[11]

The twin effects of stagnant wages and increasing costs restricts the amount of money that people are able to save. As a result, fifty-six percent of US citizens have less than $1,000 in the bank; one in three families have no savings at all.[12] More than three-quarters say they are living paycheck to paycheck.[13] In addition, millions of Americans actually have *negative* wealth due to loans, credit card debt, negative equity on homes after the 2008 housing crash, and so on.[14] Even when the economy is supposedly doing well, millions remain unemployed (which, as Upton Sinclair noted, immensely benefits capitalists, as it provides a large pool of cheap labor).[15] Victor Hugo, author of *Les Misérables*, bluntly told the wealthy in England that "the workers of this world whose fruits you enjoy live in death."[16]

In addition to the lack of savings, living in poverty also deeply affects people's physical and mental well-being—the life expectancy of the poor is over a decade shorter than their wealthier counterparts.[17] Factors that lead to this are many, including: less access to healthy food; unhealthy air and environments (companies and cities often dump hazardous waste or pollutants in poor and minority areas);[18] extreme stress and depression; lack of healthcare; and smoking (cigarette companies target poor people).[19] One in four US children are food insecure, missing meals or eating cheap, unhealthy food—ketchup sandwiches, for instance.[20] "Every empty belly," Orwell declared, "is an argument for Socialism."[21] Among advanced democracies, the US has the highest rate of poverty, and among the lowest living standards for the impoverished.[22] This contributes to worse health outcomes, from children with extremely painful rotting teeth to adults with deteriorating mental health.[23] For instance, 10,000 suicides were linked to the last recession, spurred by job loss and home foreclosures.[24]

Poverty also affects where people live, with low-income people residing in dilapidated apartments or houses infested with roaches, mice and feces, rot, and mold, sometimes without heating or air conditioning or hot water. Many are at the whims of negligent landlords. And if you have a month where you can't pay a utility bill, your water or electricity will be cut off; if you can't pay rent, you will be evicted. Remember, human needs are only met under capitalism if you have enough money. Each year, 3.5 million Americans will experience homelessness. A quarter to a third of these are children; about 13 percent are veterans, another 13 percent disabled; 20 to 25 percent suffer from mental illness; most homeless women are domestic abuse victims.[25] The homeless suffer humiliation, from being denied service at businesses to cities criminalizing begging, loitering, and sleeping in public places or even private vehicles.[26] Benches and sidewalks are redesigned, at times with spikes, to drive away the homeless looking for rest.[27] When the temperature gets too extreme, homeless people die outside.[28] This is all while millions of homes stand empty, waiting for citizens who can afford them.[29] "In the face of its enormous wealth," Jack London wrote, "capitalistic society forfeits its right to existence when it permits widespread, bestial poverty."[30]

For many of our poorest, their only hope is the social safety net. Thus, forty million Americans rely on food stamps.[31] (This number includes many current and former US soldiers.)[32] Overall, 65 percent of Americans will use welfare at some point in their lives.[33] Obviously, unemployment and the low wages offered by capitalists are what make welfare necessary. That's one of many contradictions present in free market, conservative thought: advocating against both decent minimum wages and decent welfare makes no sense, as a successful assault on one only makes demand for the other grow.

Is this widespread hardship due to laziness, as many free market advocates believe? The idea that welfare and other social programs make people lazy and thus unwilling to work has long been put forth, and not just by conservatives. It was one of the main ideas behind President Bill Clinton's desire to "end welfare as we know it" in the 1990s. But it has remained a bedrock principle of the right-wing, which has long advocated for slashing social programs.[34] As conservative philosophy posits, aren't people responsible for their own choices? If you want to save more money, change your spending habits; if you want a better wage, get a degree or some training and make yourself more valuable. In other words, pull yourself up by your bootstraps and don't rely on government handouts.

However, is the real reason that so many people struggle in our capitalist society due to laziness, or is it low wages, the fierce competition for jobs, the overall availability of work, and the rising cost of living? Charles Dickens—no socialist, but critical of the horrors of industrial capitalism—wrote that the laziness motif was a "fiction" believed by the characters in one of his novels:

> Any capitalist . . . who had made sixty thousand pounds out of sixpence always professed to wonder why the sixty thousand nearest Hands didn't each make sixty thousand pounds out of sixpence, and more or less reproached them every one for not accomplishing the little feat. What I did you can do. Why don't you go and do it?[35]

The simplistic demand for the poor to just be more responsible and work harder ignores basic economic and social realities. Obviously, individuals earning low wages must spend most of what they make on necessities such as groceries, electricity, water, rent, and gas. "To recommend thrift to the poor is both grotesque and insulting," Oscar Wilde wrote. "It is like advising a man who is starving to eat less."[36] Even if those earning low wages are somehow able to save a little money, those savings are often wiped out by the typical hurdles of life that better-off people consider to be mere inconveniences, such as broken-down cars or doctor's visits.

In addition, the poor typically cannot afford to pay for college. Even with grant and scholarship opportunities available—which some poor people can and do take advantage of—obstacles like low test scores, a family that cannot go without the potential student's income as a worker, or a necessary second or third job taking up nights and weekends rule out the possibility of higher education for many low-income earners. As a result of their immobility due to lack of education, most poor people will remain stuck where they are economically—not because of lack of willpower or effort, but because they have fewer opportunities and less flexibility than those with more money.

Even college graduates are often left behind in the capitalist economy, as over 40 percent of young graduates work in a job that does not require a degree.[37] Half a million people with bachelor's or associate's degrees make minimum wage.[38] If hard-working graduates can be crowded out of opportunities, what can we expect for those *without* degrees, the so-called "lazy" citizens? They can seek higher positions at their workplaces or elsewhere, but there aren't always enough spots available for everyone. The number of higher positions is limited, determined by capitalists' needs, not workers' needs. Further, telling someone to start their own business, another conservative rallying call, isn't much help either, as 80 percent of new businesses fail during the first year,[39] and most entrepreneurs come from high-income families.[40] Poorer people just don't have the wealth, connections, higher education, and other advantages that make it easier to start and grow a business, or try something new after a venture fails (the typical path of the successful entrepreneur).[41]

As we can see, one's economic opportunities are affected by factors beyond one's control. Dr. King once said of the black man in America: "He is deprived of normal education and normal social and economic opportunities. When he seeks opportunities, he is told, in effect, to lift himself up by his own bootstraps, advice which does not take into account the fact that he is barefoot."[42] Socioeconomic realities like racism were ignored; laziness was the answer. Today the same language is used for low-income or unemployed people in general (although people of color still remain special targets).

Consider the disadvantages you face if you come from a poor family. You're more likely to be born underweight or sick because poor mothers are less healthy; you're more likely to grow up around pollution and toxic lead; less likely to have high-quality daycare; and you will see your parents less frequently than better-off children see theirs.[43] This harsh environment can harm your physical and psychological development. We know that for a fetus, infant, or child, malnutrition impacts brain development, hurting attention span, memory, and other learning systems.[44] Lead poisoning, most prevalent in inner cities, harms intelligence and learning abilities, and poor housing causes depression.[45] Children in poverty are more likely to experience high-stress homes, neglect and abuse, abandonment, displacement, homelessness, hunger; exposure to crime and violence; chronic illness, depression, developmental delays, emotional and behavioral disorders, decreased concentration and memory capabilities, and a host of other problems.[46] A 2015 study showed that the parts of the brain tied to academic performance is 8 to 10 percent smaller in children from very poor households.[47] Being poor has similar stress effects on the adult mind as sleep deprivation, or suddenly losing thirteen IQ points.[48]

You will also enter the education system at a disadvantage not only because of the effects of poverty on your developing mind and body, but also because your parents, working long hours and likely less educated, will have spent less time reading to you and interacting with you than rich parents do with their children, meaning you will have a much smaller vocabulary.[49] You probably won't be attending costly pre-school, a vital leg up during the most important years of intellectual development.[50] And, once you start school, your educational environment won't be what better-off children experience either, which will affect your outcomes.[51] In the US, most local public school funding is based on property taxes, which ensures that poor neighborhoods have underfunded schools (at times it is also based on test scores, which also ensures that low-performing schools stay poorly funded).[52] So not only do you face the stress of poverty at home, but your place of learning offers fewer opportunities than the higher performing schools in wealthy (and usually majority-white) neighborhoods, frequently just a couple of blocks away.

Attending an underfunded school, you will likely experience less-qualified teachers, crumbling facilities, overcrowded classes, and a lack of books, supplies, and physical and mental health care.[53] Poor students also have to worry about being bitten by mice, buildings with no heat or air conditioning, water and gas leaks.[54] You might even be looked at differently compared to how teachers in more prosperous places look at their students, viewed as someone who won't amount to much, and will therefore be offered less attention, active learning, advanced knowledge, and college preparation.[55] Thus, you are far more likely to do poorly academically than your affluent peers.[56] (The poorest school districts lag many grade levels behind the richest in this country.)[57] You likely won't be able to take advantage of ACT or SAT prep courses that are available in better schools. On top of your development being damaged by poverty and learning in unequal schools, the framing and language biases of the standardized tests themselves, which are created by wealthier people, can put you at a disadvantage.[58] Many poor schools can't even afford the books that train students for standardized tests.[59] Thus, the poorest students score on average 400 points below the wealthiest students on the SAT; many score so low they will not be admitted to four-year colleges, much less get scholarships.[60] Many poor students are therefore either truly unprepared for college, or *feel* unprepared, unintelligent, or simply defeated due to the daunting educational challenges they face.

With all these negative factors, you are more likely to drop out of high school, and less likely to attend college if you do graduate (where you would in fact be less likely to finish your degree).[61] This is not to say that some poor students don't ace standardized tests, maintain perfect GPAs, graduate college with honors, and find high-paying careers or launch successful businesses. But these things are much less likely to happen for them than for wealthier people.

Being born poor will also severely limit your ability to rise out of your social class when you enter the world of work. In the United States, wealth and social connections are more closely linked to success than talent or smarts.[62] It's been found that even geniuses, with IQs approaching 200, who come from poor homes, are less successful than those with similar IQs who come from wealthier homes.[63] This has to do with opportunity. For instance, consider the idiom "It's all about who you know." Well, people who grow up poor mostly know other poor people, meaning they have access to fewer opportunities stemming from networking and similar types of connections. Low-wage work is the future for most poor children, who won't be able to purchase a home (vital for passing on wealth) in a richer, safer area with great schools, won't have decent medical care (note that poverty, by creating worse health outcomes, only makes it harder to get healthcare coverage from insurers) and so on.

The "rags to riches" story is largely a myth of capitalism. Indeed, rising from a lower- or middle-class family into the upper class is extraordinarily rare. Studies indicate a child of a low-income family has a 1 percent chance of making it into the wealthiest 5 percent, and a child from a family of middle-quintile income has a 1.8 percent chance (and is slightly more likely to fall to a lower quintile that rise to a higher one).[64] Those born in the lowest, second, and middle income quintiles have below a 5 percent chance of making it to the top 10 percent of income earners—in the fourth quintile, it's about 8 percent. Only those in the highest income bracket have a good chance, at over 40 percent.[65]

What about just rising a little bit, into a more comfortable life? Here the mobility is better, but hardly something to celebrate. Only a minority, 34 percent of Americans, manage to reach a higher income quintile (for example, moving from the lowest to the second quintile). Once again, children of middle-income families have a roughly equal chance of falling or rising; 42 percent of people born into the lowest quintile die in the lowest quintile; and the vast majority of those who escape the lowest quintile die in the second lowest. The very poorest and the very richest are those least likely to leave the social class in which they were born.[66] Your parent's income is a strong predictor of your own, and the relationship between parent and offspring in terms of income is even closer than in terms of physical attributes like height.[67] And it's not getting better. In the past several decades, Americans have even become less likely to make the same income as their parents.[68] When we step back and look at family trees over centuries, social class can persist for 10 to 15 generations.[69] That's how well class, whether for the very poor or very rich, perpetuates itself. "The game had never been fair," Upton Sinclair wrote. "The dice were loaded."[70]

Despite the evidence, many people in this country can't accept that moving up in class from where they begin is something they likely won't be able to do. They're too enamored with the propaganda of the American Dream—which for most is just that, a dream. As John Steinbeck said in his last book, *America and Americans,* "We didn't have any self-admitted proletarians. Everyone was a temporarily embarrassed capitalist."[71] Thus, it's time we put aside the old slander about irresponsible and lazy poor people, and recognize that the poor often work harder than anyone—multiple jobs, long hours. Instead, it's time to acknowledge the root causes of poverty and what is truly necessary to end it.

Six

CAPITALIST POLITICS

POLITICAL POWER, WEALTH, AND BUSINESS interests are all intimately linked in a capitalist society. Rarely do we see one without the others, which has a devastating effect on democracy. In a system where money is power, a small group of wealthy people end up having a much larger say over the direction of the country than the vast majority. Albert Einstein wrote in 1950 that there existed an

> oligarchy of private capital the enormous power of which cannot be effectively checked even by a democratically organized political society. This is true since the members of legislative bodies are selected by political parties, largely financed or otherwise influenced by private capitalists who, for all practical purposes, separate the electorate from the legislature.

To become part of the government requires a great deal of money. Of course, it helps if you have a personal fortune to spend in the first place, which can give capitalists a leg up over other candidates. In the history of our nation, the president has nearly always been a millionaire—or a billionaire, in the case of Donald Trump—and half the members of Congress are millionaires.[1] But just as significant is the amount of money a politician can raise from wealthy donors and corporations. While there are occasional upsets, the best-funded candidates win congressional elections about 90 percent of the time. The same is true of presidential races.[2] Big donors and large businesses therefore have a tremendous amount of power over who runs the government in the capitalist system. Helen Keller, when asked about whether the voice of the people was ever heard at the polls, said that money was simply too loud for that.[3]

It is true that some recent candidates for office, such as Bernie Sanders, have demonstrated the power of grassroots campaigns, rejecting corporate money and thriving on small donations from large numbers of ordinary people. Despite these occasional examples, rich individuals and large corporation still exert great control over campaigns and the votes of politicians. This influence was enshrined into law in 2010, with the Supreme Court's decision in *Citizens United v. Federal Election Commission*, which freed corporations and individuals to give unlimited money to super PACs, which support political campaigns and parties. (Super PACs can spend unlimited sums, too.) This ruling gave the richest corporations and their owners disproportionate power to help decide elections—much more power than a poor person, small business, or local union or organization. As an example, during the 2014 midterm elections, forty-two ultra-wealthy Americans gave one-third of all super PAC donations, $200 million.[4] In the 2018 midterms, super PAC spending on congressional candidates was over $800 million (regular PACs, which are limited in how much they can receive and give, spent over half that amount).[5] The 2013 *McCutcheon v. F.E.C.* decision, while preserving contribution limits to a single candidate or party, abolished the cap on a donor's total contributions, further empowering the rich to back as many candidates as they wished.

It reminds one of what Adam Smith once said: "Civil government . . . [is] instituted for the defense of the rich against the poor . . ."[6] It also reflects what Jack London wrote about the only alternative to socialism being "industrial oligarchies . . . the moneyed class controlling the State and its revenues and all the means of subsistence, and guarding its own interests with jealous care."[7]

Capitalists also do not worry too much about which party will win an election, as they frequently give money to *both sides* to ensure that whoever emerges victorious will serve their interests, at times speaking openly about it.[8] The Democratic and Republican governors associations, which work to elect party candidates, have many of the same big donors. Corporations like Comcast, Walmart, Hewlett-Packard, AT&T, Coca-Cola, AFLAC, and Verizon give about the same amount to both sides.[9] Boeing, Allstate, Ford, General Electric, Home Depot, Lockheed Martin, Microsoft, and others give to the congressional campaign committees of both parties, and CEOs like Apple's Tim Cook mimic this giving with their personal funds.[10] Companies often favor Republican candidates for their devotion to free markets, but will make sure Democratic candidates get something too, just in case. There would be little point in doing this if it wasn't seen as a valuable investment, a method of securing favorable policies. The result of all this, Einstein said, is "the representatives of the people do not in fact sufficiently protect the interests of the underprivileged sections of the population."

Research published in *Political Research Quarterly* has shown that both political parties follow the whims of their wealthy constituents and donors.[11] Other studies reveal that the rich are more likely to see policies they support enacted, even if the other classes are against it.[12] In 2017, Republicans openly admitted it was urgent to pass a new tax law or their donors would abandon them.[13] Democratic politicians who supported tighter regulations on the big banks in the wake of the 2008 recession had a 14 percent greater chance of reversing their position with every $100,000 the financial sector donated to them—and the best paid did indeed switch their votes.[14] Members of both parties are more likely to support Big Tobacco according to how much they receive in donations.[15] No one believes it's a coincidence that Democrats who oppose Medicare For All get the most money from the health insurance industry, or that the Republican leadership got huge corporate donations mere days after slashing taxes for corporations and the rich in 2017.[16] Capitalists also target with cash the members of key congressional committees that regulate them.[17] The same goes for political bodies that hire them. From 1979 to 2006, every $201,000 a corporation spent on campaign contributions resulted in 107 more government contracts, meaning millions of dollars in return for their donations.[18] A sizeable body of research leaves no doubt that the interests of big business and the rich come first, regardless of party, largely due to financial contributions.[19] Lawmakers respond best to those with the deepest pockets, meaning that under capitalism, even legislation is "distributed" according to wealth. The term *representative government*, Ralph Waldo Emerson wrote, is a misnomer.[20]

Helen Keller once asked, "Are not the dominant parties managed by the ruling classes . . . solely for the profit and privilege of the few . . . ? They toss crumbs of concession to make us believe that they are working in our interest."[21] She went on to call voting a choice between two parties that serve big business and the wealthy. Upton Sinclair echoed this when he wrote that voters were forced to decide between two candidates controlled by their own exploiters.[22] The business and political classes, he added, worked together to take and take from the working class.[23] This "system," Malcolm X observed, made people have to choose lesser evils, serving the "shrewd capitalists, the shrewd imperialists, [who] knew that the only way people would run toward the fox would be if you showed them a wolf."[24] And while there are unquestionably real differences between America's major political parties, especially on social issues (which don't really threaten capitalists' power), the influence of the wealthy business class helps explain why the Democratic Party isn't the aggressively progressive force many liberal Americans desire. Corporate donors simply won't tolerate higher minimum wages, universal healthcare, union rights, and so on.

Beyond funding candidates, businesses—from real estate giants to healthcare insurers, from the financial sector to law firms—also employ teams of lobbyists to pressure politicians to enact favorable policies. While it is true that smaller groups, like grassroots organizations and unions, also engage in lobbying, those who possess the most wealth wield disproportionate influence. So for example, while $48 million was spent on labor lobbying in 2017, that's a small piece of the $2.5 billion in total lobbying, especially when compared to $561 million from the healthcare industry or $524 million from the financial, insurance, and real estate sectors.[25] Jack London lamented that there exist "strong lobbies and bribery in every legislature for the purchase of capitalist legislation."[26]

If you're a business or organization with fewer resources, your lobbying efforts will not be as effective as it is for the bigger players. You won't be able to send as many representatives to lobby politicians on Capitol Hill, and you won't be able to spend as much time advocating for your goals as wealthier groups can. Former congressman and current Trump administration chief of staff Mick Mulvaney spoke in 2018 of a lobbying hierarchy, saying that lobbyists from entities that hadn't donated money wouldn't get meetings with him.[27] Lobbyists themselves say the same thing.[28] The statistics back this up, as public officials are three to four times more likely to meet with donors.[29] The result, according to countless studies, is that lobbying has a direct impact on legislation.[30]

Capitalist lobbying influence is so pervasive that corporate attorneys often literally write our laws.[31] In 2013, seventy of the eighty-five lines in a financial reform bill came straight from a draft created by Citigroup lobbyists.[32] In an even more extreme example, not a single word was changed in a 2016 bill written by the tobacco industry.[33] The list goes on. Groups like the American Legislative Exchange Council bring together local lawmakers and business titans to draft legislation.[34] National Rifle Association lobbyists often create and edit firearm legislation.[35] Oil companies in Colorado write laws which representatives faithfully introduce.[36] Uber has written bills that end up on the Ohio governor's desk.[37] At the top of the political food chain, the Trump administration follows oil and gas industry scripts when opening protected land for drilling.[38] Researchers have found that for every dollar spent on lobbying, companies received $220 in tax breaks—a return of 22,000 percent.[39] The 200 top companies receive $760 in State support for every dollar they spend on lobbying.[40] Overall, $4.4 trillion in tax breaks, subsidies, contracts, and other forms of corporate aid is handed over by the federal government each year.[41] And, of course, there is a significant disconnect between the agenda of lobbyists—i.e. big business—and the desires of the public.[42] Upton Sinclair wrote that the "masters" who "own . . . the labor of society" have "bought the governments" to "dig wider and deeper the channels through which the river of profits flows to them!"[43]

This corporate grip on our public policy has existed since the beginning of our nation and throughout its history. Thomas Jefferson, no anti-capitalist (but at least noticing the "enormous inequality producing so much misery to the bulk of mankind"),[44] denounced "the aristocracy of our monied corporations which dare already to challenge our government to a trial of strength and bid defiance to the laws of our country." He added that these same "aristocrats . . . fear and distrust the people, and wish to draw all powers from them into the hands of the higher classes," creating for themselves a "government of an aristocracy, founded on banking institutions, and moneyed incorporations."[45] During the nineteenth century construction of the transcontinental railroad, one of the most important steps in the economic development of this country, railroad companies spent $200,000 on bribes and received millions of dollars in loans and land in return. The Union Pacific Railroad sold shares to congressmen at discounted rates to, as it admitted, encourage favorable legislation.[46] After Ronald Reagan removed controls on oil prices, essentially awarding $2 billion to the oil industry, twenty-three industry executives donated over a quarter-million dollars to redecorate the White House living quarters. The owner of the Core Oil and Gas Company explicitly made it clear this was a *quid pro quo*.[47] Today, elected officials are allowed to own stock in companies they regulate, a blatant conflict of interest.[48] Upton Sinclair once said that "one of the necessary accompaniments of capitalism in a democracy is political corruption."[49]

Corporate influence even prompts the government to act against its own interests. The Obama administration pushed the Trans-Pacific Partnership, a trade deal which allowed corporations to sue governments—including the US—if their policies interfered with corporate profits.[50] Arthur Miller, best known for *Death of a Salesman* (which implicitly criticized "the bullshit of capitalism")[51] and *The Crucible* (which implicitly criticized McCarthyism), wrote that "we've become a corporate state. It has become the function of the state to make it possible for immense corporations to carry on their activities, and everything else is incidental."[52]

Obviously, deregulation is a primary goal for big business. These efforts can be so glaringly dangerous, it's remarkable anyone calling himself a public servant could allow them to succeed. In 1966, for instance, auto industry lobbyists managed to get the people's "representatives" to remove the criminal penalty for the often-deadly act of willfully selling defective cars.[53] In the 1980s, after much lobbying, the Reagan administration loosened penalties for workplace safety violations; as a consequence, employee days lost due to injury nearly doubled over the course of just three years.[54] In 2014, Congress yielded to pressure and changed the safety rules for truck drivers, raising the number of hours per week that someone could legally drive from seventy to eighty-two—despite recent deaths on the roads caused by exhausted drivers.[55] More recently, during the opioid crisis, pharmaceutical companies made a killing by ignoring government requirements to report suspiciously large orders of opioids, which were going to shady pain clinics and thus to addicts. When the Drug Enforcement Agency started cracking down on this negligence, the pharmaceutical industry used its lobbying arm to successfully convince Congress to scale back the agency's regulatory and enforcement powers.[56] As Malcolm X put it, if you think "being a capitalist or being a socialist is a crime, first you have to study which of those systems is the most criminal. And then you'll be slow to say which one should be in jail."[57]

Capitalist lobbyists also work hard to have business taxes slashed, regardless of the consequences to social programs, while their lawyers and accountants ensure effective use of government handouts in the tax code. Today, the largest companies pay no income taxes, and many get refunds. In 2014, thirteen major Fortune 500 companies, including Time Warner, Priceline, Prudential, Mattel, and CBS, paid $0 in federal taxes, and received refunds. Two others, General Electric and JetBlue Airways, paid less than 1 percent in taxes. These companies made $23 billion in profit during the same year.[58] In the second quarter of 2014, twenty large companies, such as Merck and News Corp., paid $0 in taxes, despite earning huge profits. Merck's income soared 52 percent during the quarter.[59] Amazon made nearly $6 billion in 2017, but paid no federal income taxes.[60] Of the 258 top US companies, eighteen firms, including GE and Priceline, paid no federal taxes from 2008 to 2015, with 100 companies enjoying at least one tax-free year. Averaged, their actual tax rate was close to 21 percent—instead of 35 percent, the top corporate tax rate during this period. The tax dodging activities of these companies amounted to well over half a trillion dollars in lost tax revenue for the nation.[61] In 2016, the top fifty US companies alone had $1.4 trillion hidden in tax havens outside the country.[62] The top 500 firms keep $2.1 trillion overseas to avoid taxation.[63] We're talking $718 billion in lost tax revenue from all firms added together.[64] Under the Trump administration, the top corporate tax rate was reduced to 21 percent. (It used to be over 50 percent.)[65] This means the actual tax rate will probably fall as well. This all echoes what Dr. King once said about who the government really serves: "This country has socialism for the rich, rugged individualism for the poor."[66]

The national tax burden disproportionately benefits corporations. The federal government collected $3.3 trillion in revenue in 2016; 81 percent came from individual income taxes and payroll taxes, while only 9 percent came from corporate taxes.[67] In 2015, the government took in $1.5 trillion in individual income taxes and $1 trillion from

Social Security and Medicare taxes, but only $342 billion from corporate taxes.[68] Sixty years ago, revenue from corporations was 5 to 6 percent of the Gross Domestic Product. In 2010, it was a mere 1.3 percent.[69] Therefore, corporate taxes are equivalent to a much lower percentage of the total national wealth than ever before.

Capitalists have also had their tax burden eased when it comes to individual income taxes. In 2013, any income over about $400,000 was taxed at a rate of 39.6 percent, down from 70 percent in the 1960s and 94 percent during World War II, averaging 81 percent from 1932 to 1980.[70] (This country has marginal income tax rates, meaning 39.6 percent is not the rate on *all* of someone's income, only the income after $400,000.)[71] In reality, however, the 400 richest Americans—billionaires—only paid 18 percent in taxes.[72] And a third of these 400 paid less than 15 percent, the same rate as someone earning just $36,000 a year.[73] Fifteen percent is in fact the average real tax rate for the richest half of citizens, and that rate doesn't get significantly higher in the upper quintiles.[74]

Not only is the system not progressive enough on paper (the $400,000 earner and $100 million earner should not be taxed at the same rate, nor should giant corporations of varying profits), but in practice it becomes regressive as you approach the top of the income ladder.[75] Once you pass $5 million in income, your effective tax rate falls.[76] Where state taxes are concerned, the lower your income, the higher your effective tax rate.[77] Some wealthy people pay no tax at all on their yearly income due to special provisions in the tax code.[78] Further, much personal wealth exists in tax havens, alongside corporate profits.[79] Meanwhile, the IRS focuses its auditing efforts on low-income people, even though the rich are both bigger prizes and more likely to illegally hide what they owe.[80]

•

Big companies also routinely threaten to move to other cities, states, or countries if politicians don't enact laws that benefit them; their departures could mean ruin for local or national economies and working families. Boeing, the largest employer in Wichita, Kansas, infamously held that city—and state—hostage in the early 2000s.[81] In 2018, Seattle quickly repealed its new tax on big businesses, which would have funded affordable housing, because Amazon hinted it would abandon the city.[82] Amazon also canceled plans in 2019 for a new headquarters in New York when the city refused to cough up billions, after much activist organizing.[83] Coca-Cola threatened to exit Brazil if tax breaks weren't restored.[84]

Capitalists can also use the government, and taxpayer money, as a life raft when they run into serious trouble. Many prominent companies would not exist today if not for public bailouts.[85] In the wake of the 2008 recession, Congress and the Federal Reserve handed over trillions to save the auto companies and the big banks from collapse.[86] Not doing so would have been disastrous for the nation. In the case of the financial institutions, taxpayer money was given to the very CEOs and boards of directors responsible for the crisis that decimated the economy.[87]

These bailouts were not surprising, as former financial executives held many of the top positions in the treasury department during the Great Recession.[88] Phone records have revealed that the heads of financial institutions like Goldman Sachs, Citigroup, and JP Morgan can get the treasury secretary on the phone several times a day, something no ordinary American is able to do.[89] In essence, capitalists got capitalist-bureaucrats to save their banks, and awarded themselves huge bonuses for good measure.[90] Today, many of the same people still control the financial sector and the governmental body in charge of overseeing it.

Wealthy corporate executives are also regularly installed in other influential government positions, where they set about serving the interests of private capital. It really is a case of the fox guarding the hen house, as these unelected individuals work to undo the restraints on businesses their departments are supposed to preserve—to protect the well-being of ordinary people. For instance, President Nixon appointed a businessman to head OSHA who hated the department's mission.[91] Things of course have reached an absurd level under Donald Trump. His Federal Communications Commission chair, Ajit Pai, axed net neutrality; Pai was a former lawyer for Verizon, one of the companies pushing for that deregulation. Trump's energy secretary, Rick Perry, was on the board of directors of Energy Transfer Partners and earlier said he wanted to abolish the Department of Energy. Trump's first head of the Environmental Protection Agency, Scott Pruitt, didn't believe in climate change and was in fact *suing* the EPA over environmental and health regulations when he was appointed. Trump's National Economic Council director, chief strategist, and treasury secretary were all Goldman Sachs alumni. His education secretary, Betsy DeVos, favored private schools, less government oversight over public schools, and was in no way qualified for the job, but donated huge sums to the Republican Party. The man Trump wanted for the Department of Labor was a fast food CEO who looked forward to robots replacing workers. Trump's original Health and Human Services director was a Big Pharma exec.[92] And so on. "Politics," John Dewey said, "is the shadow cast on society by big business."[93]

The term "revolving door" describes well a political system in which corporate players enter politics and politicians become corporate players. Raising this issue is simply to demonstrate, as many studies have, another way that business interests have a disproportionate influence over lawmaking.[94] Many senior staff members to Congress are former lobbyists.[95] In 2018, the Trump administration included 164 former lobbyists.[96] Some lobbyists even run for office and are elected.[97] The White House, Congress, agencies, and virtually every other political body is infected with people with close ties to corporations.[98] Not only do corporate executives and lobbyists become powerful politicians, department heads, and aides or advisors, but many public officials retire and join corporations and lobbying firms. The politicians who once at least put up a façade of serving the public then make millions using their political connections to influence legislation to the benefit of corporations. It is a two-way street of client politics, and it's growing worse. In 1974, only 3 percent of retiring congressmen became lobbyists, but now it's 50 percent of senators and over 40 percent of house members.[99] By law, politicians can keep job negotiations secret, so when a lawmaker is promised a lobbyist or other corporate position when she leaves office, she can serve a future employer while in Congress without anyone knowing it.[100] The average increase in salary for a lawmaker-turned-lobbyist is 1,452 percent.[101] As Emerson wrote, the American political party is "the party of capitalists."[102]

Seven

WAR

THERE ARE MANY CAUSES OF WAR. Religious and ethnic hatred, nationalistic fervor, and the desire for wealth, land, and power are among the reasons why nations engage in warfare. All these things preceded capitalism. However, the unceasing pursuit of new resources and markets for private profit—the hallmark of capitalism—has unquestionably been a leading cause of conflict throughout the world.

On a basic economic level, many businesses in the capitalist system benefit from warfare. For example, weapons manufacturers. The use of Raytheon's missiles in a 2018 US strike on Syria raised the value of the company's stock $5 billion in a single day.[1] On the other side of the coin, talk of more peaceful relations with North Korea that same year sent the stocks of military contractors tumbling.[2] Simply put, war is good for business—reminding one of the "military industrial complex" that Dwight D. Eisenhower spoke of in 1961. The United States is the world's leading supplier of weapons, reaping tens of billions a year for companies like Lockheed Martin, Boeing, BAE Systems, and Raytheon.[3] These companies frequently lobby for government spending on weapons systems or war machines that the Pentagon doesn't even want or need, all in the name of increasing profits.[4] On the eve of World War I, Helen Keller wrote that "behind the active agitators for defense you will find J.P. Morgan & Co., and the capitalists who have invested their money in shrapnel plants, and others that turn out implements of murder."[5] Langston Hughes agreed:

> Oh, the bankers they all are planning
> For another great big war.
> To make them rich from the worker's dead,
> That's all the war is for.[6]

Historically, corporations have often been willing to assist the government in its crimes, from the ITT Corporation offering a million dollars to help the US government overthrow Chile's democracy in 1973 to AT&T working with the National Security Agency to view billions of phone and email records under the administration of George W. Bush.[7]

War also opens new markets, allowing nations and corporations access to natural resources, cheap labor, and consumers in previously closed-off countries. George Orwell wrote that "capitalism leads to . . . the scramble for markets, and war." Helen Keller wholeheartedly agreed.[8] Upton Sinclair said that war serves capitalism by securing both raw materials and buyers.[9] Many Western nations grew more rich and powerful through the conquest and enslavement of other societies and the theft of their natural resources. It is no coincidence that the wealthiest nations today were—and, in some cases, are—largely imperialist powers, and the poorest those which were formerly occupied, oppressed, and exploited. "Under the capitalist system," Orwell wrote, "in order that England may live in comparative comfort, a hundred million Indians must live on the verge of starvation—an evil state of affairs."[10] Langston Hughes, in "Always the Same," wrote of the worldwide exploitation of blacks due to imperialism:

Black:
Exploited, beaten and robbed,
Shot and killed.
Blood running into

Dollars
Pounds
Francs
Pesetas
Lire[11]

At the end of the nineteenth century, there was much discussion among US business elites and politicians on the need to open foreign markets, by force if necessary. These leaders complained that American industry was creating more products than the people in this country could use. Future president William McKinley said that the US needed a foreign market for its surplus goods. Steel executives and commercial farmers demanded more foreign trade, while arms dealers and the iron industry supported war for the same reasons. (Voices like the *Leather Workers' Journal*, which pointed out that higher wages for American workers would increase purchasing power and thus consume the surplus, making war unnecessary, were ignored.) This fueled expansionist sentiment that quickly took the American military into Hawaii, the Philippines, Cuba, Puerto Rico, and other nations. Following the military into these places were railroad, lumber, fruit, sugar, and mining corporations.[12] Jack London wrote in 1905 that

never has the struggle for foreign markets been sharper than at the present. They are the one great outlet for congested accumulations. Predatory capital wanders the world over, seeking where it may establish itself. This urgent need for foreign markets is forcing upon the world-stage an era of great colonial empire. But this does not stand, as in the past, for the subjugation of peoples and countries for the sake of gaining their products, but for the privilege of selling them products.[13]

Woodrow Wilson stressed in his 1912 presidential campaign that foreign markets were needed for US products, while Secretary of State William Jennings Bryan later explicitly praised Wilson's imperialism for opening foreign nations to American capital.[14] These imperialistic attitudes continued to serve free market capitalism during the rest of the twentieth century and beyond. In 1950, the National Security Council flatly suggested that military spending was an economic stimulus.[15] Even after the US lost the war in Vietnam, there were calls in Congress for foreign investment in the country in the name of corporate profits, taking advantage of cheap labor.[16] Secretary of State Hillary Clinton wrote in 2011 of the need to open new markets for American corporations, and that a stronger military presence in East Asia would prove advantageous.[17]

Some thinkers have even noted that there is a capitalist incentive to keep other countries poor, whether through war or other means, as it preserves cheap labor and ensures a growing, but non-competitive, industrial sector. Malcolm X touched on this in 1964 when he said that allowing poorer nations to industrialize "will threaten the standard of living" in the West because it would hurt its global market share. He continued:

European factories can't produce unless they have some place to market the products. American factories can't produce unless she has some place to market her products. It is for this reason that the European nations in the past have kept the nations in Latin America and in Africa and in Asia from becoming industrial powers. They keep the machinery and the ability to produce and manufacture limited to Europe and limited to America. Then this puts America and the European nations in a position to control the economy of all other nations and keep them living at a low standard.[18]

While there are many pros and cons to free trade for poor nations, one serious issue is the damage it can do to local industries.[19] When poor countries are opened to cheap goods from wealthy countries, the developing industrial sectors originally offering the products can be wiped out. For instance, when Mexico was opened to cheap corn from the US in the wake of the North American Free Trade Agreement (NAFTA), millions of Mexican farmers were ruined.[20] This pushed many people to head north to the United States.

Free trade policies are often conditions for foreign aid and loans by rich nations, in order to feed their powerful, developed markets at the expense of weak, emerging economies in Africa, Latin America, and Asia. The World Bank and the International Monetary Fund, largely controlled by the US, frequently make poor nations cease agricultural production in exchange for aid and loans. These countries are also coerced into buying food from rich nations, which can leave hungry communities surrounded by their own fertile, untouched land.[21] The World Bank has also enforced product patents on developing nations, which eliminates competition for huge multinational corporations by banning businesses from making the same product in a cheaper or more efficient way in their own countries.[22] Like war, these sorts of actions swell the coffers of corporations in advanced nations, at the expense of economies and human beings in developing countries.

Even when the pursuit of profits, resources, and markets doesn't spark aggression, it can stall opposition to the aggression of others. (This could also be an example of what Arthur Miller called the "self-destroying capitalist system."[23] The pursuit of profit of a national economy can put the nation itself in harm's way.) Take a resource like oil. When Italy invaded Ethiopia in 1935, the former was getting most of its oil from the United States—a resource vital to fueling the invasion. While the US eventually cut off arm sales to Italy, it did not do the same with oil.[24]

On December 8, 1941, the United States declared war on Japan after the attack on Pearl Harbor. For the previous decade, beginning with its invasion of northern China in 1931, the Japanese military raped and murdered millions of innocent people. This slaughter was largely fueled by the United States: Japan imported 80 percent of its oil from US companies, before the Roosevelt administration finally enacted an oil embargo in August of 1941. By that time, Japan was moving beyond China into Southeast Asia, where much of America's tin, rubber, and other raw materials came from. A State Department memorandum warned that if Japan conquered Southeast Asia, the US would lose the Japanese market for its exports because Japan would gain vast natural resources, in the process inhibiting American access.[25] Similarly, US oil companies illegally supplied the Nazis throughout World War II, even after the Allied blockade and embargo was established.[26] George Orwell wrote about the relationship between British businesses and Germany on the eve of the war:

> Right at the end of August 1939 the British dealers were tumbling over one another in their eagerness to sell Germany

tin, rubber, copper and shellac—and this in the clear, certain knowledge that war was going to break out in a week or two. It was about as sensible as selling somebody a razor to cut your throat with. But it was "good business."[27]

When the Spanish people rose up against fascist dictator Francisco Franco, who was supported by Hitler and Mussolini, Orwell wrote that

the whole world was determined upon preventing revolution in Spain . . . It hardly needs pointing out why "liberal" capitalist opinion took the same line. Foreign capital was heavily invested in Spain. The Barcelona Traction Company, for instance, represented ten millions of British capital; and meanwhile the trade unions had seized all the transport in Catalonia. If the revolution went forward there would be no compensation, or very little; if the capitalist republic prevailed, foreign investments would be safe.[28]

Nothing demonstrates the bloody link between the politico-capitalist class and war better than oil. The government and the fossil fuel industry—often made up of the same people—have a shared goal: to extract more of that long-time lifeblood of civilization for the sake of a stronger national economy and bigger profits. During the early twentieth century, foreign powers had little interest in the desert regions of the Middle East; the increasing economic importance of oil and the discovery of "black gold" in the area changed all that. As British forces conquered much of the Middle East during World War I, the country's secretary of war declared controlling the region's oil a major goal.[29] Britain and France cooperated in the brutal occupation and exploitation of the Middle East after the defeat and division of the Ottoman Empire. "Every modern war has had its roots in exploitation," Helen Keller said at the time. "The few who profit from the labor of the masses want to organize the workers into an army which will protect the interests of the capitalists."[30] In 1958, the British Foreign Office warned that allowing Arabs to control their own oil would give them too much power over Britain.[31]

The United States has long been preoccupied with concerns about oil, as well as other commodities. A 1952 National Security Council memo worried about how communism in Southeast Asia would threaten American access to rubber, tin, oil, and other resources.[32] That same year, a congressional study mission declared Indochina to be a key to the rest of the region due to its abundance of rubber, coal, and iron.[33] John F. Kennedy's Undersecretary of State, U. Alexis Johnson, said that Southeast Asia was desirable for its fertile soil and crops, and its natural resources like tin, oil, and rubber.[34] During the Vietnam War, the leaked Pentagon Papers revealed government preoccupation not with democracy or freedom in Southeast Asia, but rather with those same resources.[35]

Of course, the top prize has always been the Middle East, home to half of the world's oil. After the US government reached an agreement with Britain in the 1940s that would allow American oil firms to operate in the region, a committee made up of State, Interior, Commerce, Navy, and Army department members crafted a confidential "US Petroleum Policy" that aimed to eliminate barriers to American oil companies in foreign nations.[36] By August 1945, a State Department officer admitted that of all commodities, oil had the biggest influence on US foreign policy.[37] Dwight Eisenhower called the Middle East the most strategically important place on Earth; the State Department agreed.[38] The

CIA helped overthrow a democratically-elected government in Iran in 1953, and installed the shah, a brutal dictator, partly over oil contracts.[39] Secret government memos reveal that when Arab nations cut off oil to Western powers in 1973, President Nixon was prepared to send paratroopers to seize oil fields in Saudi Arabia, Kuwait, and Abu Dhabi.[40]

Fast forward to more recent times, and nothing has changed. In 1999, Dick Cheney told oil industry leaders that the Middle East was still the top prize. As vice president, Cheney set up a secret energy task force to plan how the US could best control the world's oil.[41] The Pentagon foresaw an attack on Iraq, followed by wars in Syria, Lebanon, Libya, Somalia, Sudan, and Iran, as a means of establishing greater influence over the region.[42] In 2003, the US invaded Iraq, its former ally, justified by lies concerning weapons of mass destruction and links to the 9/11 terrorists.[43] The Bush administration then announced that American companies would rebuild the Iraqi oil industry; Halliburton (Cheney's old company), Baker Hughes, and other US drillers raked in hundreds of billions in profits.[44] British oil companies like BP also reaped the spoils.[45] Bush even issued a signing statement to the 2008 National Defense Authorization Act that declared he wouldn't obey parts of the bill that forbade spending taxpayer money to establish permanent military bases in Iraq or control the country's oil.[46]

There has been no need to invade Saudi Arabia, a fundamentalist dictatorship and the home nation of nearly all the 9/11 terrorists; the country is still a close ally of America, and its second-most profitable oil partner.[47] (As Osama bin Laden—a Saudi Arabian—wrote, he and the 9/11 terrorists were motivated to violence by this cozy relationship, which included American military bases in the Saudi Kingdom near Islam's holiest sites, and deadly US military intervention in Muslim lands.)[48] Despite popular rhetoric in opposition to fundamentalist

Islamic theocracies, the United States has historically supported many oppressive regimes like Saudi Arabia, spending much of the twentieth century helping to crush people's movements within Arab nations that might have "nationalized" oil industries, meaning taken control of oil away from foreign corporations. Often, those movements had socialist leanings, and aimed to overthrow dictators, reject political Islam, broaden human rights, and establish democracy.[49] Such things are unacceptable when they threaten US access to resources. As a very recent example of violence and the lust for oil going hand-in-hand, in 2019, former Trump administration National Security Advisor John Bolton publicly stated that it would benefit the US economy if our oil companies could go in and extract the resource in Venezuela, a nation with the world's largest proven oil reserves. His comments were made at the same time that talk circulated of possible US military intervention in the country.[50]

Overall, American foreign policy has much to do with preserving and growing its global power and economic interests. The State Department said in 1948 that to maintain its wealth, the US would need to forget about altruism; the objectives shouldn't be spreading democracy or human rights, but increasing American power.[51] In order to rebuild post-World War II Europe, the State Department said it would need to maintain access to Latin America's raw materials and exploit Africa; US planners cheered that America would be able to dominate Europe and restrict the power and autonomy of area countries.[52] Diplomat George Kennan called resources in Latin America "our" resources, and said the answer to securing them might be police repression and strong regimes.[53] (Kennan was the one who suggested we talk about power as our objective.)[54] Concerned about independent thought and action in Central and South America, the National

Security Council in 1971 warned that if the US could not control Latin America, it would be difficult to control other parts of the globe.[55]

All this continues. The 1994 Clinton Doctrine, which was used to justify American involvement in the Yugoslav Wars, claimed that the US had the right to unilateral use of military force to maintain access to markets and resources.[56] The following year, the US Strategic Command said in a report that we should appear irrational when it comes to the use of nuclear weapons if our interests are threatened.[57] After 9/11, the Bush administration declared it had the right to launch pre-emptive wars against any nation it perceived to be a future threat, and that no nation should be allowed to challenge America's global dominance.[58] A 2017 US Army War College study, while lamenting the decline in our global dominance, emphasized that the US must prevent any disruption of access to key markets, resources, and nations.[59] At the same time, the Trump administration was considering remaining in Afghanistan over mineral deposits that could be extracted by American companies.[60] Helen Keller wrote that war "compels the present society to admit that it has no morals it will not sacrifice for gain."[61]

When or whether war can be justified is a matter of debate among socialists. Some see violent revolution against capitalism, or war against imperialist and fascist states, as morally acceptable. Others are more pacifistic. In his April 4, 1967 "Beyond Vietnam" speech in New York City, Dr. King said that

> this way of settling differences is not just. This business of burn-
> ing human beings with napalm, of filling our nation's homes
> with orphans and widows, of injecting poisonous drugs of
> hate into the veins of peoples normally humane, of sending

men home from dark and bloody battlefields physically hand-
icapped and psychologically deranged, cannot be reconciled
with wisdom, justice, and love.[62]

There are many reasons to reject war. Rather than protecting our
freedoms, war typically abolishes them, leading to mass surveillance,
censorship—or worse—for dissenters, imprisonment of citizens without trial (and then torture), the draft, execution for desertion, and so on.
War also, of course, kills innocent people, usually broadening the death
toll far beyond whatever crime or tragedy instigated the initial conflict.
War leaves people maimed, blind, burned, brain-damaged, traumatized,
suicidal, homeless, orphaned, alone. War can at times lead to more war,
the continuous cycle of violence Dr. King famously warned of, as with
the unending War on Terror. It also inspires the dehumanization of and
attacks upon "the enemy" here at home, from Japanese Americans during
World War II to Muslim Americans today. War is often justified with propaganda and lies (the Rio Grande affair that sparked the US-Mexican
War, the Gulf of Tonkin incident used to justify the invasion of Vietnam,
the West Berlin discotheque bombing falsely blamed on Libyans before
the US bombed the country in 1986, weapons of mass destruction and
the false Iraqi link to 9/11 that launched the Second Gulf War, and more).
Gandhi once said, "I object to violence because when it appears to do
good, the good is only temporary; the evil it does is permanent."[63]

While we cannot expect to resolve here the varying viewpoints on
war on the left, there are a few important points that should be universal,
because to disagree with them would contradict the ideals of socialism.

1) War must never be waged for resources, profit, or capitalistic ends.

2) Whether or not to participate in war must be a decision of the people.
3) The priority use of national wealth must be human needs, not war or empire.
4) Internationalism must replace nationalism.
5) Wars of aggression and imperialism must end.

We've already considered the first point in the first half of this chapter. Let's look briefly at the problems inhibiting the others.

Regarding the second point, the decision to go to war has never been made by the people. War is declared by the few, or the one: the president. In fact, World War II was Congress's last declaration of war, and there have been fewer than ten congressional authorizations of military force since then, despite hundreds of military incursions.[64] Those who declare war are those who will suffer least from its consequences. The soldiers, their families, and innocent civilians do not make the final decision; instead, it is the wealthy politicians and capitalists, who are safe from, and even profit from, conflict. Helen Keller wrote that

> the burden of war always falls heaviest on the toilers. They are taught that their masters can do no wrong, and go out in vast numbers to be killed on the battlefield . . . Nothing is to be gained by the workers from war. They suffer all the miseries, while the rulers reap the rewards. Their wages are not increased, nor their toil made lighter, nor their homes made more comfortable.[65]

To address the third point, on how this nation spends its money, it is incredibly expensive to maintain some 800 military bases around the globe, and to keep a military presence in over 170 nations, as the United States currently does.[66] Some $600 billion a year is spent on the military; Donald Trump would like to increase that amount to $750 billion.[67] The War on Terror cost $5.6 trillion from 2001 to 2017.[68] Imagine what those funds could have accomplished domestically. "Why are millions spent on the war each day," asked Anne Frank in her diary in 1944, "while not a penny is available for medical science, artists, or the poor? Why do people have to starve when mountains of food are rotting away in other parts of the world?"[69] President Eisenhower—no socialist, but a war general and a proponent of a strong military—put it best when he famously declared that every weapon made and used by the United States was a theft from the poor.[70] Dr. King said that

> A nation that continues year after year to spend more money on military defense than on programs of social uplift is approaching spiritual death . . . There is nothing, except a tragic death wish, to prevent us from reordering our priorities, so that the pursuit of peace will take precedence over the pursuit of war.[71]

Then there's the scourge of nationalism. From a young age, Americans—like citizens of other countries—are indoctrinated with the patriotic worship of country, the unshakeable belief that our motives are pure, and the narcissistic view that we are the greatest nation in the world. This notion of national superiority serves an important function for the State. With the blind glorification of one's country inherent in nationalism and patriotism comes the belief that the lives of foreigners are less valuable than those of your own countrymen. In this way of thinking, because your country is good and right, it doesn't matter how many innocent people perish in the pursuit of its goals. This attitude is even stronger in the United States when those innocents are not white or Christian. The brown Muslim is of little concern, of little real value. That's the attitude nationalism creates, further fueled by racism, religious intolerance, and war fever.

Were this not the case, the American people would not tolerate the War on Terror for a moment longer. The citizens of this country are rightly horrified when innocent Americans die in terror attacks, but when US bombs tear apart innocent people in the Middle East and Africa, we look the other way—or celebrate. After all, they're only "towelheads," "sand niggers," "goat fuckers," or "potential terrorists." By 2015, it was estimated that 1.3 million people had died because of US wars in Afghanistan, Iraq, and Pakistan.[72] Surely, these deaths are worthy of the same grief and outrage as the three who died in the Boston Marathon bombing in 2013 or the 3,000 who died in New York on September 11, 2001.

To remain mute over the deaths of non-American men, women, and children, you have to consider those people less worthy of life. That attitude sustains war. "I don't believe the war is simply the work of politicians and capitalists," Anne Frank wrote. "Oh no, the common man is every bit as guilty; otherwise, people and nations would have rebelled long ago!"[73] Consider a drone strike. A collection of classified documents known as the "Drone Papers," leaked by a whistleblower in the US intelligence community, revealed that nearly nine in ten people killed in drone bombings across the Middle East and Africa are unintended deaths.[74] In an ethical society, it would be unacceptable to kill so many innocent people in the course of killing the enemy. Would it be acceptable for anyone to bomb a group of American innocents if it also took out a terrorist? Some will object, saying, "Well, that's war." Indeed it is—and a good reason to reject it.

Jack London wrote that people should care "more for men and women and little children than for imaginary geographical lines."[75] Thomas Paine agreed. While Paine lived just before socialism appeared as a concept, he inspired many later radicals, like Charles Fourier and Robert Owen, with his ideas on social security, guaranteed income, free public education, public work programs, taxes on the rich, and more.[76] He declared, "My country is the world."[77] Helen Keller said the same, adding that patriotism means service to all human beings.[78] Woody Guthrie famously sang: "This land is your land, this land is my land." (The original version, modified over fear of McCarthyism, included lines about private property, relief offices, and hunger.)[79] "With all my heart," Einstein said, "I believe that the world's present system of sovereign nations can only lead to barbarism, war, and inhumanity."[80]

Finally, let's consider the fifth point, wars based on imperialism. Patriotic Americans of course believe their country exclusively uses force for benevolent purposes: to expand democracy, establish peace and save foreigners, or to protect US citizens and their freedoms. However, the actual history of American foreign policy is darker and more complex, as the country has frequently used military force for the sake of its economic interests and global power—that is, imperialism. The United States has launched hundreds of attacks on foreign nations (usually weak and defenseless ones), particularly in Latin America. This has included invasions and occupations, bombings, terror attacks, massacres and intentional targeting of civilians, assassinations, forcing open markets, and enacting trade blockades using naval and air power. Other methods based on American imperialistic philosophy have included secretly arming and training rebel and terrorist groups, instructing in methods of torture, supplying or aiding in the design of weapons of mass destruction, organizing or supporting coups, rigging ballots, enacting deadly sanctions, and arming and funding brutal dictators and genocidal regimes. Targets have included popular socialistic and communistic groups or governments (the best-known cases being Salvador Allende in Chile and the Russian revolutionary government of 1917). These actions killed millions, and led to civil war, totalitarianism, genocide, and dire poverty in many countries. Over ninety percent of our nation's existence has been marked by war, and surveys indicate people around the world view the United States as the single greatest threat to world peace.[81]

Examining the full history of US wars and military interventions around the globe raises an important question: would Americans deem it permissible for other powers to do to us what we have done to them, for identical purposes and using identical violence? What if: Vietnam had bombed millions of Americans to prevent us from electing a democratic government; Mexico had conquered half the US for more land and resources; Guatemala had helped overthrow our democracy in the interest of fruit corporations; or the Philippines had invaded the US during a war with a third power, killing 600,000 Americans, including women and children?[82] Mark Twain had this to say of that last conquest, the Philippine-American War:

> We have pacified some thousands of islanders and buried them; destroyed their fields; burned their villages, and turned their widows and orphans out-of-doors; furnished heartbreak by exile to some dozens of disagreeable patriots; subjugated the remaining ten millions by Benevolent Assimilation, which is the pious new name of the musket; we have acquired property in the three hundred concubines and other slaves of our business partner, the Sultan of Sulu, and hoisted our

protecting flag over that swag. And so, by these Providences of God—and the phrase is the government's, not mine—we are a World Power.[83]

While some of this nation's many conflicts can be justified ethically, most cannot. We look favorably upon the American Revolution (even though Britain taking steps to abolish slavery in its colonies was a motivating factor), the Civil War, and the two world wars.[84] But do we remember our destruction of Native American nations, our bloody violence in Haiti, Cuba, Nicaragua, Panama, Chile, Honduras, Hawaii, Puerto Rico, Cambodia, Laos, China, Lebanon, and scores more? It is easy to see why Dr. King said America's soul was "totally poisoned" and that the US was "the greatest purveyor of violence in the world."[85]

PART TWO

SOCIALISM

Eight

WORKER OWNERSHIP

NOW THAT WE HAVE DISCUSSED THE numerous problems with capitalism, it is time to focus on solutions. Before we get to specifics, however, it is important to note that many of the historical figures in this book held varying views on what kind of system should replace capitalism. Most fall under three main ideologies—communism, anarchism, or socialism. Let's examine the first two briefly, then dive into the third.

Communism destroys capitalism from the top-down. In this system, the government, as an instrument of the people, owns all workplaces and organizes workers and the economy according to a central plan that meets citizen needs. Under communism, the competitive element of the free market is abolished entirely, ending capitalism's emphasis on putting profits over people. Wasteful work is eliminated, leaving more resources—and workers—for the important tasks that build a better society. The national wealth, in the form of public sector salaries, is divided up evenly among the people.

The idea of communism intrigued many leaders, thinkers, and artists. Gandhi voiced support for it in *India of My Dreams*.[1] "I have become a Communist," Pablo Picasso explained, "because our party strives more than any other to know and to build a better world, to make men clearer thinkers, more free and more happy."[2] (He also declared that his paintings were communist paintings.)[3] Another famous painter, Frida Kahlo, wrote, "I'm more and more convinced it's only through communism that we can become human."[4] "Yes, I am a Communist," wrote activist icon Angela Davis, "and I consider it one of the greatest honours, because we are struggling for the total liberation of the human race."[5]

Despite this support, communism comes with many problems. First, worker power and autonomy are insufficient. Under communism, workers are supposed to "own" their workplaces because they "own" the State, but this is a very indirect form of control. In addition, such a system requires giving up the freedom to choose your line of work. An economic production plan will fail if not enough workers want to do the specific tasks. You may have some options regarding the work you do, but those options will be limited, for the sake of the larger plan. If you wish to work in a bookstore, for example, but your community or national plan only allows for a specific number of bookstores or bookstore workers, you will have to pursue another line of employment. In opposition to this idea, Oscar Wilde said that "every man must be left quite free to choose his own work."[6]

Another question is whether communism could break free of representative government and give ordinary people power over their own destinies in the form of direct democracy. In contrast with examples from history where communism has been linked with authoritarianism, it is possible for communism to function with elected leaders, separation of powers, constitutional rights, and so on. However, it is unlikely to work without keeping power away from the populace through systems like representative government. In the traditional vision of communism, the people would elect members of their worker councils to participate in the design and execution of the national plan. So, for example, if you worked in auto manufacturing, you would elect someone to represent auto workers on the national planning committee. Essentially, you'd be joining all the other auto workers in the country to vote for representatives, like how you vote today with others in your geographic community to select members of Congress. The elected representatives, using a broad array of data on what goods and services are needed, and what resources and workers will be required, would then craft a central plan.

As we have seen, there are big risks with representative governance, in that it concentrates power in the hands of the few, who can more easily be influenced and corrupted. In this communist model, a small group of decision-makers would still be in charge, facing pressure from countless localities, people, and organizations, or simply doing as they pleased after getting elected, much like in our current capitalist system. While the people could theoretically participate in an up or down vote on the central plan after it is crafted by the representatives, eliminating the representative structure in favor of direct democracy seems impossible. After all, how can a national economic plan be created by popular vote?

For some real-world examples, imagine the daunting task of voting on how much corn the United States should grow in a given five-year period, how many more workers are needed to produce EpiPens, or the number of houses that should be built in a city. Can the voting public devote the time and study to make educated decisions on what to produce, their quantities, prices, and required manpower and resources, for an entire country? Would not voting itself, on countless economic details, take an inordinate amount of time? If the people cannot be expected to plan the economy via direct vote, how can they be expected to make an informed up-down vote on a plan formulated by others? And, after each municipality democratically decided on its individual, local needs, everything would then have to be reconciled at the national level, as there may not be enough resources to do everything that every community wants. Reconciliation of these local needs would have to be the duty of national officials, bringing back the representative government model. It might be possible to divide up the national wealth according to regional needs, and let each region democratically decide how to use allotted funds, but how much each city or town should get would be difficult to sort out without representative government.

Overall, organizing an economy is a monumental task requiring mountains of accurate, up-to-date data, which carries a high risk of costly mistakes and turmoil. It can be done—authoritarian communist governments used central planning to launch gigantic economic growth and rapid technological advancement (while of course crushing ordinary people to do so). But what is difficult for an elected body of experts would be impossible for the voting populace. There seems to be no escaping representative government with communism. All these challenges suggest that communism is not preferable.

Anarchism does away with capitalism from the bottom-up. In this system, workplaces are owned and run by workers (or workers and consumers) who coordinate their activities, rather than compete with one another. In addition, local communities make all decisions democratically, without elected representatives. The State, as a hierarchical structure—similar to capitalist firms—is abolished, as are nations. In this way, the people are as free as possible from compulsion, authority, and the concentration of power. You have equal power to make decisions that affect you, joining your local resident assembly and worker council. Anarchism harkens back to the era of "primitive communism" we explored in the first chapter.

Anarchists have differing views on whether capitalism or the State should be dismantled first. Does the State have a vital role to play in capitalism's eradication? Or do you do away with capitalism after eliminating the government? Anarchist H.G. Wells seemed to agree with the former idea, saying that only socialism could make anarchism possible:

> Socialism is the preparation for that higher Anarchism; painfully, laboriously we mean to destroy false ideas of property and self, eliminate unjust laws and poisonous and hateful suggestions and prejudices, create a system of social right-dealing and a tradition of right-feeling and action. Socialism is the schoolroom of true and noble Anarchism, wherein by training and restraint we shall make free men.[7]

Anarchists likewise do not always agree on whether violence is necessary to end the State. Anarchist Leo Tolstoy, author of *War and Peace*, certainly didn't think so.[8] Albert Camus, anarchist sympathizer and author of *The Stranger*, was largely against violence, except in extreme circumstances.[9] Belief in this social system doesn't require belief in violence. The term anarchism connotes order, organization, and voluntary cooperation, unlike anarchy, which means disorder, lawlessness, and violent revolution.

The challenge with anarchism is that it leaves communities to fend for themselves, potentially creating inequality. With no higher entity to address the issue, poorer regions would exist beside richer ones. True, communities could cooperate, sharing workers and resources, but there would be no guarantees. Further, extensive collaboration may require joint administration, over time weakening local control and creating larger political units—steps toward a State. Anarchism may also lead to factionalism and violence between municipalities, especially if they differ in wealth, habitability, and so on—like the cities of ancient Greece. Loyalty to one's community—"nationalism" on a smaller scale—seems more likely than a universal embrace of human oneness. At the least, such a world seems more prone to conflict than one with a single government spanning all continents and serving all people.

Another question concerning anarchism has to do with criminal justice. Crime is unlikely to end completely with the disappearance of capitalism. The relevant task of anarchism (or socialism or communism) is to build a humane, fair justice system that does not morph into what came before—a current system of countless horrors. But is it possible to have a functioning society, with just consequences for wrongdoing and real protection for others, without the State? Dr. King and George Orwell didn't think so, and thus rejected anarchism.[10] Anarchists, of course, think it is possible, embracing a vision—of community policing, restorative justice, rehabilitation, and so on—that does not require a State. These things can indeed be done on an intimate, local level, but whether they would function well enough in a global human society of independent anarchist communities is up for debate. If a murderer or rapist flees one city, will there be tight coordination between communities around the world to catch and extradite him? Or will he be allowed to escape justice and victimize others elsewhere, due to communities being too isolated, independent, or unhelpful? Overall, due to the difficult questions concerning inequality, tribalism, and justice, anarchism is not the way forward.

Finally, the subject of this book. Socialism also eliminates capitalism from the bottom-up. As with anarchism, workers collectively own their workplaces, making decisions democratically and equitably sharing the profits of their labor. The State exists to serve the various needs of the people, and is in fact under the people's direct control (we will explore this in the next chapter). Under socialism, the exploitation of labor and authoritarian power are consigned to the dustbin of history, replaced by cooperation, equity, and democracy. Workers control their own destinies, deciding together how they should use the profits created by their collective labor, be it improving production through technology, taking home bigger incomes (Jack London said socialism at its heart simply allows people to afford more food),[11] hiring new workers, lowering the price of a service, producing something new, and all other conceivable matters of business. W.E.B. Du Bois wrote that socialism is "an attempt to rearrange work and industry, wages and income on a basis of reason, need and desert, rather than leaving it to chance and the rule of the strong . . ."[12]

In comparison, women's rights icon, suffragette, and socialist Elizabeth Cady Stanton wrote that under capitalism, "the law is each for himself, starvation and death for the hindmost." But under "philosophical Socialism," we would have "co-operation, a new principle in industrial economics . . . The few have no right to the luxuries of life, while the many are denied its necessities . . ."[13] The classes, she said, needed to be more equal. Similarly, after pointing out the authoritarian hierarchy of the capitalist workplace—with the capitalist chief at the top wielding ultimate decision-making power and owning the wealth created by the workers—John Stuart Mill envisioned instead the "association of laborers themselves on terms of equality, collectively owning the capital with which they carry on their operations, and working under managers elected and removable by themselves."[14] Socialism is how the producers will get what they produce, as one of Upton Sinclair's characters phrased it.[15]

In the socialist model, worker cooperatives are the humane alternative to capitalist businesses. In a cooperative, all workers share equal ownership of the firm. This translates to equality in power (all decisions are made democratically) and in wealth (company shares and incomes are the same for everyone). Gandhi said that the worker must "become a co-sharer with the capitalist instead of remaining his slave."[16] Elizabeth Blackwell wrote that Christian socialism would mean labor receiving a "fair and increasing share in the profits it helps to create."[17]

With the disappearance of hierarchy and wage theft comes the great alleviation of many of the crimes of capitalism. The resulting increased wealth for workers reduces poverty. Victor Hugo wrote in *Les Misérables* that we need an "equitable distribution" to do away with "monstrous opulence" beside "monstrous wretchedness." We'd have to establish ownership that is "democratic . . . making it universal, so that every citizen, without exception, may be a proprietor . . ."[18] In turn, greater purchasing power for the people will ease the economic throes of recession and depression. With the elimination of capitalism, workers won't be fired on the whim of an individual owner or manager. Instead, letting someone go for whatever reason, from poor performance to budgetary restrictions, is a democratic decision. Worker-owners will also not outsource their own jobs to Bangladesh or China, and won't fire themselves after investing in new technologies that increase productivity and require less human labor. Instead, they can make more money and/or work fewer hours, bettering their standard of living and spending more time with family or doing things they enjoy. Orwell declared that socialism was "better wages and shorter hours and nobody bossing you about." It represents "justice and liberty."[19]

Transparency and democracy will make a firm less likely to commit profit-driven abuses against people, planet, and the peace, because there are more players influencing decisions; the wider the field, the less likely everyone will feel comfortable with, say, poisoning the biosphere to make a buck. This is not to say that a law prohibiting the use of fossil fuels, for example, would be unnecessary in a socialist system. It would—just like anti-monopoly, minimum wage, worker safety, and other laws, as competition for customers would still exist between worker co-ops. However, there would be more room for dissent (or whistleblowing) in the workplace and greater opportunity for more moral or safer alternatives to be pursued. We can't think of socialism, Orwell said, as a cure-all; it only makes the world better.[20]

Worker cooperatives in their modern form have existed around the world since the Industrial Revolution. Currently, there are 11.1 million worker-owners worldwide.[21] When we include folk who work for cooperatives but are not owners, the total rises to twenty-seven million. This is "the coming of the new cooperative society" that Jack London desired.[22]

The United States has a rich history of cooperative enterprises that continues to this day.[23] While some exemplify precisely the socialist vision, others were and can be more egalitarian or democratic (some elected managers and executives have significantly larger salaries, other co-ops are slow to grant ownership rights, etc.). But they are all a giant step up from capitalist firms. The US has an estimated 300 to 400 true cooperatives, everything from the 4th Tap Brewing Co-Op in Texas to Catamount Solar in Vermont, in total employing 7,000 workers (the average size is fifty people) and earning $400 million in revenue each year. Twenty-six percent of US co-ops used to be capitalist-structured businesses.[24] Converting to a cooperative is a great way to preserve a business and protect people's livelihoods. Statistically, when small business capitalists retire, they are usually unable to find a buyer for their business or pass ownership on to family members. As a result, the enterprise simply ends, and the workers are out of a job.[25] Dr. King said, "True compassion is more than flinging a coin to a beggar; it comes to see that an edifice which produces beggars needs restructuring." He recognized that poverty was due to lack of ownership of the means of production, saying we can't "question the capitalistic economy" without asking "Who owns the oil?" and "Who owns the iron ore?"[26]

American cooperatives represent all economic sectors, and have annual profit margins comparable to top-down businesses—such firms are also of the same size, if not bigger, than comparable capitalist companies.[27] Many co-ops are members of the US Federation of Worker Cooperatives, a growing organization. Because people are put before profits, cooperatives place a special focus on community improvement and development. One study found that food co-ops reinvest more money from each dollar into the local economy than standard food businesses.[28] "Oh, we'll live to see it yet," Langston Hughes penned, "When the land belongs to the farmers / And the factories to the working men." Woody Guthrie likewise wrote that the workers "ought to own and run every mine, factory, timber track."[29]

America's largest co-op, the Cooperative Home Care Associates (CHCA) in New York, has grown to 2,300 employees, about half of whom are owners (to become an owner, one pays $1,000 in installments). The co-op is 90 percent owned by minority women. With $64 million in profits in 2013, the CHCA provides wages of at least $16 an hour (twice the market rate), a highest to lowest-paid worker ratio of 11:1, flexible hours, and good insurance. Its governing board is elected; profits are shared. The company has a turnover rate that is a quarter of the industry standard. Some of the co-op's workers left behind minimum wage jobs and are now making $25 an hour. People say they stay because the co-op lifted them out of poverty, and as owners, they have decision-making power.[30] On the opposite coast, workers who join the Women's Action to Gain Economic Security (WAGES) co-ops in California see their incomes skyrocket 70 to 80 percent.[31] Ralph Waldo Emerson wrote in *The Conduct of Life* that "the socialism of our day has done good service in setting men to thinking how certain civilizing benefits, now only enjoyed by the opulent, can be enjoyed by all."[32]

As one might expect, workers are more invested in a company when they are also owners, which translates into better business outcomes. Being an owner empowers the individual—a fact some thinkers used to turn a traditional conservative platitude on its head. Gandhi said, "My concept of socialism implies that people should be self reliant. That is the only way they can be prevented from being exploited."[33] Oscar Wilde argued that, for a host of interesting reasons, "individualism will be far freer, far finer" under socialism.[34] Rather than trying to take advantage of the hard work of others, workers in co-ops are self-starting and driven. Indeed, a review of the extant research reveals that co-ops have the same or greater productivity and profitability than conventional businesses, and thus tend to last longer; workers are more motivated, satisfied, and enjoy greater benefits and pay; and resignations and layoffs decline.[35]

Co-ops are also quite innovative. Some readers may believe the contrary, that without the free market structure of capitalism, there exists no incentive to innovate, but this is not the case. In truth, the mechanisms and incentives that drive technological, systematic, and other forms of change remain in place in co-ops. Outside inventors can still sell or license their creations to cooperative businesses; start-up founders, while sacrificing total power and wealth hoarding, can still bring their creations to the world, doing what they love and making money off it; established co-ops benefit significantly from horizonal idea sharing (more open communication and better information flow), teamwork, and the individual incentive to improve their own company, all fostering innovative change at a rate on par with capitalist business-es.[36] Co-ops also frequently network, a competitive advantage in spur-ring innovation.[37]

Co-ops are also more stable than capitalist firms, even during eco-nomic crises.[38] Overall, their survival rates are 20 to 30 percent higher.[39] In Canada, worker cooperatives last on average four times longer than traditional businesses.[40] Many studies come from Europe, where cooper-atives are more widespread and more data has been collected. Research on France's cooperatives revealed that worker-owned enterprises were more productive and efficient, and over a four-year period cooperative startups actually outnumbered capitalistic startups.[41] French capitalist-turned-cooperative businesses have better survival rates than capital-ist businesses by significant margins.[42] Analyzing businesses across the United Kingdom, Canada, Israel, France, and Uruguay, one study found that co-ops had similar survival rates to traditional businesses over the long term, but better chances of making it through the crucial early years. Italy and Germany experienced the same.[43] Italian co-ops are 40 percent more likely to survive their first three years; Canadian co-ops are about 30 percent more likely to make it through the first five years and 25 percent more likely to make it through the first ten years; in the UK, twice as many cooperatives survive the first five years than traditional firms.[44] In Italy's Emilia Romagna region, an economic pow-erhouse of that nation and Europe, two-thirds of residents belong to worker cooperatives.[45] In Spain, one study of a retail chain that has both top-down and cooperative stores revealed that the latter have much stronger sales growth rates because worker-owners have decision-making authority, a financial stake, and earn higher pay.[46]

In the United States, while not much research has been done on worker cooperatives, there is a great deal of data on businesses with Employee Stock Ownership Plans (ESOPs). These plans are called "employee-owned" because employees are given stock, but most are not democratic nor totally owned and run by the workers (Publix and Hy-Vee are examples). Contrary to popular belief, owning stock is not actual ownership of a business, even if it comes with some voting rights.[47] Employee Stock Ownership Plans nevertheless reveal the benefits of giving workers at least a bit more control and wealth, and have even been praised and supported by prominent conservatives.[48] Overall, there's greater happiness, motivation, productivity, profitability, and longevity with ESOPs.[49] They are only one-third as likely to fail compared to publicly traded businesses, suffer less employee turnover, and are more productive.[50] A meta-analysis of over one hundred studies of 57,000 firms found that those with employee ownership perform (relating to growth and efficiency) slightly better than those without it.[51] Similarly, one rare study on American plywood worker cooperatives found they were 6 to 14 percent more efficient in terms of output than conventional mills.[52] When the economy declined, conventional mills attacked worker hours and employment, whereas the worker-owners agreed to lower their pay to protect hours and jobs.[53]

Given the benefits of worker cooperatives, places like New York City, California, Madison, and Cleveland are investing in their development, recognizing the ability of co-ops to lift people out of poverty and thus strengthen the consumer economy, as well as alleviating systemic barriers to work and wealth that minorities, former felons, and others face.[54] This is no small matter. The egalitarian structure and spirit of solidarity inherent in co-ops can help win equality for the oppressed and disadvantaged. Women tend to have more equitable pay and access to more prestigious positions in co-ops.[55] Sixty percent of worker-owners in new American co-ops in 2012 and 2013 were people of color.[56] It's the same around the world. Ninety percent of worker-owners at one of Spain's co-ops are people with disabilities.[57] Italian cooperatives are more likely to hire folks who have been unemployed for long periods, often a major barrier to work.[58]

Spain has one of the strongest cooperative enterprises, no surprise to those who know its Marxist history.[59] (In the 1930s, George Orwell marveled at Barcelona, where "every building of any size had been seized by the workers . . . Every shop and cafe had been collectivized . . .")[60] Mondragon Cooperative Corporation is a federation of over one hundred socialistic workplaces around the globe and in many economic sectors, from retail to agriculture. It is one of Spain's largest corporations and the largest cooperative experiment in the world, with over $10 billion in annual revenue and 74,000 workers. Those who are worker-owners have shares of the business and the ability to run for a spot in the General Assembly, the federation's democratic body of power, which elects a Governing Council. However, each cooperative is semi-autonomous, having its own, smaller democratic body. The manager-worker pay ratio is capped at 6:1.[61] In rough economic times, worker-owners decide democratically how much their pay should be reduced or how many fewer hours they should work, with managers taking the biggest hits. This stabilizes the entity during recession, avoiding layoffs. Further, Mondragon has the ability, as a federation, to transfer workers or wealth from successful cooperatives to ones that are struggling.[62]

Due to these flexibilities, Mondragon cooperatives going out of business is nearly unheard of. When it does happen, the federation finds work for the unlucky workers at other member co-ops and retrains them.[63] During the Great Recession of 2008, Mondragon's number of workers held steady, and the Spanish county where it is headquartered was one of the least troubled in the nation.[64] The enterprise, however, does have its faults. It actually owns more subsidiary companies than cooperatives—capitalistic, exploitive businesses in poor countries where the workers are not owners. Indeed, less than half of all Mondragon employees are owners.[65] Nevertheless, the business is a step in the right direction, indicating that socialistic workplaces can function on a large scale. Remember, on average, co-ops tend to have more employees than top-down firms.[66]

Imagine living in an America like this. Where the sharing of power and profits is the normal, natural way of doing things. Is there any doubt that such a change in our societal environment, in our organizational structures, would be beneficial to our attitudes and character? Might we grow, collectively, less greedy and more caring? Less individualistic and more attuned to the needs of all, the common good? Orwell saw what a socialist society was like in the Aragon region of Spain, where workplaces were cooperatively owned and residents experienced equality of wealth: "Many of the normal motives of civilized life—snobbishness, money-grubbing, fear of the boss, etc.—had ceased to exist." It was a "community where hope was more normal than apathy or cynicism . . . One had breathed the air of equality."[67]

Our historical figures knew that the first step toward a socialist society full of worker cooperatives was simply realizing that another world is possible. That is, breaking out of old capitalistic mindsets. Upton Sinclair marveled in *The Jungle* that people didn't realize they could make more money by simply taking the owner's place and running things together.[68] Mark Twain once wrote, "Many a time, when I have seen a man abusing a horse, I have wished I knew that horse's language, so that I could whisper in his ear, 'Fool, you are master here, if you but knew it. Launch out with your heels!' The working millions, in all the ages, have been horses" but could "be master."[69] Victor Hugo used the same imagery when he wrote that the capitalist is a king who sits on a horse, the people—the king could easily be thrown off.[70] John Lennon, a socialist sympathizer, when asked how the capitalist system could be destroyed, replied:

> I think only by making the workers aware of the really unhappy position they are in, breaking the dream they are surrounded by. They think they are in a wonderful, free-speaking country. They've got cars and tellies and they don't want to think there's anything more to life. They are prepared to let the bosses run them, to see their children fucked up in school. They're dreaming someone else's dream, it's not even their own . . . As soon as they start being aware of all that, we can really begin to do something. The workers can start to take over. Like Marx said: "To each according to his need . . ."[71]

Nine

SOCIALIST DEMOCRACY

THE BASIC IDEA BEHIND SOCIALISM IS that power should be made "social"—i.e. spread among the people. In practice, this means strengthening the democratic foundations of society. "Call it democracy, or call it democratic socialism," Dr. King said, highlighting the synonymic relationship between democracy and socialism.[1] George Orwell posited that socialism is "political democracy, social equality, and internationalism."[2] Jack London wrote that socialism's

> ultimate aim is pure democracy . . . a form of government in which the supreme power rests with and is exercised directly by the people instead of the present form, which is a republican form of democracy, in which the supreme power rests with the people, but is indirectly exercised by them, through representatives. Representatives may be corrupted, but how could the whole people be bribed?[3]

The solution to our troubled political realm today, where the will of the people is often overruled by elite, free market forces, is more democratic—that is, socialist—structures. We saw an example of a more democratic structure for workplaces in the previous chapter when discussing worker cooperatives, which rely on representative democracy (elected, removable managers and executives) or direct democracy (decisions made by workers on a one-person one-vote basis), as opposed to the authoritarian structures of capitalist businesses. In the same vein, we need a governmental system with more popular participation.

The democracy of socialism would allow the people to have a direct say in public policy, giving them the ability, like Congress has now, to vote yes or no on proposed laws. There is more than one reason for America's abysmal voter turnout, but a large part of it is that people do not believe that their vote will bring about meaningful change.[4] With politicians mostly representing the interests of the rich individuals and corporations that fund them, this attitude is understandable. However, this could change if the people had real power—if they controlled the State, rather than the reverse. "Political rulership of the state," du Bois wrote, "must eventually rest [with] the people."[5]

As Jack London pointed out, it would be difficult for special interests to influence policy as they do now under a people-centered system. Since citizens would not be running for office, they could not, for example, be bribed with campaign contributions, or be lobbied the way politicians are today. Thus, the money-based corruption that is so prevalent under our current system would be greatly reduced. This is not to say that there should be no elected officials, or no laws that shield such officials from the influence of cash—such as severe limits on campaign contributions, or the establishment of publicly-financed elections. It simply means that incorporating the popular vote into our political system can help reduce the power of money in the system as a whole. John Dewey asserted that democracy would be strengthened by the people's control of business institutions in the form of worker ownership, because the interests of firms would more closely align with the interests of ordinary people:

> Power today resides in control of the means of production, exchange, publicity, transportation and communication. Whoever owns them rules the life of the country . . . In order to restore democracy, one thing and one thing only is essential. The people will rule when they have power, and they will have power in the degree they own and control the land, banks, the producing and distributing agencies of the nation.[6]

There are two fundamental pathways to increasing democratic participation under a socialist system. The first would be to allow the people to place legislation on a national ballot, and then vote on it. Congress would still exist to also craft laws and place them before the people for a vote—but the institution itself would no longer have voting power. This is what is known as a semi-direct, referendum democracy. The second option would be to simply replace Congress with the people, a true direct democracy. Whatever path is chosen, citizens would need direct initiative rights, which allow people to place a proposed law on a ballot for everyone to vote on.

Where direct initiative rights exist, individuals work together to draft legislation, file it with local officials, and then gather the required number of signatures to get it on the ballot. After the vote takes place, if the measure passes, government departments enact and enforce the new law in the same way they do today after Congress passes a bill. "Imagine everybody governing!" exclaimed Victor Hugo. "Can you imagine a city governed by the men who built it? They are the team, not the coachman."[7] F. Scott Fitzgerald, a self-described socialist,[8] created a character in *This Side of Paradise* who called socialism "the theory that people are fit to govern themselves."[9]

Such a proposal can cause consternation, especially among the wealthy capitalists who control this country. The first objection often has to do with tradition: the US was founded as a representative democracy and must remain that way. What's forgotten in this argument is that political systems and practices have been changed in substantial ways throughout American history. The country was birthed in revolution against monarchism. The new United States scrapped its first constitution, the Articles of Confederation, after seven years because its designed governmental structure was flawed and ineffective. The Twelfth Amendment got rid of a system where the losing presidential candidate automatically became vice president. Only in 1856 did North Carolina become the last state to do away with property requirements to vote for members of the House of Representatives. In 1913, the American people were allowed for the first time to elect their senators; formerly, only state legislatures could do that. The Twenty-Second Amendment created presidential term limits. Add in the broadening of voting rights for subjugated groups like women and people of color, and it's clear that altering political mechanisms to create a better government, often with increased popular participation, is not a foreign concept to the US.

Another major objection to direct democracy is that it's a bad idea to give the people so much power, as it would result in so-called "mob rule" or a "tyranny of the majority." Most of the founders of this country detested direct democracy and its majority rule, because they saw it as a threat to their wealth and power.[10] Thus, they made sure that ordinary voters could not elect Supreme Court justices, nor directly choose their senators, or the president (the Electoral College). Initially, only members of the House of Representatives were directly elected, and only property owners (white and male) could vote.

However, those who fear majority rule do not realize that that is how the system works today. While on occasion the bar is higher, a simple majority decides the fate of most bills in Congress. A majority similarly carries the day in city councils, state legislatures, and in every election across the country (except the presidential election at times, such as in 2000 and 2016). Direct democracy simply alters which majority makes decisions, giving ordinary people power over the decisions that affect them. True, the majority can—and will—make poor decisions sometimes, but the same is true with Congress and other bodies backed by or full of wealthy capitalists. As with worker cooperatives, it is better that the many stumble together by their own hand than be destroyed by the few from above.

In addition, under a semi-direct, referendum democracy or a direct democracy, there would be limits to the laws the popular will could enact, as systems of checks and balances would still exist. To establish the people as a new branch of government or as a replacement of the congressional branch is not to do away with shared, co-equal political authority. There would still be a president to veto legislation. There would remain a Supreme Court, and lower courts, to declare laws unconstitutional. Only a supermajority of the people could change the Constitution or overrule a presidential veto, like how a supermajority is required in Congress to do so today. As a result, fears about prejudiced majorities oppressing smaller groups can be put aside. It's possible, but no more likely than it is now, because checks and balances will be preserved. There is simply no evidence that direct initiatives lead to tyranny and oppression, and much evidence to the contrary. And it goes without saying that greater popular participation gives the people power to end injustices that have long been ignored by capitalist, representative government. As Arthur Miller said, "Socialism was reason."[11]

Another concern about popular democracy is how well the system would work. For instance, today bills are introduced by politicians and go through multiple committees, where representatives of different political views research, discuss, and modify them. If a bill makes it out of committee, it goes to the House or Senate floor for debate and more changes, amendments, before finally being voted on. With direct initiative rights, aren't we sacrificing this crucially important vetting and compromise process? Furthermore, are ordinary people knowledgeable and experienced enough to craft laws?

Let's address the first point. While a "vetting and compromise process" is valuable in theory, in practice all it means today is congressional gridlock and the resultant death of most bills. Only 1 to 5 percent of the many thousands of bills introduced in each Congress become law.[12] Most bills die in committee, never making it to the debate floor.[13] This is not because they are all bad bills, but because the two political parties can't agree on anything. The system is so broken that a congressional majority leader—one person—can simply refuse to schedule a vote on a bill.[14] The direct initiative process does in fact have its own vetting mechanisms, but they are much simpler and align far better with the will of the people. If an initiative petition cannot garner enough support, it dies. If a question makes it to the ballot and is not reflective of what most people want, it will fail. Overall, vetting lies in the discussion and debate surrounding proposed legislation before the vote, as citizens of different opinions study the bill, weigh in, and try to convince others to vote this way or that.

The second question, concerning the competencies of the people to design law, is not a significant concern when we consider the initiative process.[15] Because filing the legal paperwork, gathering enough petition signatures, and getting out the vote is not an easy task, it is usually undertaken by political advocacy groups, grassroots organizations, non-profits, and so on. It's a serious undertaking, and all involved must be careful to craft legislation that will not immediately be thrown out by the courts as unconstitutional. Thus, those launching an initiative typically have help from lawyers and allies with political experience to write sensible, and legible, legislation for the people to vote on. It's a collaborative effort. This functions well in practice, both in this country and around the world.

The United States already uses initiative rights and the popular vote to pass or reject legislation at the city and state levels. State-wide ballot questions are legal in twenty-four states, some of which are quite large, such as California (40 million people) and Florida (21 million).[16] (Some states use indirect initiatives, which force a legislature to vote on citizen-crafted bills.) In the November 2016 election, 150 ballot measures were voted on, representing a wide range of topics. California, Nevada, and Massachusetts approved recreational marijuana use, while voters in Arizona rejected it; Arizona, Colorado, Maine, and Washington raised their minimum wages; Nebraska restored the death penalty, while California kept it and Oklahoma made it harder to get rid of; Colorado legalized medically assisted suicide; California, Washington, and Nevada tightened gun laws, while Maine shot down stricter gun control; Oregon, Washington, Colorado, Missouri, and North Dakota rejected tax increases.[17] (It's no surprise when looking at this list that even some conservatives favor popular democracy.)[18] The US is not alone in this, as the Canadian province of British Columbia, German and Indian states, and countless other states and cities around the world also enjoy initiative rights.[19]

And this is not a new phenomenon, as popular democracy has existed in local government throughout human history, from the city-state of Athens, Greece in the fifth century B.C. to the town hall meetings of American colonial times to Porto Alegre, Brazil, today.[20] In fact, since 1989, Porto Alegre, a Brazilian city of 1.5 million people, has allowed participatory budgeting. Citizens there are involved in the design of the annual city budget, and everyone has the right to vote to approve or strike down the finished product. Since this idea—pushed forward by socialists—was enacted, funds have shifted dramatically to poorer, high-need areas of the city. The process is also marked by transparency and lack of corruption.[21] Participatory budgeting has also been launched in varying degrees in large US cities such as New York and Chicago, and in many other municipalities around the globe.[22]

There are even countries that use direct initiatives at the federal level. Switzerland, a nation of nine million, began its national initiative process in 1891. Since then, twenty-two initiatives have been passed, from over 200 ballot questions. In 2016, for instance, the populace rejected a law to give each citizen a guaranteed income. The country also has a parliament that passes laws; the country is a semi-direct democracy (the people, however, can veto legislation parliament passes). Popular votes take place at most four times annually. Changes to the nation's constitution require majority support from the people and from the cantons (states).[23] While the Swiss majority has at times passed prejudiced, oppressive laws, the Human Freedom Index, published by conservative and libertarian institutes, nevertheless ranks the country as the freest nation in the world.[24] It is also among the most stable countries, and has more wealth per adult than any other nation, including the US.[25] The Philippines, the European Union, and other federal bodies likewise have initiative rights—while not without challenges, they are steps in the right direction.[26] Overall, 113 of the world's 117 democracies give citizens the right to vote on national initiatives or referenda (questions sent to the people by the legislature); some of these nations, like Brazil, have hundreds of millions of citizens. One of the four democracies without these rights is the United States.

Many studies point to the benefits of popular democracy, and dispel the myth that it is ruinous for a nation.[27] For example, the process itself boosts the belief of the people that they can make a difference and that government works for them, which leads to a happier and more politically engaged and educated populace (which in turn correlates with higher voter turnout).[28] Citizens who choose to vote are typically competent and well-informed, and those who are not tend to use information shortcuts that lead them to vote the same way as better-informed persons.[29] It is at times suggested that voters are too ill-informed to vote directly on public policy, but this is not the case—and if voters cannot be trusted to make such decisions, how can they be trusted to choose policymakers to adequately represent them?

The initiative mechanism also pushes legislatures to better align with constituent wishes—representatives know that if they don't act according to the public will, the people may enact policies on their own.[30] There is even evidence the initiative system can lead to more efficient, less wasteful government and faster economic growth.[31] Government officials are more careful and cost-effective with resources when decisions are made by the people, or when the threat of being overruled by the people exists.[32] More efficient State services and projects benefit the economy as a whole.[33] Further, while some critics of expanded democracy believe voters will pass laws without paying for them—such as directing more money to public schools without a tax increase—studies suggest voters are in fact more conservative with public funds than representatives. (Perhaps that's because it's their money.) In Switzerland, the expansion of democracy has been linked to decreases in government spending.[34] The same is true for US states with initiative rights.[35] In California, initiatives have not impeded the state's ability to raise revenue to cover costs.[36] (At the end of 2018, the state had a massive surplus.)[37] In short, such a political system doesn't automatically mean runaway spending (also, with this country's current $22 trillion debt, it's hard to say our representatives are preferable in this area).

While you won't always get what you want with a popular vote, you will, no matter your beliefs, have a voice. And things will get done. No politicians gridlocked in committee. No representatives on the voting floor following the whims of their biggest donors. Just ordinary people creating real change for themselves. "I'm a socialist," one of H.G. Wells' characters from *In the Days of the Comet* said. "I don't think this world was made for a small minority to dance on the faces of every one else."[38]

Participatory democracy is not perfect, by any means. For example, though the influence of money is weakened, individuals and organizations with more resources and time may nevertheless have an easier path to placing something on the ballot for a popular vote.[39] Likewise, more powerful special interests can better use media platforms to argue their case or even to try and deceive the populace. Rules for the length and readability of bills would need to be enforced, especially for referenda from Congress. Yet despite its imperfections, popular democracy gives the people the ability to achieve the societal changes we are exploring in this book: worker ownership; protection of the planet; rejection of war; abolition of poverty, and so on. As Mark Twain once asked, "Why is it right that there is not a fairer division of the spoil all around? Because laws and constitutions have ordered otherwise. Then it follows that laws and constitutions should change around and say there shall be a more nearly equal division."[40]

Establishing a semi-direct, referendum democracy or a true direct democracy would be revolutionary. Regarding the first option, allowing citizens to introduce and vote on their own bills, alongside approving or rejecting all bills crafted by city councils, state legislatures, and the US Congress, would be an enormous change after nearly 250 years of representative democracy. A direct democracy would go further, abolishing these institutions as we know them and leaving the people as the sole designers of the law—while necessarily preserving support institutions, like the Congressional Budget Office, General Accounting Office, and Library of Congress, to aid the people, and shifting some oversight responsibilities to the executive cabinet. Both systems eliminate one check and balance: today a bill must pass both House and Senate to see the light of day, while these new systems replace them with one chamber, the people. (There are countries, such as Denmark, Luxemburg, Sweden, Finland, Israel, and New Zealand, which function just fine with one house, a unicameral congress.)[41] Importantly, either system is possible—as with Orwell and his motor cars, or those who could never envision the end of monarchism, it's unwise to find the impossible in the unknowable future.

Support for and use of popular democracy is already climbing quickly in the United States, with the number of citizen initiatives doubling from 2014 to 2016, and 67 percent of Americans regarding direct votes on national issues to be a good way of running the country.[42] The more dissatisfied people become with the unresponsive, dysfunctional system of today, the more they desire the "open democracy" Ralph

Waldo Emerson observed in Concord, Massachusetts, which gave "every individual his fair weight in government . . . Here the rich gave counsel, but the poor also."[43]

It is important to note that the end of representative government under socialism does not mean the end of all representatives. Rather, it eliminates representative voting power in the legislative branch. The judicial and executive branches will remain comprised of appointed or elected public officials like Supreme Court justices, federal judges, cabinet members, and intelligence agency leaders, who can be confirmed by the people instead of Congress, after public hearings. This is necessary not only to preserve checks and balances, but also for a functioning government that can carry out the public policies the people vote on.

However, some reforms are needed in that area to create more accountability and ensure a government of, by, and for the people. For instance, the Electoral College must be abolished to ensure that the presidential candidate with the most support wins, as with every other election in the US, and presidential elections in the majority of the world's democracies. Candidates for president, governor, mayor, and so on will either enjoy publicly financed elections, receiving equal taxpayer funds to run their campaigns, or rely on small donations from individuals. Co-ops and organizations should not be able to give to candidates, to avoid quid pro quo politics. Personal donations would be strictly limited, so all citizens would have the same influence. A $50 cap for each American adult during the presidential race, for instance, means almost $12 billion for candidates to compete for.

Under a semi-direct, referendum democracy, this principle would also apply to House and Senate members—they may not have voting power, but special interests cannot be allowed to influence the design of legislation. As with elections for executive offices, multiple parties would have equal ballot and debate access, and candidates would be voted on via ranked-choice systems, in districts free of gerrymandering and voter suppression. Under a direct democracy, we may be forced on special occasions to elect representatives for investigative committees and other non-legislative tasks the populace cannot complete, and these representatives will also run publicly financed campaigns or receive small donations from individuals.

Finally, the people must be given recall rights, allowing a supermajority to remove an elected or appointed official for poor behavior. In the same way Congress has the power to impeach and remove presidents, Supreme Court justices, federal judges, cabinet members, and other civil officers today, the citizenry will have that authority under socialism. Nineteen US states already allow constituents to recall elected state officials; city and county politicians can be kicked out of office in thirty states.[44] This mechanism likewise exists around the world. The threat of recall will keep public officials in line at every level of government, from mayors and sheriffs to state supreme court justices and governors to intelligence agency heads and presidents. That gives, as John Lennon sang, "Power to the People."

Ten

THE SOCIALIST LIFE

WHILE LIVING IN A SOCIALIST SOCIETY would mean awakening each workday and heading to your co-op, while also regularly visiting your voting place to help decide local and national policies, government services are still necessary to fill in any potential economic or social gaps. What if, for instance, you could not find a job? Just because all workplaces are democratic and share profits does not mean there will always be enough jobs for everyone. Thus, some State mechanism is required if the dream of prosperity and dignity for all is to be achieved. We need, as Oscar Wilde insisted, to make it so poverty is impossible, and to end the horrors of what Arthur Miller labeled "failing capitalism."[1] Jack London proposed we "socialize distribution."[2] We will begin with the two paths forward that Dr. King boldly outlined: "We must create full employment, or we must create incomes."[3]

Let's first consider a guaranteed income, or a universal basic income (UBI). A UBI entails using tax revenue to send a regular check to each citizen; in short, it's a simple redistribution of wealth to eradicate poverty and provide security during times of unemployment or underemployment. There has been support for some form of UBI in America since colonial times. Thomas Paine advocated for a one-time universal payment for young people, wanting "to create a National Fund, out of which there shall be paid to every person, when arrived at the age of twenty-one years, the sum of fifteen pounds sterling."[4] He also said that ten pounds should go to each person over fifty every year. This was the right thing to do, Paine believed, because land used to be "the common property of the human race," but the system of land ownership had stolen that "natural inheritance" from most everyone, and therefore owners owed "ground-rent" to non-owners to compensate for the loss.

To a degree, a UBI already exists in the United States. For example, Alaska has given $1,000 to $2,000 a year to every resident without condition since 1982.[5] Hawaii may soon follow suit.[6] The Eastern Band of the Cherokee Nation launched its own UBI in 1996, and today gives $10,000 annually to each of its members.[7] On the global stage, Iran, from 2010 to 2016, had the world's first national UBI, giving each family the equivalent of $16,300 a year.[8] In 2011, Kuwait gave $3,500 to each citizen.[9] In 2017, Macau, a region of China, gave over $1,100 a year to each permanent resident.[10] That same year, experiments with UBI launched or were preparing to launch in Finland, Canada, Kenya, Uganda, the Netherlands, Scotland, Spain, and the US.[11] Canada has also had prior experience with such trials, as have India, Brazil, Namibia, and other countries. The models range from everyone getting the same amount of money to poorer recipients getting more. Even some prominent conservative and libertarian economists support a UBI program, because its simplicity could do away with more complex welfare systems.[12] Charles Murray, a conservative social scientist, has written about giving everyone $10,000 a year.[13]

The benefits of a UBI have been clearly demonstrated. Trials in some of India's towns that began in 2011 show huge success in improving children's education, access to food and healthcare, as well as the number of new business startups.[14] Becoming an entrepreneur or going back to school is easier with supplemented income, loosening the restraints of social class. A basic income also provides greater freedom to care for children (especially among single parents), the sick, and the elderly. Parenting and housework are at last compensated. Studies indicate that when people have the financial security that a UBI can provide, they spend more time taking care of family and focusing on education, and are able to win higher raises at work because they have a real alternative to employment.[15] This bargaining power can in turn improve working conditions in general, from hours to safety. When citizens are given money, crime and drug and alcohol use decrease, while more people invest in schooling, medical care, and other needed services.[16] (Contrary to myth, giving poor people cash tends to have no impact on, or even reduces, alcohol and tobacco consumption.)[17] We need, as John Stuart Mill said in his praise of socialism, to manage "distribution [and ensure] a certain minimum is first assigned for the subsistence of every member of the community, whether capable or not of labour."[18]

In terms of expense, Dr. King made a point about our national priorities in 1967 when he said that "a guaranteed annual income could be done" for less than the cost of the war in Vietnam and the moon landing.[19] The cost of a UBI in today's America would depend on several factors: how much would be guaranteed, whether everyone would receive it (should it be truly universal, with even the wealthy getting something?), if those living in more expensive areas would receive more, and the like. Ten thousand a year for all 240 million American adults would come to $2.4 trillion, whereas $5,000 a year to the poorest 75 million would be $375 billion. (The actual structure must be progressive, with a graduated scale of payments that provides the poor with the most and the better off with the least.) The net cost of such a program, however, would likely be lower, as giving citizens billions or trillions of dollars' worth of purchasing power would put the economy into over-drive, enriching co-ops (leading to more jobs and even more consum-ers) and thus increasing government tax revenues. Dr. King believed that guaranteed income or work would create more and stronger con-sumers, and many of today's economists agree with him.[20] One study estimated giving each American adult $1,000 a month would grow the economy 12 to 13 percent over eight years, if employment remained steady.[21] A UBI may seem expensive, but it also increases State revenues for the program as a result of economic growth, through taxes on work-place profits, sales taxes on consumers, and other mechanisms.

Now, a common concern raised by those who oppose a UBI is that it will cause people to stop working, leaving the worker-owners stuck supporting the easy lifestyle of the "lazy." Regarding this issue, most studies show no effect or only a small decline in employment under a UBI.[22] A study of Alaska found that employment levels weren't affect-ed.[23] In France, the disincentive to work among guaranteed income recipients was gone after several months.[24] A study of Iran's massive UBI revealed that while some people worked a bit less, others actu-ally worked more.[25] (The extra income circulating in the economy means more hiring and additional hours offered to workers.) India's basic income grants led to more labor participation, as did Uganda's.[26] Namibia saw no negative effects on labor participation.[27] Granted, most of these studies looked at small UBIs, just supplemental incomes, but they suggest the size of the problem may not be as great as some predict.

More importantly, however, as we saw in chapter three, at some point in the human future, automation will essentially make labor a thing of the past, highlighting the need for collective ownership of the machines and State-provided incomes or work. So we will eventually have to give up our agitation over people who do not work (rather, poor- or middle-income people who do not work; critics seem less concerned about wealthy individuals who already enjoy work-free lives). A future where technology can serve our every need is one where work is optional and done solely for enjoyment. Therefore, if a UBI is enacted, there is going to be a transition period over the decades or centuries. As technology advances and the UBI increases, fewer human beings will be needed to do society's tasks and more will choose to enjoy lives without work.

Guaranteed work is a more complex program than a universal basic income, but avoids the concerns associated with lower labor participation, as there would be a job for everyone. In a society offering guaranteed work, tax revenue would be transferred to municipalities to create salaries for unemployed or underemployed people. Local governments would then use these funds to launch public work projects to improve their communities (what projects are chosen would be a local democratic decision, of course). So, for example, if a city has 50,000 people looking for work at the start of the year, it might receive $2 billion, to offer a $40,000 salary to each person. If the US had eight million unemployed people, a standard number, it would cost $320 billion to employ them—half our modern military budget. As with a UBI, broadening purchasing power would reduce the net cost of guaranteed work through increased tax revenues. A well-structured program could be wholly funded by the revenues it creates from a more dynamic economy.[28] Thomas Paine advocated public buildings with "as many kinds of employment as can be contrived, so that every person who shall come may find something which he or she can do."[29] He understood that guaranteed work could empower the individual and reduce crime, as did Ralph Waldo Emerson, who urged the government to give each person "a pair of acres, to enable him to get his bread honestly," and Jack London, who said socialism meant everyone was born "free and with equal opportunities to earn by honest labor—mental or physical—a livelihood."[30]

Under a guaranteed work system, employment could be directed toward tasks that are essential to societal well-being, such as rebuilding crumbling inner cities, installing solar panels on homes, planting trees, tutoring struggling students, spending time with neglected seniors—literally any task that betters society in some way. This would orient "production to the needs of the community, would distribute the work to be done among all those able to work and would guarantee a livelihood to every man, woman, and child," as Albert Einstein wanted. Under capitalism, needed work often goes undone because it's not profitable—even while millions of people need a job. Guaranteed work corrects this. Further, because not all positive tasks require physical labor, the program would be inclusive of persons with disabilities or seniors who want to work (though this is obviously not intended to replace social security or disability insurance, which could only be replaced by a UBI). Nelson Mandela wrote that he "subscribed to Marx's basic dictum, which has the simplicity and generosity of the Golden Rule: 'From each according to his ability, to each according to his needs.'"[31]

Cities and other municipalities will need more funds than just those for salaries, however. Some projects under a guaranteed work program will be relatively cheap, like cleaning trash off the streets or caring for children, while others will be more costly, like renovating an old school or building a new library. Extra funds could be fixed to unemployment levels, so that the areas with the most need have the greatest capacity to create change. Using their allotted monies, communities could contract with local co-ops to supply equipment and raw materials for necessary ventures. As projects wrap up, public workers could receive help securing employment at cooperatives. Co-ops could also receive government contracts to do certain projects, as capitalist businesses receive today, with increased employment stipulations. Alternatively, local governments could organize unemployed persons into new cooperatives, helping fund endeavors during the critical first few years until they became self-sustaining. If there was a need for greater production in a certain sector, from agriculture to social work, that need could be met with new co-ops. This could also help address monopolizing sectors.

Overall, one should not think of guaranteed public work as dooming private business. This is not the nationalization of industries, as State enterprises are competing alongside private worker cooperatives or doing tasks that businesses aren't interested in because little financial reward is possible. In addition, rather than shrink the private sector, guaranteed work programs can actually expand it and increase its wages—fewer unemployed persons means more spenders, benefiting businesses and allowing them to expand; one prediction estimated a public jobs program for eleven million to sixteen million people would increase private sector jobs by a count of four million, while increasing the GDP by up to $560 billion.[32] "I am a socialist," Helen Keller said, "because I believe that socialism will solve the misery of the world— give work to the man who is hungry and idle ..."[33]

Of course, there is already a prominent historical precedent for guaranteed work in the United States, the New Deal under President Franklin Roosevelt. During the Great Depression, Roosevelt's Works Progress Administration, Civil Works Administration, and Civilian Conservation Corps hired some 15.5 million people to build roads, bridges, schools, hospitals, museums, and zoos; to garden, plant trees, fight fires, reseed land, save wildlife, and sew; and to undertake art, music, drama, education, writing, and literacy projects. Resuming a program of this type would certainly please the ghost of socialist Jules Verne, who envisioned a dystopian capitalist future where only corporate concerns had any value to human beings, and thus the arts, literature, and music have disappeared: an "instrument no longer suffices to feed the instrumentalist! Talk about a trade that's not practical. Ah, if we could use the power wasted on the pedals of a piano for pumping water out of coal mines!"[34] H.G. Wells saw the New Deal as true socialism in action.[35] Woody Guthrie praised the building of the Grand Coulee Dam, in a song by that name: "Uncle Sam took up the challenge in the year of '33 / For the farmer and the factory and for all of you and me." While not without its challenges, the New Deal saved many people from hunger, strengthened the consumer class and thus the economy, and beautified the country.[36]

Similar federal initiatives have occurred since the time of FDR. Construction of the Interstate Highway System in the 1950s and 1960s entailed the federal government providing funding to the states, which either expanded their public workforces or contracted with private companies. The Comprehensive Employment and Training Act, approved by President Nixon in 1973 to aid the poor and jobless, employed 750,000 people by 1978.[37] Today, at the local level, cities like San Diego, Albuquerque, Tempe, Fort Worth, Reno, Chicago, Denver, Portland, and Los Angeles offer jobs to the homeless to help them out of the social pit.[38] There's currently much excitement over Alexandria Ocasio-Cortez's "Green New Deal" proposal. Speaking more generally, however, government employment is something we take for granted. Local governments across the US already employ 14.1 million people, in education, healthcare, fire and policing, financing and administration, transportation, library services, utilities, environment, recreation—and public works. States employ another five million, and the federal government employs over 2.5 million civilians and over two million military personnel.[39]

In addition, many local and national governments around the world run similar jobs programs. India is pouring billions into the Mahatma Gandhi National Rural Employment Guarantee Act (MGNREGA), which gives residents of poor, rural states one hundred days of guaranteed work annually.[40] Fifty million households and 170 million people are involved in what is the largest public works program in world history.[41] The program has been very successful, hugely alleviating poverty.[42] Argentina's Jefes de Hogar program paid the heads of households with children, persons with disabilities, or pregnant women to do construction, maintenance work, or community service. Two million Argentinians, 5 percent of the country's population, were employed at the program's height.[43] South Africa's Expanded Public Works Program includes government jobs in infrastructure, tourism, environment, early childhood education, and more.[44] There is nothing to stop the US from developing "a federal program of public works, retraining, and jobs for all," as Dr. King envisioned.[45]

One criticism of guaranteed work is that it will cause unemployment to drop too low, creating inflation. The thinking goes that if unemployment is eliminated, businesses will have to compete for fewer workers, driving wages up, which will in turn increase costs to compensate, which will lead to higher wage demands, creating an unending upward wage-price spiral. However, this is not actually a grave concern. First, the correlation between unemployment and inflation is not terribly strong: sometimes they move in opposite directions, sometimes they move together.[46] Many mainstream economists have acknowledged that the relationship is weak or nonexistent.[47] More workers doesn't necessarily mean higher prices. Rather, the increased profits from more consumer spending (less unemployment) allows firms to absorb higher wage costs without raising prices by any significant degree. This is similar to how increases in the minimum wage create only miniscule increases in prices, if any, and don't increase unemployment: extra money is spent at businesses, boosting their profits, balancing the system out.[48] Many economists have argued persuasively that, contrary to William Phillips, Milton Friedman, and others, full employment can be achieved without inflation.[49] Some among them even argue it has a stabilizing effect on prices.[50] After all, we'd have more stable demand, without long stretches of unemployment hurting consumer spending.

There are other realities that would keep inflation in check under a guaranteed work system. For example, more production of goods and services through the public sector would increase supply and thus pull prices down.[51] In addition, the various tactics the State currently uses to control inflation would still exist.[52] In practice, skyrocketing inflation has been a nonissue in places where a guaranteed work program has been put in place. The Reserve Bank of India found that the MGNREGA program did not raise food prices.[53] Programs in the US, Sweden, France, and Argentina likewise did not lead to inflation.[54] Such efforts are not incompatible with declines in inflation, either—again, the correlation is not strong. Argentina's inflation rate was extremely high in 2002, the year its works program began, but declined and remained relatively low past 2007, when the program ended, until 2013.[55] South Africa's ongoing program began in 2004; inflation grew by over 10 percent by 2009, during an economic crisis, but then fell and remained low through 2019.[56] We should also note that studies of Alaska, Kuwait,

Lebanon, Mexico, India, and African nations have shown that a small UBI does not cause inflation, either.[57]

A UBI or guaranteed work system would have other significant effects on society, too, such as replacing many forms of welfare, and freeing people from the fear of quitting a job they do not enjoy or is unsafe.[58] Further, like the broader prosperity that comes with worker ownership, always having access to a paycheck serves as an "economic shock absorber" that can reduce the effects of economic crises.[59] But no effect compares to the total abolition of poverty. Coretta Scott King, who once gave her husband the utopian socialist novel *Looking Backward*, declared: "Every man deserves a right to a job or an income."[60] "Overcoming poverty is not a task of charity, it is an act of justice," Nelson Mandela said. "Like Slavery and Apartheid, poverty is not natural. It is man-made and it can be overcome and eradicated by the actions of human beings."[61]

"Doesn't anything socialistic make you want to throw up?" quipped socialist Kurt Vonnegut. "Like great public schools or health insurance for all?"[62] H.G. Wells said leaving medical care and education to the free market was a recipe for disaster.[63]

As we've seen, the problem with capitalism is that goods and services are distributed according to purchasing power, not need. Demand is based on consumer spending, with supply going to those who can afford the commodity. Those who cannot afford it are ignored by the entire system. For example, while the world produces enough food to feed everyone, dire hunger persists; the United States has more than enough empty homes, yet a large homeless population; and so on.[64] In short, there's a massive waste of available necessities under capitalism. (It should also be noted that the system's supply doesn't even follow the monetary demand that efficiently; for instance, US grocery stores throw away some forty-three billion pounds of food each year.)[65] This is the "economic anarchy" that Einstein bluntly called "evil." H.G. Wells asked if it was true that there "isn't enough food or care to go round, and hence the unavoidable anxiety in the life of every one (except in the case of a small minority of exceptionally secure people) . . . ? The Socialist says, No! He asserts that our economic system is . . . chaotic and wasteful . . ."[66] Ralph Waldo Emerson found it "cruel that every man . . . saint though he be . . . should find himself in this most awkward relation to loaves of bread. And the promise of Socialism is to redress this distorted balance."[67]

Guaranteed income or work, coupled with a strong minimum wage, make this problem largely disappear, as everyone has purchasing power. However, healthcare is one service that could remain prohibitively expensive, as an exorbitant medical bill could still cause financial ruin or leave someone with the inability to pay—even if healthcare providers are co-ops. It would be best, as Bernie Sanders advocates, to make private insurers obsolete and have State-run universal coverage in which taxes cover everyone's medical needs. This does not mean the State will own the hospitals and employ the doctors. Instead, the reverse would be true—the doctors, nurses, receptionists, and janitors (the workers) would own the clinics and hospitals. Under socialism, an individual in need of care would simply go to a healthcare co-op of their choosing, which would then send his or her bill to the government.

Critics of universal healthcare don't always understand that there are multiple paths to achieving it. There's the Beveridge Model, in which the government owns and runs hospitals (Britain, Spain, Hong Kong, and others operate under this system, as well as US Veterans

Affairs hospitals). The Bismark Model entails private insurance funds that employers and employees pay into, like in the US, but insurers are strictly not-for-profit and compelled to cover all citizens and their medical needs (a system used in Germany, Japan, and Switzerland). With a National Health Insurance Model, or single-payer system, the government operates an insurance pool funded by taxes and pays the healthcare bills of citizens (Canada, South Korea, and Taiwan).[68] This is how popular, efficient, and effective US programs like Medicare and Medicaid operate, hence the recent calls for "Medicare For All." In some single-payer countries, like Denmark, Sweden, and Finland, everything is done locally, with taxes for healthcare going to city and county governments, not the federal government.[69] Many nations even provide free care to visitors, such as Germany, which has had a universal system for 125 years.[70] Universal healthcare systems are far more popular in the nations that have them than the free-for-all system US citizens currently endure.[71]

Now, a myth exists that healthcare costs for providers—everything a hospital needs to purchase, like MRI machines or anesthetics or scalpels—will rise if consumer care is subsidized. It's said that manufacturers will charge more because they think hospitals will simply pass any bigger bill on to the State. However, even under socialism, manufacturers will still need to offer competitive prices because hospital budgets will not be unlimited—they will still depend on how many people come through the door for help, which determines State funding. Hospitals and clinics will still seek the best quality products at the lowest price to stay within budget. Also, if hospital funds still rely on the number of patients, the incentive will be to keep quality of service up and innovation going. This is also why public schools don't face skyrocketing prices for pencils, paper, desks, computers, and smartboards—they do not have a blank check, and must still seek out affordable purchases, forcing manufacturing companies to compete for their dollars.

Evidence from around the world has shown that it is not more expensive to care for people in single-payer systems. In fact, it's cheaper. Hospitals in comparable advanced democracies with universal care spend far less per patient than US hospitals.[72] They also spend less on needed purchases, like pharmaceuticals and medical devices—and citizen use of hospitals is essentially the same; the systems are not being overloaded.[73] By contrast, healthcare spending—all the goods and services proffered by the industry to keep people healthy and alive—is nearly 18 percent of GDP in the US, higher than nations with universal healthcare.[74] And not everyone is covered under the free market American system.

The current US system is in fact the world's most expensive per person—and underperforms in areas like efficiency, equity, access, and many other health outcomes compared to nations that spend less on healthcare and insure every citizen.[75] Entities like the World Health Organization, the Legatum Institute, and the Commonwealth Fund that rank healthcare systems consistently put the US below Europe, Canada, Japan, and others.[76] Hospitals, individuals, and employers are paying more in this country for healthcare, and getting less than they would under a tax-based State insurance system. That's why some Americans leave the country for more affordable care. An Indiana man, Michael Shopenn, underwent hip replacement surgery in Belgium in 2007, which cost just under $14,000—airfare included—compared to the $100,000 the same procedure would have cost in the US.[77] In total, 1.4 million Americans went abroad for medical care in 2017, saving between 20 to 90 percent on their healthcare bills. Even members of Congress do so: the free market libertarian Rand Paul went to Canada to have hernia surgery in 2019.[78]

All this is not to say that rising healthcare costs are not a serious concern. It is simply to recognize that the problem is less severe under universal healthcare. Cost increases are caused by multiple factors in private and public systems alike, but there are significant ways universal healthcare can lower costs for hospitals and patients. For one, research comparing the American and Canadian health care systems reveals that having a single place where all bills are sent saves colossal amounts of money in administrative and overhead costs.[79] The US devotes a much higher percentage of its healthcare spending to administrative and governance costs than comparable nations.[80] However, Medicare's administrative costs are just 2 percent of total costs; American private insurance companies pay over six times more.[81] Universal care also frees providers from having to spend so much on advertising: private insurers spend 15 percent of their budgets on advertising, whereas a public system spends almost nothing.[82] In terms of prescription drugs, the US spends two to six times more for the same medicines because of the lack of government regulations other nations have.[83] Finally, some problems can be caught earlier and more expensive solutions avoided when people aren't afraid to see a doctor due to cost or lack of insurance.

Some advocates of capitalism also believe that innovation will be lost with universal healthcare. The US is indeed a leader in pharmaceutical and medical technology research and development, churning out the most patents, Nobel Prize winners, and so forth. But the population of this country is enormous, so such a comparison is inappropriate. Of course a country with 325 million people will create a larger collection of useful innovations than one of sixty-seven million (France) or nine million (Switzerland), and spend more collectively. If you examine Nobel Prizes in physiology and medicine in terms of awards per one million citizens, however, the US is beaten out by Denmark,

Switzerland, Sweden, Austria, the UK, Norway, and Germany.[84] It's also behind these nations and several others in terms of all science awards, which include physiology and medicine, per capita.[85] The UK, Switzerland, and a few other countries actually outperform the US in developing new pharmaceuticals when you compare research and development spending as a proportion of GDP.[86]

Other countries are also just as innovative. The European Union's ratio of pharmaceutical patents to all patents is slightly higher than that of the US.[87] Regarding applications for international patents of medical technologies, in 2015, two of the three companies that filed for the most were in Japan and the Netherlands (the third being in the United States).[88] A Swiss pharmaceutical company filed for more patents than any company in any industry. The previous year, Japan filed for half the number of medical technology patents the US did, with less than half the population.[89] In 2013, the Netherlands filed for one-tenth the medical tech patents of the US, despite having less than one-eighteenth the population.[90] In 2014, the Swiss to American drug patents ratio was 1:12; the population ratio was 1:40.[91] With the same population disparity, Israeli to American drug patents was 1:26.[92] In all industries, the World Economic Forum ranks the US as the second-most innovative nation, beat out by Switzerland and followed closely by Israel, northern and central Europe, and Japan; Bloomberg puts the US at number eleven, behind a host of "socialist" countries.[93]

All this makes a great deal of sense, as the individual motives and larger structures for advances in the field still exist in a universal healthcare system. Pioneers at research universities still seek to better the world or make names for themselves, companies still want to sell new medicines, equipment, and software (even if using taxpayer reimbursement dollars), and so forth. In addition, Research & Development funding from the government and private investors don't vanish when the State pays citizen medical bills.

In other areas of medicine, like quality and effectiveness of care, things are essentially even. Some duties the US does better, some duties other countries do better—and sometimes there are no differences.[94] For instance, hospital wait times. While the US typically has shorter wait times in some areas of healthcare, like elective surgery and specialty care, in other areas they are far longer, such as getting an appointment with your doctor when you're sick, a key to fixing problems before they worsen.[95] So, while you can get quick elective surgery and specialty care in the US—quicker than in Canada or the UK—you can get it fastest in Germany or France.[96] Access to after-hours care is also superior elsewhere.[97] There are plenty of countries with universal care where wait times are not a serious issue, while others that are struggling have taken steps to reduce wait times, quite successfully.[98] Like costs, wait times are impacted by many factors in both private and public systems (for instance, US wait times for cancer treatment increased between 1995 and 2005 as hospital caseloads increased.)[99] It is not the case that universal healthcare automatically means longer waits than free market systems, even with increased utilization. In the US, most expansions of Medicaid have not resulted in increased wait periods or worse quality of care.[100] Even Veterans Administration wait times, despite the extra media attention on the frustrations, are the same as for non-VA care.[101] Longer waits increase mortality rates in any healthcare system, and while some people do die from preventable deaths in countries with universal care, the point is that many countries with universal healthcare have wait times shorter or equal to the United States—and a higher percentage of the US population dies from preventable problems compared to other countries (whether with long wait times or not) because they have no insurance.[102] The free market system, which rations care based on purchasing power or how decent a job you have, is simply a deadlier system—and the goal of socialism is not a perfect world, but a better one.

It's estimated that universal healthcare would cost the US $3 trillion per year, less than the $3.5 trillion Americans spend annually on healthcare today in the forms of out-of-pocket care, private insurance purchased by individuals and businesses, and taxes for Medicare, Medicaid, etc.[103] Converting spending in the private sphere to new taxes for comprehensive coverage is a trade-off that can save individuals and companies money, resulting in an economic stimulus.[104] Even a Koch-funded libertarian think tank like the Mercatus Center calculated that Medicare For All would save $2 trillion over ten years compared to the current state of affairs.[105] This finding has been backed up by other analyses and studies, one putting the savings of the same Medicare For All plan at $5 trillion over ten years.[106] (Research of single-payer plans for California, New York, Minnesota, and many other states found the same cost-saving effects.[107] New York City is now enacting a universal program.)[108] What this means is that while your taxes may go up under a universal system, the more expensive insurance costs would be abolished, resulting in a net income gain for most people.[109]

Indeed, the common hysteria among ordinary people over crushing universal healthcare taxes is largely misplaced. If you look at other advanced democracies with universal coverage, some indeed have higher income tax rates than the United States (20 to 24 percent higher in places like Germany, Denmark, and Belgium), but many are about the same or lower. An individual making an average salary in the UK has a rate only 3 percent higher than one in America. A single person in New Zealand pays 4 percent less; 7 percent less in Israel. In the Czech Republic, couples with two children pay a tax rate half of what a US couple pays. South Koreans owe a tad less than Americans whether citizens have children or not. Higher-income earners in Germany and South Korea actually take home larger portions of their income than higher-income Americans.[110] If you made the equivalent of $100,000 a year, your income and social security taxes would be lower in Switzerland, the Czech Republic, and Hong Kong; if you made three times that, you'd still be better off in the last two nations—and get guaranteed healthcare.[111]

Further, other prosperous societies like Canada and New Zealand have lower top income tax rates than the US.[112] Nearly every nation in Europe, and around the world, has a lower corporate tax rate.[113] (And lower debt-to-GDP ratios; they don't just borrow to fund the programs.)[114] Of course, there are many forms of taxes beyond income and corporate, so if you look at all forms together, US citizens pay more in taxes as a GDP percentage (26 percent) than countries like Ireland and South Korea, just a couple percentage points less than Switzerland and Australia, and six to eight percent less than Israel, Canada, Japan, the UK, New Zealand, and Spain.[115] In other words, there are countries with quality universal healthcare that pay less, the same, or just slightly more than the United States in taxes.

Overall, the conversation on costs cannot end without the obvious being stated: the United States is the richest nation in the history of the world. If other countries can survive and thrive while providing medical care to their entire population, so can America. This country must simply start siding with ordinary people, not profit-hungry insurance companies. John Lennon believed that

> there are only two things to be, basically: You are either for
> the labor movement or for the capitalist movement. Either

you become a right-wing Archie Bunker if you are in the class I am in, or you become an instinctive socialist, which I was. That meant I think people should get their false teeth and their health looked after, all the rest of it.[116]

Like healthcare, education should not be a commodity that people cannot access due to lack of income. After all, two years at a community college and two at an in-state university in the US costs $30,000 on average, just for tuition.[117] Even with a UBI or jobs guarantee, sending a family member to college without incurring large debts would be difficult—imagine sending two, three, or more. And while public K through 12 schools are already free, because of discrepancies in property taxes, test scores, and state funding, poor inner-city neighborhoods often get dismal schools, while rich suburban neighborhoods get very fine ones, as we saw earlier. Under socialism, schools would be funded equitably, according to need.

A socialist society would include free K through 12 education, preschool (which offers significant individual and societal benefits),[118] and college. Countries like Brazil, Denmark, Germany, Finland, Greece, Ireland, Mexico, Norway, and Poland have already done away with university tuition; other nations, like France, Columbia, Austria, and Switzerland, barely charge anything.[119] Danish students are in fact paid to attend college.[120] Understandably, some Americans move to Europe for a free or near-free degree.[121] As with healthcare, free college in other countries is not used to such an extent that the system is overwhelmed; rather, utilization is often similar to the United States.[122]

Many states in the US are moving in this direction. New York State now has tuition-free public college, with California and New Mexico drawing close. Eight other states, including some in the conservative

South, are eliminating the cost of community college, among other efforts.[123] Making America's public colleges and universities tuition free would only cost an additional $30 billion to $63 billion per year on top of the state and federal funding already in place.[124] Abolishing tuition costs and current student loans would also be a massive economic stimulus—money currently spent on those things cannot be spent on goods and services in the private sector.[125] Most importantly, though, free college would end a massive waste of human talent—to think of the gifted individuals who could have advanced society in fields they were passionate about but were dissuaded by empty bank accounts or thoughts of crushing debt. "All this beneficent socialism is a friendly omen," Ralph Waldo Emerson wrote, "and the swelling cry of voices for the education of the people indicates that Government has other offices than those of banker and executioner."[126]

Under socialism, democracy would enter education. Teachers, paraprofessionals, librarians, janitors, and other workers would own their schools, and federate with neighboring schools to form districts. Scores of successful US schools have already done away with principals. Teachers make all decisions collectively; there is no one above them calling the shots while making six figures.[127] Similarly, professors, adjuncts, groundskeepers, and other staff will own and run colleges—current students will have decision-making authority, too. None of this should be mistaken for privatization, however. Private schools are for-profit entities with religious or ideological focuses, and are largely free from regulation. In contrast, public schools will remain tax-funded and neighborhood-based, following a democratically determined national curriculum. The ownership simply changes under socialism. Today, public schools are owned by school districts, which are regulated by state and federal governments; colleges are owned by states, likewise regulated from above. (The State only owns military colleges.) With socialism, ownership passes to the workers.

Here it's important to note that there isn't something particular about public schools that results in worse student performance. It's well known that the United States underperforms in math, science, and reading compared to dozens of countries also dominated by public schooling.[128] Those who use the struggles of US students to argue for dismantling public education often forget that there's much room for improvement within the system. To praise countries like Finland for educational excellence and advancement, which indeed put the US to shame, is to praise places where nearly all schools are public, and even the few private ones are publicly financed, by law.[129] Comparable countries with larger shares of private schools do not perform better on benchmark tests.[130] Private schools only produce consistently superior results when they're compared to public schools where students are much poorer; when you compare the two systems in the same socioeconomic contexts, student performance is the same, or even a bit better, in public schools.[131] It's American public schools in poor areas that underperform, not those in rich areas.[132] Thus, our problem is not public education—it's poverty. "I am firmly convinced," Nelson Mandela once said, "that only socialism can do away with the poverty, disease, and illiteracy that are prevalent amongst my people."[133]

The shift to a more cooperative society would involve a similar shift within our classrooms. One can imagine many changes the philosophy of socialism will bring about. We might finally do away with merit pay, high-stakes testing, class rankings, and even grades, while embracing active learning, cooperative testing, democratic classrooms, and emphases on learning for learning's sake and changing society for the better. Elizabeth Cady Stanton wrote that "the co-operative idea will remodel codes and constitutions, creeds and catechisms, social customs and conventionalism, the curriculum of schools and colleges. It will give a new sense of justice, liberty and equality in all the relations of life."[134] Einstein lambasted how schools taught students to compete and worry only about their own successes, envisioning instead the instruction to serve others. Schools, he thought, should have "social goals." One such goal would be preparing students to help decide public policy and run a cooperative. John Dewey emphasized the need to develop, through education, "intelligent initiative, ingenuity and executive capacity as shall make workers, as far as may be, the masters of their own industrial fate."[135]

That is socialism. It is more democracy at work and in government. It is the collective care of all who need a paycheck, medicine, and schooling. "Socialism is a beautiful word," Gandhi declared, under which "there will certainly be no have-nots, no unemployment, and no disparity between classes and masses such as we see today."[136]

Eleven

REVOLUTION

THOUGH OSCAR WILDE WROTE THAT SOCIALISM "touches the heart of one and the brain of another, and draws thus man by his hatred of injustice, and his neighbour by his faith in the future,"[1] many practical questions need to be addressed if we are going to make socialism a reality in America.

The first question is financial. How will the country pay for universal healthcare, education, work or income, and other tenets of socialism? The answer is partly through budget reprioritization and partly through increased taxes on the rich. Let's say, for example, we wanted to devote $400 billion to a UBI for the poorest third of American households ($9,500 for forty-two million households), plus $70 billion to make college free for all citizens. Where would we get $470 billion? First, we could shift resources away from the military, the largest annual discretionary expenditure in the US budget. Suppose we decided that we would spend $350 billion on the military per annum, rather than the $600 billion we currently spend. That would get us over halfway to our $470 billion goal, and still leave more than enough for our national defense—in fact, the US would still have the largest military budget in the world.[2] Second, we could take $220 billion of the $360 billion currently granted to safety net programs (unemployment insurance, food stamps, Earned Income Tax Credits, Child Tax Credits, housing and energy bill assistance, etc.) and give it to this UBI program instead. Just like that, America has a UBI for a third of its families—a good start— and free college for all students. States and cities can help fund socialism, too, through budget reprioritization; the federal government may have a $4 trillion budget, but these entities spend $3 trillion collectively.

Universal healthcare, on the other hand, will not only require changes in how we spend current tax revenues, it will also require tax increases. However, these tax increases won't cost the majority of Americans one extra cent. As we saw in the preceding chapter, the cost of universal healthcare in the US will be $3 trillion. Half of that cost is already covered in the form of federal, state, and local taxes that fund current healthcare programs (Medicare, Medicaid, CHIP, and so forth).[3] Under a socialist system, these revenues and programs would be merged into Medicare For All. That leaves $1.5 trillion more to raise—and individuals and businesses will collectively spend this amount on taxes, rather than in the private healthcare sphere as they currently do.

Under the tax system of socialism, rich citizens and larger businesses, as the possessors of nearly all the money in this country, will pay higher proportions of their incomes—and indeed all wealth, including inheritances, investments, property, and so on. This, coupled with the elimination of tax loopholes and a crackdown on tax evasion, makes universal healthcare easy to afford. For instance, a new 5 percent tax on individual wealth over $5 million—affecting just 2 percent of US households—would add $1.5 trillion in annual tax revenue.[4] Thus, Medicare For All is paid for, and we haven't even gotten to corporate taxes or a progressive structure for the wealth tax. In short, the socialist solutions proposed in this book in no way require crushing taxes on low or average income people, and even the wealthy, with massive sums left over after taxes, will be just fine. In addition, as prosperity spreads and grows more equitable due to worker ownership, a UBI, guaranteed work, and so on, the tax burden will likewise grow more equitable. Rising numbers of healthy, educated citizens with strong incomes is a huge economic stimulus; economic growth increases tax revenues, meaning these programs help pay for themselves.

Many of the world's advanced democracies have used their taxes on the wealthy to enact universal healthcare, universal education, and strong social safety nets—and some are trying guaranteed work and universal basic income programs. These nations are closer than the United States to understanding that the horrors of capitalism will not end until capitalism does. They realize that the mechanism of government must be used for the common good, because private charities and non-profits are not collectively powerful enough to handle the scope of our societal problems, as is sometimes postulated by free market advocates. Charity, Oscar Wilde wrote, is "a ridiculously inadequate mode of partial restitution" for the wealth lost to capitalists. "Why should [the poor] be grateful for the crumbs that fall from the rich man's table? They should be seated at the board."[5]

Another question has to do with whether these socialist solutions will lead to totalitarian communism. Obviously, expanding democracy moves a society away from authoritarianism, not toward it. There's no evidence that Switzerland or other sovereignties with national initiatives or referenda are more likely to fall into totalitarianism. Same for all the advanced democracies around the globe with free healthcare and college, or guaranteed work or income programs. In fact, American conservative organizations rank many of these nations as freer than the United States; these countries also typically

enjoy greater citizen happiness, better stability, and stronger, less corrupt democracies.[6] Also, workplace organization under socialism has
no bearing on the national political structure. The State's only involvement is granting the legal right to equal ownership, in the same way
it grants the legal right to a minimum wage, workplace safety, equal
opportunity, and so on.

Communism's top-down dismantling of capitalism necessarily
puts it in conflict with the bottom-up approaches of socialism and anarchism. Thus, throughout history, many socialists and anarchists, including many historical figures in this book, opposed communism. There
is no contradiction there, as these philosophies are fundamentally
distinct. In 1946, Orwell said, "Every line of serious work that I have
written since 1936 has been written, directly or indirectly, against totalitarianism and for democratic socialism."[7] This would include *Animal
Farm*, his allegory criticizing the Soviet Union.

Overall, it's time to put aside the old fears over socialism, and step
boldly into that next, more "advanced stage" of human life, as Nelson
Mandela phrased it.[8] We can create a more decent, equitable, and fair
society, if we so choose.

This brings us to the most important question of all: How do we bring
these changes about? How can we strip capitalists and their representatives of their power, and establish services that fully meet human needs?
How exactly do we change a capitalist society into a socialist society?

Well, there is a word that has stirred countless souls in the US in
recent years, as ordinary people watched or participated in the great
upheavals of the past decade, from the 2011 beginnings of the Occupy
Wall Street movement to the 2016 Dakota Access Pipeline protests at
Standing Rock. That word is *revolution*. Langston Hughes wrote:

Listen, Revolution,
We're buddies, see—
Together,
We can take everything ...
And turn 'em over to the people who work.
Rule and run 'em for us people who work ...

That's our job!
I been starvin' too long
Ain't you?

Let's go, Revolution![9]

People don't realize the power they possess. They feel help-less in the face of injustice and misery, not understanding the simple truth: that they have the ability to take whatever they want. By join-ing together, the people—the workers—can radically transform soci-ety, through revolutionary direct action.

There are many tools in the toolbox of social change, all of which are valuable at creating a better society. First, creating or voting for social-istic ballot initiatives, and voting for self-avowed socialist candidates (or running for office yourself), can help bring us closer to this new world. Since 2016, a surge of socialist candidates have won local, state, and national races—continuing a long tradition of radicals in American office.[10] While some on the radical left frown upon any participation in the current system, it can do a great deal of good, as the right public officials can push forward more ethical policies and make government more pliable to the demands of a socialist mass movement. Electoral politics should be viewed as simply one strategy among many; attacks from outside the system can only be aided by having allies chipping away from within. Also, one cannot discount the tool of education—showing others the true nature of capitalism and the enduring promise of socialism. "The battle for Socialism," wrote H.G. Wells, "is to be fought not simply at the polls and in the market-place, but at the writing-desk and in the study."[11]

From there, the tools of social change grow more agitational. You harass the powerful in business and politics with petitions, messages, and phone calls. Organize—work together—with fellow citizens to boycott businesses. Protest and march outside workplaces, or the offices and homes of CEOs and politicians. Go on strike, refusing to return to work until your demands are met. Engage in acts of civil disobedience: sit in and occupy your workplace or a political chamber, block streets that members of the ruling class use to get to work, and commit other illegal acts, facing the risk of arrest or violence by police, private security, or bystanders. Orwell urged us to be active, not passive, socialists.[12] Emerson said, "If you act, you show character; if you sit still, if you sleep, you show it." If you "have spoken nothing . . . on socialism . . . your silence answers very loud."[13] One must join Woody Guthrie's "militant worker on his long hard fight from slavery to freedom."[14] Malala Yousafzai, the famous Pakistani human rights advocate who faced down the Taliban, declared, "I am convinced Socialism is the only answer and I urge all comrades to take this struggle to a victorious conclusion. Only this will free us from the chains of bigotry and exploitation."[15] These types of confrontational tactics have done incalculable good in the US and around the globe, weakening or defeating occupation, war, white supremacy, patriarchy, starvation wages, and countless other evils; many socialists, including some of the heroes of this text—like Gandhi, fighting to free India from Britain—were on the front lines. Progress comes on the backs of the troublemakers. Revolution is simply a bigger way to stir up trouble, a sustained, nation-wide mass action of non-cooperation against the powerful.

Though violent revolutions have resulted at times in freer, more democratic societies—including our own, to an extent, after the 1770s—a revolution doesn't require violence. In fact, nonviolent mass action has grown increasingly successful in recent times. When political scientists examined violent and nonviolent revolutions between 1900 and 2006, they found nonviolent campaigns were twice as likely to be successful at toppling dictators and ending foreign occupations. Since the 1940s, the success rate of nonviolent efforts has jumped about 30 percent, while the success rate of violent efforts has fallen by about the same amount.[16] The latter are also more likely to result in unstable, anti-democratic regimes or bloody civil wars. The researchers also found that nonviolent campaigns never failed when at least 3.5 percent of the population was involved. Many won with far less than that. In addition, only nonviolent revolts reached that threshold, as more people are willing to join peaceful campaigns, and more are physically able to, such as children, the sick, the elderly, persons with disabilities, and so on. Gandhi wrote that socialism would be achieved through "non-violent non-co-operation."[17] He explained further that:

> My socialism was natural to me and not adopted from any books. It came out of my unshakable belief in non-violence. No man could be actively non-violent and not rise against social injustice, no matter where it occurred . . .

> Impure means result in an impure end. Hence the prince and the peasant will not be equalized by cutting off the prince's

head, nor can the process of cutting off equalize the employer and the employed . . . Therefore, only truthful, non-violent and pure-hearted socialists will be able to establish a socialistic society in India and the world . . .[18]

Economic and political systems survive only through mass cooperation. Gandhi said what we need to do to build a better world is to simply disobey the exploiters and the powerful.[19] Helen Keller wrote, "All you need to do to bring about this stupendous revolution is to straighten up and fold your arms."[20] Then, she said, not even the full might of the police or the military could prevent the fall of capitalism.[21] Three and a half percent of the US population is a mass action— say, a general strike—of 11.5 million people. Victory could probably be accomplished with fewer. A general strike means skipping work and school, marching through the streets, and not leaving until your demands are met. Imagine a million people bringing Washington, D.C., to a standstill, with millions more paralyzing cities across the rest of the country. When workers come together, they can shut down a street, a city, a state, or an entire nation. That's how you win. Oscar Wilde wrote in "The Soul of Man Under Socialism" that "[d]isobedience, in the eyes of anyone who has read history, is man's original virtue. It is through disobedience that progress has been made, through disobedience and through rebellion."[22] No violence is necessary; you simply stop producing and bring society to a halt until power yields.

True, there is always the risk of being fired, expelled, arrested, beaten, or killed. There is no revolution without danger. Mass action also requires solidarity and support networks, to help those who cannot last long without an income or necessities. But prior generations faced the same dangers, and with fewer numbers secured lasting victories against our darkest and most oppressive systems. There is truly nothing the people cannot do, if they unite and refuse to cooperate with power, from the Montgomery, Alabama, boycott that ended local segregated busing in 1956 to the Arab Spring protests that drove out Tunisia's dictator in 2011. These events were not entirely peaceful. Whites bombed Dr. King's house.[23] Some Tunisians willfully clashed with police, though most of the violence was just the predictable acts of a repressive State—which resulted in deaths.[24] It is difficult to foresee or control the actions of all involved, whether enemies or allies. But these disruptions nevertheless showed how direct action, in general nonviolent, can accomplish huge goals.

The US has seen what mass action can do in recent years, through the resurgence of the strike. In 2012, Fight for $15 began organizing nationwide strikes, and within four years, nearly 20 million workers had earned a pay raise, as cities, states, and businesses across the US yielded to the pressure, many adopting the full $15 minimum wage.[25] In 2016, nearly 40,000 Verizon workers went on strike and largely won their demands.[26] In 2018, tens of thousands of West Virginia teachers went on strike, forcing every public school in the state to close, winning higher pay in just nine days.[27] Then Arizona teachers, also after just nine days of work refusal, won a 20 percent raise. Oklahoma teachers won the largest pay raise in state history in the same amount of time.[28] The strikes continued to spread, as 8,000 hotel workers went on strike across the country and won a raise.[29] In 2019, Los Angeles teachers, working in the country's second-largest school system, went on strike for a week and won a host of demands.[30] Denver teachers won $26 million in pay raises in three days.[31] At the time of this writing, 50,000 workers at General Motors are on strike. Capitalists and governments need the people to survive and maintain legitimacy. When the steed begins to buck, they cannot hold on for long.

We have also seen the success of protest movements in marshalling huge numbers of people for a cause. Dr. King's 1963 March on Washington for Jobs and Freedom brought 250,000 to the capital, helping push forward the 1964 Civil Rights Act and the 1965 Voting Rights Act. Two million Americans in various cities marched against the war in Vietnam on October 15, 1969. Later, about one million people came to D.C. to support LGBT rights, and again for denuclearization. The spring of 2006 saw millions of Latinos, Hispanics, immigrants, and allies protest in 160 cities against anti-immigrant legislation. That May Day, the "Day Without Immigrants," saw 1.5 million people refuse to go to work or school. In January 2017, in perhaps America's largest single-day protest, 4 million people participated in the Women's March in 600 cities. In 2018, 800,000 descended on Washington D.C. for the March for Our Lives, with over two million marching in municipalities throughout the country to support gun control. In 2019, half a million citizens in Puerto Rico swarmed the streets of San Juan for two weeks, quickly forcing their governor to resign over corruption, homophobia, and sexism. As these examples show, millions of Americans participating in revolutionary direct action isn't too far-fetched an idea. What's key is to organize non-cooperation and agitation. That is, instead of millions gathering in public places for a few hours of speeches, they would instead stage sit-ins at seats of power and strategic locations indefinitely, as brave Americans did at the Wisconsin state capitol in 2011 over attacks on union rights and at Standing Rock. The authorities can arrest a couple of hundred people; they cannot so easily disperse millions.

A people's movement can eradicate capitalism and democratize the political system. Nelson Mandela wrote, "[t]he transition from capitalism to socialism and the liberation of the working class from the yoke cannot be effected by slow changes or by reforms as reactionaries and liberals often advise, but by revolution."[32] Langston Hughes urged us in his beautiful little poem "If You Would" to make the choice to bring society to a screeching halt, in order to transform it.[33] Mark Twain said that, "I am always on the side of the revolutionists, because there never was a revolution unless there were some oppressive and intolerable conditions against which to revolute."[34] He also believed that great power was slumbering within the workers, and that they would one day rise up.[35] Steinbeck warned in *The Grapes of Wrath* that those who "hate change and fear revolution" may try to keep struggling people apart, "make them hate, fear, suspect each other," but the thoughts of the poor will inevitably go "from 'I' to 'we.'" Like Twain, he knew poor conditions led to rebellion and change: "Paine, Marx, Jefferson, Lenin, were results, not causes."[36] Ordinary people are going to have to come together, organize, and engage in revolutionary direct action to win worker ownership, direct democracy, universal healthcare and education, and guaranteed work or income. They are going to have to strike—and occupy—until this new world is realized.

The seeds of American socialism have long been planted. As we have seen, worker co-ops and direct democracy already exist in this country. There are growing universal healthcare and tuition-abolition movements—partly rekindled by Bernie Sanders—with some success at the state level. Even mainstream Democratic presidential candidates are calling for UBI programs and work guarantees.[37] One may be quite surprised to learn just how close the US came to universal healthcare, universal early childhood education, UBI, and guaranteed jobs under Nixon and Carter, among others, after they felt some pressure from the people.[38] We may find that tipping points arrive sooner than expected.

Elsewhere in the world, national direct democracy, free healthcare, and free college are all taken for granted. UBI and the State as the employer of last resort have been successful at the federal level. Co-ops are growing even more common, and workers in capitalist firms are gnawing at power from the inside. For example, German unions fought for and won the right to have representatives on the boards of directors of large corporations.[39] The right to ownership is a logical next step. "The Socialist," Jack London said, must work to "make illegal the capitalist's ownership of the means of production, and make legal his own . . ."[40] Abraham Lincoln called it "wrong" that "some have labored" while "others have without labor enjoyed a larger proportion of the fruits," and thus "to secure to each laborer the whole product of his labor, or as nearly as possible, is a worthy object of any good government."[41] Other countries are often ahead of the US in the march toward a better world because they have stronger mass movements. For example, in 2016, over a million South Koreans shut down their capital, demanding the impeachment of a corrupt president, which quickly followed; in 2016 and 2019, anti-labor policies in India sparked the largest strikes in world history, with 150 to 180 million people participating in each—well over 10 percent of the population.[42] Victor Hugo told the rich to "tremble," for the "hungry show their idle teeth" and will "ascend" to create a society where "there will be no more lords; there will be free, living men. There will be no more wealth, there will be an abundance for the poor. There will be no more masters, but there will be brothers. They that toil shall have. This is the future."[43]

International solidarity and coordination are also growing. Six to fifteen million people around the world protested the planned US invasion of Iraq on February 15, 2003, the world's largest single-day protest at the time. In October 2011, nearly 1,000 cities across the globe rose up to protest economic inequality and the corporate corruption of democracy during Occupy Wall Street. Cities on every continent, including Antarctica, joined in America's Women's March. In March 2019, 1.4 million people went on strike or marched around the world to push for global environmental protections; in September 2019, the number went up to 4 million.[44] Human beings are uniting for sanity and justice. We may yet achieve what Helen Keller, Jack London, and others envisioned, a global revolution for workers' freedom from capitalism.

And internationalism is crucial, as many problems described in this book—workplace exploitation, authoritarianism, war, anti-democratic political systems, corruption, poverty, inequality, and lack of healthcare, education, work, decent shelter, and nourishment—are far worse in many countries, whether capitalist or communist. Natural resources and wealth alike remain unevenly distributed across the globe, to devastating effect. It's not just America that needs socialism. All citizens of this world deserve the prosperity and opportunities described herein. This can only be achieved by letting go of nationalism, recognizing that all Earth's people are one—and coming together to organize the world accordingly.

There's no question where our famous historical figures stood on this issue. Gandhi envisioned a human government where "all the states of the world are free and equal, no state has its military. There may be a world police to keep order in the absence of universal belief in non-violence."[45] It would be a "world federation."[46] He said, "Real socialism has been handed down to us by our ancestors who taught: 'All land belongs to Gopal [God], where then is the boundary line? Man is the maker of that line and he can therefore unmake it.'"[47] Einstein likewise called for a world government.[48] Orwell wrote: "Socialism aims, ultimately, at a world-state of free and equal human beings."[49] H.G. Wells said the exact same thing.[50] Du Bois and Camus agreed.[51] Victor Hugo said he belonged to "the party of revolutionary civilization" that would create a "United States of the World."[52] Dr. King wanted to "bring about universal disarmament and set up a world police force through the United Nations that could handle any problems that arise . . . I would also consider some form of a world government. [We must] come to see the oneness of mankind and the geographical oneness of the world . . ."[53]

John Lennon and Yoko Ono (another self-described socialist) captured this vision when they wrote a song Lennon described as "virtually the Communist manifesto"[54]:

> Imagine there's no countries
> It isn't hard to do
> Nothing to kill or die for
> And no religion too
> Imagine all the people living life in peace . . .

The United Nations' global democratic body and peacekeeping forces, the European Union's open borders policy and integrated military, and other systems are the foundation on which the human nation will grow. Whether in one hundred years or 1,000, at some point the Earth will be one big democracy, with borders and nations disappearing, opening up a world where war is unheard of, protecting the environment is coordinated, and all people enjoy ownership, political power, and the rights and services required for a free, happy life. Many of us may not live to see the new society, but while we are here, we will fight for it. We end with the words of Helen Keller:

Slowly man is waking up. The people—the great "common herd"—are finding out what is wrong with the social, political and economical structure of the system of which they are a part. This is not a time of gentleness, of timid beginnings that steal into life with soft apologies and dainty grace. It is a time for loud voiced, open speech and fearless thinking; a time of striving and conscious manhood, a time of all that is robust and vehement and bold; a time radiant with new ideals, new hopes of true democracy.[55]

NOTES

INTRODUCTION

1. David Garrow, *Bearing the Cross* (New York: HarperCollins, 2004), 382.

1: HUMAN NATURE

1. Albert Einstein, "Why Socialism?," *Monthly Review*, May 1949. All quotes from Einstein in this work come from this article, unless indicated by another footnote.

2. Elizabeth Blackwell, "Christian Socialism: Thoughts Suggested by the Easter Season, 1882," in *The Socialist Reader*, ed. Eric v.d. Luft (North Syracuse: Gegensatz Press, 2015), chap. 7.

3. Oscar Wilde, "The Soul of Man Under Socialism," *Project Gutenberg*, accessed July 4, 2019, https://www.gutenberg.org/ebooks/1017; and how right Wilde was. See H.C. Triandis and E.M. Suh, "Cultural Influences on Personality," *Annual Review of Psychology* 53 (February 2002).

4. "Children & Youth in History," George Mason University, accessed July 4, 2019, http://chnm.gmu.edu/cyh/primary-sources/24.

5. Nirmal Kumar Bose, *Selections From Gandhi* (Ahmedabad: Navajivan, 1960), http://www.mkgandhi.org/sfgbook/seventh.htm.

6. Chris Harman, *How Marxism Works* (London: Bookmarks Publications, 1979), chap. 2, https://www.marxists.org/archive/harman/1979/marxism/index.html; John Curl, *For All the People: Uncovering the Hidden History of Cooperation, Cooperative Movements, and Communalism in America* (Oakland: PM Press, 2009), 15–17; Steve Taylor, "An Alternative View of Human Nature," *Psychology Today*, July 20, 2018.

7. Deborah Rogers, "Inequality: Why Egalitarian Societies Died Out," *New Scientist*, July 25, 2012; Harman, *Marxism*, chap. 2 and 3; Taylor, "Alternative View."

8 Hannah Devlin, "Early Men and Women Were Equal, Say Scientists," *The Guardian*, May 14, 2015; Taylor, "Alternative View."

9. Nelson Mandela, "How to be a Good Communist," *Rhodesia*, accessed July 4, 2019, http://www.rhodesia.nl/goodcom.html.

10. R. Brian Ferguson, "War is *Not* Part of Human Nature," *Scientific American*, September 1, 2018.

11. Robert W. Sussman and C. Robert Cloninger, *Origins of Altruism and Cooperation* (New York: Springer, 2011); Dacher Keltner, "The Compassionate Instinct," University of California, Berkeley, March 1, 2004, https://greatergood.berkeley.edu/article/item/the_compassionate_instinct.

12. Richard Dawkins, *The God Delusion* (Boston: Houghton Mifflin Co., 2006), chap. 6.

13. Adrian F. Ward, "Scientists Probe Human Nature and Discover We Are Good, After All," *Scientific American*, November 20, 2012; Ernst Fehr, Urs Fischbacher, and Simon Gächter, "Strong Reciprocity, Human Cooperation, and the Enforcement of Social Norms," *Human Nature* 13, no. 1 (March 2002); Alfie Kohn, *The Brighter Side of Human Nature: Altruism and Empathy in Everyday Life* (New York: Basic Books, 1992).

14. Ernst Fehr and Bettina Rockenbach, "Human Altruism: Economic, Neural, and Evolutionary Perspectives," *Current Opinion in Neurobiology* 14, no. 6 (December 2004).

15. Tom Stafford, "Are We Naturally Good or Bad?," *BBC*, January 14, 2013; Michael Tomasello, *Why We Cooperate* (Cambridge: The MIT Press, 2009); Michael Shermer, *The Moral Arc: How Science and Reason Lead Humanity Toward Truth, Justice, and Freedom* (New York: Henry Holt and Co., 2015).

16. Belinda Recio, *Inside Animal Hearts and Minds* (New York: Skyhorse, 2017); Frans de Waal, *Are We Smart Enough to Know How Smart Animals Are?* (New York: W.W. Norton, 2017).

17. Richard Wrangham, "How Humans Evolved to be Both Shockingly Violent and Super-Cooperative," *New Scientist*, February 13, 2019.

18. Mandela, "Good Communist."

19. George Orwell, "Second Thoughts on James Burnham," Orwell Foundation, accessed July 4, 2019, https://www.orwellfoundation.com/the-orwell-foundation/orwell/essays-and-other-works/second-thoughts-on-james-burnham/.

2: EXPLOITATION

1. Martin Luther King, Jr. to Coretta Scott, July 18, 1952, Stanford University, https://kinginstitute.stanford.edu/king-papers/documents/coretta-scott.

2. Martin Luther King, Jr., "Keep Moving From This Mountain" (speech,

Spelman College, April 10, 1960), Stanford University, https://kinginstitute.stanford.edu/king-papers/documents/keep-moving-mountain-address-spelman-college-10-april-1960; Martin Luther King, Jr., "America's Chief Moral Dilemma" (speech, Hungry Club Forum, May 10, 1967), *The Atlantic*.

3. Shriman Narayan, *The Selected Works of Mahatma Gandhi*, vol. 5, *The Voice of Truth* (Ahmedabad: Navajivan, 1968), https://www.mkgandhi.org/voiceof-truth/classwar.htm.

4. John Stuart Mill, *Autobiography* (New York: P.F. Collier & Son, 1909), chap. 7.

5. John Stuart Mill, *Principles of Political Economy: and Chapters on Socialism* (New York: Oxford University Press, 1998), 147.

6. "Rich Criticized by Helen Keller," *New York Times*, February 7, 1913. Cited in Keith Rosenthal, "The Politics of Helen Keller," *International Socialist Review*, accessed July 8, 2019, https://isreview.org/issue/96/politics-helen-keller; Helen Keller, "New Vision for the Blind," in *Helen Keller: Her Socialist Years*, ed. Philip S. Foner (New York: International Publishers NYC, 1967), 55.

7. Jack London, "Revolution and Other Essays," Somona State University, accessed July 4, 2019, http://london.sonoma.edu/writings/revolution/life.html.

8. George Orwell, "Review of *Communism and Man* by F. J. Sheed," in *The Collected Essays, Journalism and Letters of George Orwell*, vol. 1, *An Age Like This, 1920–1940*, ed. Sonia Orwell and Ian Angus (Boston: Godine, 2000), 383.

9. Nelson Mandela, *Long Walk to Freedom* (New York: Back Bay Books, 1995).

10. Philip S. Foner, *Mark Twain: Social Critic* (New York: International Publishers, 1958), 169.

11. Lawrence Mishel and Jessica Schieder, "CEO Pay Remains High Relative to the Pay of Typical Workers and High-Wage Earners," *Economic Policy Institute*, July 20, 2017.

12. Andrew Chamberlain, "CEO to Worker Pay Ratios: Average CEO Earns 204 Times Median Worker Pay," *Glassdoor Economic Research Blog*, August 25, 2015, https://www.glassdoor.com/research/ceo-pay-ratio/.

13. Rob Wile, "The Heirs to the Walmart Fortune Just Made $5 Billion in One Day," *Time*, October 11, 2017; "WMT Company Financials," NASDAQ, accessed October 1, 2017, http://www.nasdaq.com/symbol/wmt/financials?query=income-statement.

14. "NKE Company Financials," NASDAQ, accessed October 1, 2017, http://www.nasdaq.com/symbol/nke/financials?query=income-statement; "Phil Knight & Family" profile, *Forbes*, accessed October 1, 2017, https://www.forbes.com/profile/phil-knight/?list=rtb.

15. "MSFT Company Financials," NASDAQ, accessed October 1, 2017, http://www.nasdaq.com/symbol/msft/financials?query=income-statement; "Bill Gates" profile, *Forbes*, accessed October 1, 2017, https://www.forbes.com/profile/bill-gates/.

16. Rachel Abrams, "Retailers Like H&M and Walmart Fall Short of Pledges to Overseas Workers," *New York Times*, May 31, 2016.

17. Harriet Beecher Stowe, *Uncle Tom's Cabin*, Project Gutenberg, accessed July 4, 2019, http://www.gutenberg.org/files/203/203-h/203-h.htm. See chapter 19.

18. Mishel and Schieder, "CEO Pay."

19. "The Top Charts of 2015," *Economic Policy Institute*, December 17, 2015.

20. Nelson D. Schwartz, "Recovery in U.S. is Lifting Profits, but Not Adding Jobs," *New York Times*, March 3, 2013.

21. Branko Milanovic, *The Haves and Have Nots: A Brief and Idiosyncratic History of Global Inequality* (New York: Basic Books, 2012); Matthew Yglesias, "95 Percent of Recovery Income Gains Have Gone to the Top 1 Percent," *Slate*, September 10, 2013, http://www.slate.com/blogs/moneybox/2013/09/10/one_percent_recovery_95_percent_of_gains_have_gone_to_the_top_one_percent.html.

22. Jake Johnson, "'Eye-Popping': Analysis Shows Top 1% Gained $21 Trillion in Wealth Since 1989 While Bottom Half Lost $900 Billion," *Common Dreams*, June 14, 2019, https://www.commondreams.org/news/2019/06/14/eye-popping-analysis-shows-top-1-gained-21-trillion-wealth-1989-while-bottom-half.

23. Helen Keller, "Menace of the Militarist Program," in *Helen Keller: Her Socialist Years*, ed. Philip S. Foner (New York: International Publishers NYC, 1967), 73, https://archive.org/stream/helenkellerherso00hele/helenkellerherso00hele_djvu.txt.

24. Michael I. Norton and Dan Ariely, "Building a Better America—One Wealth Quintile at a Time," *Perspectives on Psychological Science* 6, no. 9 (2011).

25. "Is Capitalism Dying?," *In Defence of Marxism*, February 5, 2013, http://www.marxist.com/is-capitalism-dying.htm.

26. Adela Suliman, "82 Percent of the Wealth Generated Last Year 'Went to the Richest 1 Percent of the Global Population,'" *Time*, January 22, 2018; "Just 8 Men Own Same Wealth as Half the World," Oxfam, January 16, 2017, https://www.oxfam.org/en/pressroom/pressreleases/2017-01-16/just-8-men-own-same-wealth-half-world; Ezra Klein, "10 Startling Facts About Global Wealth Inequality," *Washington Post*, January 22, 2014.

27. Shelly Hagan, "Billionaires Made So Much Money Last Year They Could End Extreme Poverty Seven Times," *Time*, January 22, 2018.

28. Harry Belafonte, *My Song: A Memoir of Art, Race, and Defiance* (New York: Vintage Books, 2012), 328.

29. Ajay Kapur, Niall Macleod, Narendra Smith, "Plutonomy: Buying Luxury, Explaining Global Imbalances," Citigroup industry note, October 16, 2005, https://delong.typepad.com/plutonomy-1.pdf. See commentary in G.S. Griffin, "Capitalists Speaking Frankly," GSGriffin.com, November 6, 2017, https://gsgriffin.com/2017/11/06/capitalists-speaking-frankly/.

30. Deborah Boucoyannis, "Contrary to Popular and Academic Belief, Adam Smith Did Not Accept Inequality as a Necessary Trade-off for a More Prosperous Economy," The London School of Economics and Political Science, February 18, 2014, http://blogs.lse.ac.uk/politicsandpolicy/adam-smith-and-inequality; Deborah Boucoyannis, "The Equalizing Hand: Why Adam Smith Thought the Market Should Produce Wealth Without Steep Inequality," *Perspectives on Politics* 11, no. 4 (December 2013): 1051-1070; Noam Chomsky, *On Anarchism* (New York: The New Press, 2013), 36.

31. Adam Smith, *An Inquiry into the Nature and Causes of the Wealth of Nations*, Project Gutenberg, accessed July 6, 2019, http://www.gutenberg.org/files/3300/3300-h/3300-h.htm. See chapter 8.

32. Ibid., chap. 8 and 4.

33. John Nichols, *The "S" Word: A Short History of an American Tradition . . . Socialism* (New York: Verso, 2011), 66, 73, 80.

34. Abraham Lincoln, "First Annual Message," University of California, Santa Barbara, accessed July 6, 2019, http://www.presidency.ucsb.edu/ws/?pid=29502.

35. Ralph Waldo Emerson, "Napoleon; Man of the World," Emerson Central, accessed July 6, 2019, https://emersoncentral.com/texts/representative-men/napoleon-man-of-the-world/.

36. George Orwell, *The Road to Wigan Pier*, Archive, accessed July 6, 2019, https://archive.org/stream/roadtowiganpie00orwe/roadtowiganpie00orwe_djvu.txt. For instance, there's "the robbers and the robbed . . . Socialism means a fair deal" for all "manual laborers" (259); Oscar Wilde, *Oscar Wilde: The Dover Reader* (Mineola: Dover Publications, 2015), 267.

37. Gustav Janouch, *Conversations with Kafka*, Archive, accessed July 6, 2019, https://archive.org/details/in.ernet.dli.2015.187760/page/n75. See pages 86 and 77. Page numbers are from the text, not the website navigator; Michael Löwry, "Franz Kafka and Libertarian Socialism," *New Politics* 6, no. 3 (summer 1997).

38. Upton Sinclair, *The Jungle*, Project Gutenberg, accessed July 6, 2019, http://www.gutenberg.org/files/140/140-h/140-h.htm. Chapter 30.

3: THE PROFIT MOTIVE: AND PRESENT ECONOMIES

1. Frances Goldwin, Debby Smith, and Michael Steven Smith, *Imagine: Living in a Socialist USA* (New York: Harper Perennial, 2014).

2. Justin McCurry, "Japanese Company Replaces Office Workers with Artificial Intelligence," *The Guardian*, January 5, 2017.

3. Oscar Wilde, "The Soul of Man Under Socialism," Project Gutenberg, accessed July 6, 2019, http://www.gutenberg.org/files/1017/1017-h/1017-h.htm. See page 37.

4. Einstein, *Why Socialism?* "Technological progress . . . frequently results in more unemployment rather than in an easing of the burden of work for all"; Wilde, "The Soul of Man," 38; Orwell, *Wigan Pier*, 221.

5. Max Roser, "Working Hours," *Our World in Data*, accessed July 6, 2019, https://ourworldindata.org/working-hours; Chris Isidore and Tami Luhby, "Turns Out Americans Work Really Hard . . . But Some Want to Work Harder," CNN, July 9, 2015.

6. Howard Zinn, *A People's History of the United States* (New York: Harper Perennial, 2005), 322.

7. Erik Olin Wright, *Envisioning Real Utopias* (New York: Verso, 2010), 43–44.

8. Ibid., 48.

9. Mark Smith, "Deloitte: UK Benefiting From Automation of Work," Deloitte, http://www2.deloitte.com/uk/en/pages/press-releases/articles/uk-benefitting-from-automation-of-work.html.

10. Gustav Janouch, *Conversations with Kafka* (New York: New Directions Press, 1971), 103.

11. Carl Benedikt Frey and Michael A. Osborne, "The Future of Employment: How Susceptible Are Jobs to Computerisation?," University of Oxford, September 17, 2013, http://www.oxfordmartin.ox.ac.uk/downloads/academic/The_Future_of_Employment.pdf.

12. Michael Chui, James Manyika, and Mehdi Miremadi, "Four Fundamentals of Workplace Automation," McKinsey, November 2015, http://www.mckinsey.com/business-functions/business-technology/our-insights/four-fundamentals-of-workplace-automation.

13. Wren Handman, "You Can't Talk About Robots Without Talking About Basic Income," *Vice*, May 14, 2016, https://motherboard.vice.com/read/you-cant-talk-about-robots-without-talking-about-basic-income.

14. Tanvi Misra, "Where Robots Are Doing Factory Jobs," *CityLab*, August 18, 2017, https://www.citylab.com/life/2017/08/where-robots-are-doing-factory-jobs/537327/.

15. Richard Kozul-Wright, "Robots and Industrialization in Developing

Countries," *United Nations Conference on Trade and Development,* October 2016, http://unctad.org/en/PublicationsLibrary/presspb2016d6_en.pdf.

16. "Experts Predict When Artificial Intelligence Will Exceed Human Performance," *MIT Technology Review,* May 31, 2017.

17. T.N. Khoshoo and M.S. John, *Mahatma Gandhi and the Environment* (New Delhi: The Energy and Resources Institute, 2010), 50.

18. Bose, *Selections From Gandhi,* https://www.mkgandhi.org/sfgbook/seventh.htm.

19. Zinn, *People's History,* 322.

20. Alexander C. Kaufman, "Stephen Hawking Says We Should Really be Scared of Capitalism, Not Robots," *Huffington Post,* October 8, 2015, https://www.huffpost.com/entry/stephen-hawking-capitalism-robots_n_5616c20ce4b0dbb8000d9f15.

21. Goldwin, *Imagine,* 7; Brian Merchant, "Life and Death in Apple's Forbidden City," *The Guardian,* June 18, 2017.

22. Zachary M. Seward, "These Are the Clothing Labels Left Behind in the Bangladesh Factory Fire That Killed 112 Workers," *Quartz,* November 26, 2012; Gillian B. White, "What's Changed Since More Than 1,110 People Died in Bangladesh's Factory Collapse?," *The Atlantic,* May 3, 2017.

23. "Employers Who Put Workers & Communities at Risk," *National Council for Occupational Safety & Health,* April 2017, https://drive.google.com/file/d/0B2MOa-NgCU4ZUFNtT2hSVk9EeEk/view.

24. Martin Luther King, Jr., "Beyond Vietnam" (speech, New York City Riverside Church, April 4, 1967), Stanford University, https://kinginstitute.stanford.edu/king-papers/documents/beyond-vietnam.

25. Helen Keller, "Strike Against War," in *Helen Keller: Her Socialist Years,* ed. Philip S. Foner (New York: International Publishers NYC, 1967), 77, https://archive.org/stream/helenkellerherso00hele/helenkellerherso00hele_djvu.txt.

26. Alex Lach, "5 Facts About Overseas Outsourcing," Center for American Progress, July 9, 2012, https://www.americanprogress.org/issues/economy/news/2012/07/09/11898/5-facts-about-overseas-outsourcing/.

27. Katherine Peralta, "Outsourcing to China Cost U.S. 3.2 Million Jobs Since 2001," *U.S. News & World Report.*

28. Kimberly Amadeo, "How Outsourcing Jobs Affects the U.S. Economy," *The Balance,* June 25, 2019.

29. French politician and economist Pierre-Joseph Proudhon, the first self-described anarchist, said, "Competition kills competition." Daniel Guerin, *Anarchism* (New York: Monthly Review Press, 1970), 53.

30. George Orwell, "Review: *The Road to Serfdom* by F.A. Hayek, *The Mirror of the Past* by K. Zilliacus," in *The Collected Essays, Journalism and Letters of George*

Orwell: As I Please, 1943–1945, ed. Sonia Orwell and Ian Angus (London: Seeker & Warburg, 1968), 3:118.

31. Garrett Baldwin, "How Big Corporations Are Destroying the 'Free Market,'" *Money Morning*, May 29, 2013.

32. Nate Berg, "Radiating Death: How Walmart Displaces Nearby Small Businesses," *CityLab*, September 14, 2012, https://www.citylab.com/life/2012/09/radiating-death-how-walmart-displaces-nearby-small-businesses/3272/.

33. Noam Chomsky, *Hopes and Prospects* (Chicago: Haymarket Books, 2010), 30.

34. *The Literary Digest* 36 (New York: Funk & Wagnalls, 1908), 38.

35. Barry C. Lynn, "America's Monopolies Are Holding Back the Economy," *The Atlantic*, February 22, 2017.

36. Matt Krantz, "6% of Companies Make 50% of U.S. Profit," *USA Today*, March 2, 2016.

37. David Leonhardt, "The Monopolization of America," *New York Times*, November 25, 2018.

38. Jed Greer and Kavaljit Singh, "A Brief History of Transnational Corporations," Global Policy Forum, 2000, https://www.globalpolicy.org/empire/47068-a-brief-history-of-transnational-corporations.html#ft3.

39. Gar Alperovitz and Thomas M. Hanna, "Beyond Corporate Capitalism: Not So Wild a Dream," *The Nation*, May 22, 2012.

40. "Corporate Consolidation," *Last Week Tonight with John Oliver* (HBO), September 24, 2017, https://www.youtube.com/watch?v=00wQYmvfhn4.

41. Nicolas Rapp and Aric Jenkins, "Chart: These 6 Companies Control Much of the U.S. Media," *Fortune*, July 24, 2018.

42. Aldous Huxley, *Brave New World Revisited*, Huxley.net, accessed July 6, 2019, https://www.huxley.net/bnw-revisited/. See chapter 3.

43. John Steinbeck, *The Grapes of Wrath*, Archive, accessed July 6, 2019, https://archive.org/stream/in.ernet.dli.2015.261773/2015.261773.The-Grapes_djvu.txt. See page 44.

44. Lee Sustar, "Why Karl Marx Was Right," *Socialist Worker*, September 13, 2011, http://socialistworker.org/2011/09/13/why-karl-marx-was-right; David Wessel, "'Secular Stagnation' Even Truer Today, Larry Summers Says," Brookings Institute, May 30, 2017, https://www.brookings.edu/articles/secular-stagnation-even-truer-today-larry-summers-says/.

45. Karl Marx, *Capital*, vol. 3, Marxists.org, https://www.marxists.org/archive/marx/works/1894-c3/ch30.htm; Paul Krugman, "A Permanent Slump?," *New York Times*, November 17, 2013; Robert Reich, "What Walmart Could Learn From Henry Ford," *Baltimore Sun*, November 20, 2013; Robert

Reich, "Higher Wages Can Save America's Economy—and its Democracy," *Salon*, September 3, 2013.

46. Reich, "What Walmart Could Learn"; Michael Harrington, *Socialism: Past and Future* (New York: Arcade, 2011), chap. 1 and 5.

47. Henry Ford, *Today and Tomorrow: Commemorative Edition of Ford's 1926 Classic* (Boca Raton: CRC Press, 2003), chap. 1.

48. Jonathan D. Ostry, Andrew Berg, and Charalambos G. Tsangarides, "Redistribution, Inequality, and Growth," International Monetary Fund, February 2014, http://www.imf.org/external/pubs/ft/sdn/2014/sdn1402.pdf; Larry Elliot, "Austerity Policies Do More Harm Than Good, IMF Study Concludes," *The Guardian*, May 27, 2016.

49. Derek Thompson, "Tax Cuts Don't Lead to Economic Growth, a New 65-Year Study Finds," *The Atlantic*, September 16, 2012.

50. Jeff Kearns, "Two-thirds of U.S. Business Economists See Recession by End-2020," *Bloomberg*, September 30, 2018.

51. "Letter From W.E.B. Du Bois to Communist Party of the U.S.A.," University of Massachusetts, Amherst, accessed July 6, 2019, http://credo.library.umass.edu/view/pageturn/mums312-b153-i071/#page/1/mode/1up.

52. Milton Friedman and Anna Jacobson, *A Monetary History of the United States, 1867–1960* (Princeton: Princeton University Press, 1963), http://www.jstor.org/stable/j.ctt7s1vp.

53. Kimberly Amadeo, "Inverted Yield Curve and Why It Predicts a Recession," *The Balance*, June 25, 2019, https://www.thebalance.com/inverted-yield-curve-3305856; James McWhinney, "The Impact of the Inverted Yield Curve," Investopedia, March 26, 2019, https://www.investopedia.com/articles/basics/06/invertedyieldcurve.asp.

54. Sean Williams, "6 Signs We're Closer to the Next Recession Than You Think," *USA Today*, September 7, 2018; Joel Anderson, "10 Recession Warning Signs You Need to Know," GOBankingRates, June 28, 2019, https://www.gobankingrates.com/making-money/economy/recession-warning-signs/#2.

55. Harman, *Marxism*, chap. 6; Stuart Easterling, "Marx's Theory of Economic Crisis," *International Socialist Review* 32 (November-December 2003); David M. Kotz, "Marxist Crisis Theory and the Severity of the Current Economic Crisis," University of Massachusetts, Amherst, December 2009, https://people.umass.edu/dmkotz/Marxist_Cr_Th_09_12.pdf; John Weeks, *Capital, Exploitation and Economic Crisis* (Abingdon-on-Thames: Routledge, 2011); Howard Sherman, *The Business Cycle: Growth and Crisis Under Capitalism* (Princeton: Princeton University Press, 2014); Alfredo Saad-Filho, *The Value of Marx* (Abingdon-on-Thames: Routledge, 2007).

56. Ibid.

57. Richard D. Wolff, *Occupy the Economy: Challenging Capitalism* (San Francisco: City Lights Publishers, 2012); Bob Bryan, "There's Another Sign the US Could be Headed For Recession," *Business Insider*, April 18, 2016.

58. John Dewey, *John Dewey: The Later Works, 1925–1953*, ed. Jo Ann Boydston (Carbondale: Southern Illinois University Press, 1986), 9:61.

59. Jake Grovum, "2008 Financial Crisis Impact Still Hurting States," *USA Today*, September 15, 2013.

4: THE PROFIT MOTIVE: PEOPLE AND THE PLANET

1. Keller, "New Vision," 55.

2. "2014 Preventable Deaths: The Tragedy of Workplace Fatalities," National Council for Occupational Safety and Health, accessed July 12, 2019, http://www.coshnetwork.org/sites/default/files/uploads/Preventable_ Deaths-2014.pdf; "Death on the Job: The Toll of Neglect, 2017," AFL–CIO, April 26, 2017, https://aflcio.org/reports/death-job-toll-neglect-2017; "The Dirty Dozen 2018: Employers Who Put Workers and Communities at Risk," National Council for Occupational Safety and Health, April 2018, http://coshnetwork.org/sites/default/files/Dirty%20Dozen%202018%2C%20 4-25-18%2BFINAL%281%29.pdf.

3. "Employer-reported Workplace Injuries and Illnesses—2017," Bureau of Labor Statistics, November 8, 2018, https://stats.bls.gov/news.release/archives/osh_11082018.pdf.

4. Michael Buehler, Edmundo Werna, and Mark Brown, "More Than 2 Million People Die at Work Each Year. Here's How to Prevent It," World Economic Forum, March 23, 2017, https://www.weforum.org/agenda/2017/03/work-place-death-health-safety-ilo-fluor/; "ILO Calls For Urgent Global Action to Fight Occupational Diseases," International Labour Organization, April 26, 2013, https://www.ilo.org/global/about-the-ilo/newsroom/news/WCMS_211627/lang--en/index.htm.

5. "The Dirty Dozen 2017: Employers Who Put Workers and Communities at Risk," National Council for Occupational Safety and Health, April 2017, https://drive.google.com/file/d/0B2MOa-NgCU4ZUFNtT2hSVk9EeEk/view; "The Dirty Dozen 2018," National Council for Occupational Safety and Health.

6. "Death on the Job," AFL–CIO; Drew Desilver, "More Older Americans Are Working, and Working More, Than They Used To," Pew Research Center, June 20, 2016, http://www.pewresearch.org/fact-tank/2016/06/20/more-older-americans-are-working-and-working-more-than-they-used-to/.

7. Mary Jordan and Kevin Sullivan, "The New Reality of Old Age in America," *Washington Post*, September 30, 2017.

8. Melissa Chan, "How Working Too Much Can Actually Kill You," *Time*, October 6, 2017.

9. Jeff Pfeffer, "How Your Workplace is Killing You," BBC, May 3, 2018.

10. Jena McGregor, "Stanford Professor Says the Workplace Is the Fifth Leading Cause of Death in the U.S.," *Chicago Tribune*.

11. Goldwin, Imagine, 232; "'Poisoned' Chinese Workers Turn to Apple For Help," BBC, February 23, 2011.

12. Guy Quenneville, "Teen's Preventable Death 'Shamed' Shercom Industries into Making Safety Fixes, Says Judge," CBC, January 12, 2018.

13. Sean Cockerham, "BP 'Reckless,' 'Profit-driven' in 2010 Gulf Oil Spill, Judge Rules," *McClatchy*, September 4, 2014; "Profit Over Safety: BP Faces Billions in Fines For 'Grossly Negligent' Role in 2010 Gulf Oil Spill," *Democracy Now!*, September 4, 2014, https://soundcloud.com/democracynow/profit-over-safety-bp-faces-billions-in-fines-for-grossly-negligent-role-in-2010-gulf-oil-spill.

14. Michael Grabell, "Hummus Maker Warned of 'Extreme Safety Risk' Before Temp Worker's Death," *ProPublica*, May 21, 2014, https://www.propublica.org/article/hummus-maker-warned-of-extreme-safety-risk-before-temp-workers-death.

15. Sandy Smith, "58 Percent of Construction Workers Say Safety Takes a Backseat to Productivity," *EHS Today*, May 18, 2017, https://www.ehstoday.com/construction/58-percent-construction-workers-say-safety-takes-back-seat-productivity.

16. Stephanie Valentic, "Productivity Takes Precedent Over Employee Health and Safety, Survey Finds," *EHS Today*, June 20, 2016, https://www.ehstoday.com/2016NSS.

17. Brett Snider, "How Many Workplace Injuries Go Unreported?," *Find Law* (blog), December 20, 2013, https://blogs.findlaw.com/injured/2013/12/how-many-workplace-injuries-go-unreported.html; "The Dirty Dozen 2017," National Council for Occupational Safety and Health.

18. Ladan Nikravan Hayes, "New CareerBuilder Survey Finds 72 Percent of Workers Who Experience Sexual Harassment at Work Do Not Report It," *CareerBuilder*, January 19, 2018, http://press.careerbuilder.com/2018-01-19-New-CareerBuilder-Survey-Finds-72-Percent-of-Workers-Who-Experience-Sexual-Harassment-at-Work-Do-Not-Report-it.

19. Judson Caskey and N. Bugra Ozel, "Research: Workplace Injuries Are More Common When Companies Face Earnings Pressure," *Harvard Business Review*, May 18, 2017.

20. Jordan B. Schwartz and Eric J. Conn, "OSHA Criminal Referrals on the Rise," Epstein, Becker, and Green, December 18, 2012, https://www.

oshalawupdate.com/2012/12/18/osha-criminal-referrals-on-the-rise/; Randy Rabinowitz, "OSHA Has a Big Job, on a Tiny Budget," *New York Times*, April 29, 2013; David Barstow, "U.S. Rarely Seeks Charges For Deaths in Workplace," *New York Times*, December 22, 2003; "Commonly Used Statistics," Occupational Safety and Health Administration, accessed July 12, 2019, https://www.osha.gov/oshstats/commonstats.html.

21. "OSHA Penalties," Occupational Safety and Health Administration, accessed July 12, 2019, https://www.osha.gov/penalties/.

22. "BP History Fact Sheet," Occupational Safety and Health Administration, accessed July 12, 2019, https://www.osha.gov/dep/bp/bphistory.html; Graeme Wearden, "BP Profits Jump After Oil Price Rise," *The Guardian*, April 27, 2010.

23. Malcolm X, "Malcolm X at the Audubon Ballroom" (speech, New York City, December 20, 1964), *Teaching American History*, http://teachingamericanhistory.org/library/document/at-the-audubon/.

24. Upton Sinclair to John Reed, October 22, 1918, Spartacus Educational, https://spartacus-educational.com/Jupton.htm.

25. Michael Moore, dir., *Capitalism: A Love Story* (New York: Dog Eat Dog Films, 2009).

26. Ellen E. Schultz and Theo Francis, "Companies Profit on Workers' Deaths Through 'Dead Peasants' Insurance," *Wall Street Journal*, April 19, 2002.

27. David Gelles, "An Employee Dies, and the Company Collects Insurance," *New York Times*, June 22, 2014.

28. Shruti Singh, "Denied Breaks, U.S. Poultry Workers Wear Diapers on the Job," *Bloomberg*, May 11, 2016.

29. Shona Ghosh, "Peeing in Trash Cans, Constant Surveillance, and Asthma Attacks on the Job: Amazon Workers Tell Us Their Warehouse Horror Stories," *Business Insider*, May 3, 2018; Harriet Agerholm, "Amazon Workers Working 55-hour Weeks and So Exhausted by Targets They 'Fall Asleep Standing Up,'" *Independent*, November 27, 2017.

30. Rachel Abrams, "Walmart Is Accused of Punishing Workers For Sick Days," *New York Times*, June 1, 2017.

31. Hilary Osborne, "Amazon Accused of 'Intolerable Conditions' at Scottish Warehouse," *The Guardian*, December 12, 2016.

32. Annie Lowrey, "Jeff Bezos' $150 Billion Fortune Is a Policy Failure," *The Atlantic*, August 1, 2018.

33. Sophie Weiner, "Walmart Patents Audio Surveillance Tool to Monitor Employee Conversations," *Splinter*, July 11, 2018, https://splinternews.com/walmart-patents-audio-surveillance-tool-to-monitor-empl-1827529033; Thuy Ong, "Amazon Patents Wristbands that Track Warehouse Employees' Hands in Real Time," *The Verge*, February 1, 2018,

https://www.theverge.com/2018/2/1/16958918/amazon-patents-trackable-wristband-warehouse-employees.

34. Sara Salinas, "Tesla Factory Workers Were Reportedly Offered Free Red Bull, Walked Through Raw Sewage to Meet Model 3 Quotas," CNBC, July 12, 2018; "The Dirty Dozen 2018," National Council for Occupational Safety and Health; Brittany Shoot, "Tesla Factory Used Lyft Instead of Ambulances to Send Workers to the Hospital, Report Says," *Fortune*, November 5, 2018.

35. Scott Borchert, "Woody Guthrie: Redder Than Remembered," *Monthly Review*, May 1, 2011; Woody Guthrie, *Pastures of Plenty: A Self-Portrait*, ed. Dave Marsh and Harold Leventhal (New York: HarperCollins, 1990), 74, 207.

36. Lise Nelson, "Donald Trump's Wall Ignored the Economic Logic of Undocumented Immigrant Labor," UPI, October 26, 2016.

37. Cristina Jimenez, "Exploited: The Plight of the Undocumented Worker," *AlterNet*, August 11, 2008, https://web.archive.org/web/20170306235558/http://www.alternet.org/story/94703/exploited%3A_the_plight_of_the_undocumented_worker.

38. Travis Putnam Hill, "Big Employers No Strangers to Benefits of Cheap, Illegal Labor," *Texas Tribune*, December 19, 2016.

39. Ibid.

40. Young Park, *The Dark Side: Immigrants, Racism, and the American Way* (Bloomington: iUniverse, 2012), 169–70; "History of Labor in Hawai'i," University of Hawai'i, West O'ahu, accessed July 13, 2019, https://www.hawaii.edu/uhwo/clear/home/HawaiiLaborHistory.html; Deborah Rudacille, *Roots of Steel: Boom and Bust in an American Mill Town* (New York: Anchor Books, 2010), 63; Rodney Coates, Abby Ferber, David Brunsma, *The Matrix of Race: Social Construction, Intersectionality, and Inequality* (Thousand Oaks: SAGE Publications, 2017), 291.

41. Malcolm X, "Remarks at Militant Labor Forum Symposium on 'Blood Brothers'" (speech, New York City, May 29, 1964), Memorial University of Newfoundland, http://collections.mun.ca/PDFs/radical/TwoSpeechesbyMalcolmX.pdf. See page 17.

42. Peter Louis Goldman, *The Death and Life of Malcolm X* (Champaign: University of Illinois Press, 1979), 235; "Quotations From Rev. Dr. Martin Luther King, Jr.," Kairos Center for Religions, Rights, and Social Justice, accessed July 15, 2019, http://kairoscenter.org/wp-content/uploads/2014/11/King-quotes-2-page.pdf.

43. James Baldwin, *Conversations with James Baldwin* (Jackson: University Press of Mississippi, 1989), 131; James Baldwin, *No Name in the Street* (New York: Random House, 2007), 175.

44. Manning Marable, *W.E.B. Du Bois: Black Radical Democrat* (New York:

Routledge, 2016), 89; W.E.B. du Bois, "The American Negro and Communism," University of Massachusetts, Amherst, accessed July 13, 2019, http://credo. library.umass.edu/view/pageturn/mums312-b206-i015/#page/1/mode/1up.

45. Jane Anna Gordon and Cyrus Ernesto Zirakzadeh, eds., *The Politics of Richard Wright: Perspectives on Resistance* (Lexington: University Press of Kentucky, 2018), 25.

46. Wright, *Envisioning Real Utopias*, 74.

47. Micheline Maynard, "The $2 Billion Toll of GM's Defect Coverup," *Forbes*, September 17, 2015.

48. Russell Hotten, "Volkswagen: The Scandal Explained," BBC, December 10, 2015, http://www.bbc.com/news/business-34324772.

49. Doreen McCallister, "Takata Pleads Guilty in Air Bag Scheme, Will Pay $1 Billion in Penalties," NPR, February 28, 2017, https://www.npr.org/sections/thetwo-way/2017/02/28/517647864/takata-pleads-guilty-in-air-bag-scheme-will-pay-1-billion-in-penalties.

50. Lesley Stahl, "Life Insurance Industry Under Investigation," CBS, April 17, 2016.

51. German Lopez, "The 3 Deadliest Drugs in America Are Legal," *Vox*, January 17, 2017, https://www.vox.com/2014/5/19/5727712/drug-alcohol-deaths.

52. Ryan Jaslow, "Big Tobacco Kept Cancer Risk in Cigarettes Secret: Study," CBS, September 30, 2011.

53. Mark Fainaru-Wada, "How the NFL Worked to Hide the Truth about Concussions and Brain Damage," *Scientific American*, March 7, 2014.

54. J.B. MacKinnon, "The L.E.D. Quandary: Why There's No Such Thing as 'Built to Last,'" *New Yorker*, July 14, 2016; Nicholas Vinocur, "Italy Hits Apple, Samsung With Fines Over 'Planned Obsolescence,'" *Politico*, October 24, 2018, https://www.politico.eu/article/italy-hits-apple-samsung-with-fines-over-planned-obsolescence/.

55. Morgan Whitaker, "'Salt Sugar Fat': How Food Companies Put Profits Ahead of Public Health," MSNBC, October 2, 2013.

56. Dan Charles, "A Muscle Drug for Pigs Comes Out of the Shadows," NPR, August 14, 2015, https://www.npr.org/sections/thesalt/2015/08/14/432102733/a-muscle-drug-for-pigs-comes-out-of-the-shadows.

57. Sinclair, *The Jungle*, chap. 29.

58. Nichols, *The "S" Word*, 212.

59. Stan Dorn, "Uninsured and Dying Because of It," Urban Institute, January 2008, http://www.urban.org/sites/default/files/publication/31386/411588-Uninsured-and-Dying-Because-of-It.PDF; David Morgan, "Over 26,000 Annual

Deaths For Uninsured: Report," *Reuters*, June 20, 2012; Reed Ableson, "Harvard Medical Study Links Lack of Insurance to 45,000 Deaths a Year," *New York Times*, September 17, 2009.

60. Cathy Schoen, Robin Osborn, David Squires, Michelle M. Doty, Roz Pierson, and Sandra Applebaum, "How Health Insurance Design Affects Access to Care and Costs, by Income, in Eleven Countries," *Health Affairs*, December 2010, https://www.healthaffairs.org/doi/abs/10.1377/hlthaff.2010.0862.

61. Alison P. Galvani, David P. Durham, Sten H. Vermund, and Meagan C. Fitzpatrick, "California Universal Health Care: An Economic Stimulus and Life-saving Proposal," *Lancet* 390, no. 10106 (September 15, 2017).

62. Karen Pallarito, "17,000 Child Deaths Linked to Lack of Insurance," *U.S. News and World Report*, October 29, 2009.

63. Sabriya Rice, "Uninsured More Likely to Die During Hospital Stay," CNN, June 10, 2010.

64. Ian Millhiser, "Here's How Many People Could Die Every Year if Obamacare Is Repealed," *Think Progress*, December 7, 2016, https://thinkprogress.org/heres-how-many-people-could-die-every-year-if-obamacare-is-repealed-ae4bf3e100a2.

65. Benjamin Sommers, "Face Facts, GOP: Obamacare is a Lifeline That's Doing Enormous Good," *USA Today*, June 20, 2017; Rachel West, "Expanding Medicare in All States Would Save 14,000 Lives Per Year," Center for American Progress, October 24, 2018, https://www.americanprogress.org/issues/healthcare/reports/2018/10/24/459676/expanding-medicaid-states-save-14000-lives-per-year/.

66. Ibid.

67. Galvani, "California Universal Health Care"; Michael Hiltzik, "How Many People Will Die from the Republicans' Obamacare Repeal Bills? Tens of Thousands per Year," *Los Angeles Times*, June 26, 2017.

68. Lacie Glover, "How Much Does Chemotherapy Cost?," *NerdWallet* (blog), March 8, 2016, https://www.nerdwallet.com/blog/health/medical-costs/how-much-does-chemotherapy-cost/; "Diabetes Treatment Cost," Cost Helper, accessed July 13, 2019, http://health.costhelper.com/cost-diabetes-care.html.

69. Andrew Pollack, "Drug Goes from $13.50 a Tablet to $750, Overnight," *New York Times*, September 20, 2015.

70. Dan Mangan, "Medical Bills Are the Biggest Cause of US Bankruptcies: Study," CNBC, June 25, 2013, http://www.cnbc.com/id/100840148.

71. Michael Rainey, "Affordable Care Act Hasn't Reduced Bankruptcies," *The Fiscal Times*, February 11, 2019, https://www.thefiscaltimes.com/2019/02/11/Affordable-Care-Act-Hasn-t-Reduced-Bankruptcies-Study.

72. Molly Gamble, "Even 20% of Insured Americans Face Burdens of Medical Debt: 5 Key Survey Findings," *Becker's Hospital Review,* January 5, 2016, http://www.beckershospitalreview.com/finance/even-20-of-insured-americans-face-burdens-of-medical-debt-5-key-survey-findings.html.

73. Adrienne M. Gilligan, David S. Alberts, Denise J. Roe, Grant H. Skrepnek, "Death or Debt? National Estimates of Financial Toxicity in Persons with Newly-Diagnosed Cancer," *American Journal of Medicine* 131, no. 10 (October 2018).

74. S. R. Collins, M. Z. Gunja, M. M. Doty, and S. Beutel, "How the Affordable Care Act Has Improved Americans' Ability to Buy Health Insurance on Their Own," The Commonwealth Fund, February 2017, https://www.commonwealthfund.org/sites/default/files/documents/____media_files_publications_issue_brief_2017_feb_1931_collins_biennial_survey_2016_ib.pdf. See summary with charts at https://www.commonwealthfund.org/sites/default/files/documents/___media_files_publications_issue_brief_2017_feb_pdf_collins_biennial_survey_2016_exhibits.pdf.

75. Kimberly Leonard, "52 Million Americans Have Pre-Existing Conditions," *U.S. News and World Report,* December 12, 2016; Brittany Shoot, "102 Million People in the U.S. Have Pre-existing Conditions, Study Says. Here's Why that Figure Is Suddenly Important," *Fortune,* October 24, 2018.

76. Stephanie Kirchgaessner, "Half a Million Americans Denied Health Coverage," CNBC, October 13, 2010.

77. Collins, "Affordable Care Act."

78. Marian Wang, "Insurers Denied Health Coverage to 1 in 7 People, Citing Pre-existing Conditions," *ProPublica,* October 13, 2010, https://www.propublica.org/blog/item/insurers-denied-health-coverage-to-1-in-7-people-citing-pre-existing-condit; "Health Insurance Company Abuses," Health Care For America Now!

79. Lisa Girion, "Blue Cross Praised Employees Who Dropped Sick Policyholders, Lawmaker Says," *Los Angeles Times,* June 17, 2009.

80. "Testimony of Wendell Potter," PBS, July 10, 2009, https://www.pbs.org/moyers/journal/07102009/potter_testimony.html.

81. Lisa Girion, "Health Insurers Tied Bonuses to Dropping Sick Policyholders," *Los Angeles Times,* November 9, 2007; Girion, "Blue Cross Praised Employees"; Michael Moore, dir., *Sicko* (New York: Dog Eat Dog Films, 2007).

82. Girion, "Health Insurers Tied Bonuses."

83. "Health Insurance Company Abuses," Health Care For America Now!

84. Sarah Kliff, "An ER Visit, a $12,000 Bill—And a Health Insurer

That Wouldn't Pay," *Vox*, January 29, 2018, https://www.vox.com/policy-and-politics/2018/1/29/16906558/anthem-emergency-room-coverage-denials-inappropriate.

85. David Lazarus, "Bummer about Your Medical Emergency, But Your Claim Is Denied Because You Didn't Call in Advance," *Los Angeles Times*, September 21, 2018.

86. "Testimony of Wendell Potter," PBS.

87. George Orwell, *The Lion and the Unicorn: Socialism and the English Genius*, Orwell Foundation, accessed July 13, 2019, https://www.orwellfoundation.com/the-orwell-foundation/orwell/essays-and-other-works/the-lion-and-the-unicorn-socialism-and-the-english-genius/. See "Part II: Shopkeepers at War," chap. 1.

88. "Testimony of Wendell Potter," PBS; "Health Insurance Company Abuses," Health Care For America Now!

89. Woolhandler, "Relationship of Health Insurance and Mortality"; "Health Insurance Company Abuses," Health Care For America Now!

90. Faith Berry, *Langston Hughes: Before and After Harlem* (New York: Citadel Press, 1992), 161.

91. Melissa Bailey, "Ambulance Trips Can Leave You with Surprising—and Very Expensive—Bills," *Washington Post*, November 20, 2017.

92. Nicole Ostrow, "Hospitals Eliminate 1 in 4 U.S. Emergency Rooms Since 1990, Study Finds," *National Nurses United*, June 2, 2011, https://www.nationalnursesunited.org/news/hospitals-eliminate-1-4-us-emergency-rooms-1990-study-finds.

93. Tami Luhby, "Premiums for Popular Obamacare Plans Soar 37% for 2018," CNN, October 30, 2017, "Aetna Fully Exits Obamacare Exchanges with Pull-out in Two States," *Reuters*, May 10, 2017.

94. Jacob Passy, "Businesses Eliminated Hundreds of Thousands of Full-time Jobs to Avoid Obamacare Mandates," *MarketWatch*, November 24, 2017, https://www.marketwatch.com/story/businesses-eliminated-hundreds-of-thousands-of-full-time-jobs-to-avoid-obamacare-mandate-2017-11-24.

95. Rachel Garfield, "The Coverage Gap: Uninsured Poor Adults in States that Do Not Expand Medicaid," Kaiser Family Foundation, March 21, 2019, https://www.kff.org/medicaid/issue-brief/the-coverage-gap-uninsured-poor-adults-in-states-that-do-not-expand-medicaid/.

96. Malcolm MacDougall, "My Insurance Company Killed Me, Despite Obamacare," *The Daily Beast*, July 12, 2017, http://www.thedailybeast.com/my-insurance-company-killed-me-despite-obamacare; Sarah Kliff and Dylan Scott, "Trump's Quiet Campaign to Bring Back Preexisting Conditions," *Vox*, February 22, 2018, https://www.vox.com/

policy-and-politics/2018/2/22/17033588/trump-obamacare-preexisting-conditions.

97. Emily E. Adams, "World Forest Area Still on the Decline," Earth Policy Institute, August 31, 2012, http://www.earth-policy.org/indicators/C56/.

98. "Deforestation and Forest Degradation," World Wildlife Fund, accessed July 13, 2019, https://www.worldwildlife.org/threats/deforestation.

99. Damian Carrington, Niko Kommenda, Pablo Gutierrez, and Cath Levett, "One Football Pitch of Forest Lost Every Second in 2017, Data Reveals," *The Guardian*, June 27, 2018.

100. Duncan Brack, "Lessons from the Control of Illegal Logging," *Chatham House*, February 16, 2016, https://www.chathamhouse.org/sites/default/files/Duncan%20Brack.pdf.

101. Khoshoo, *Gandhi and the Environment*, 49; "Letter From Helen Keller to Dr. Karl Menninger Acknowledging Receipt of the Article, 'Conserving and Using Our Open Spaces,'" American Foundation for the Blind, accessed July 16, 2019, https://www.afb.org/HelenKellerArchive?a=d&d=A-HK01-03-B073-F10-029.1.1&srpos=16&e=-------en-20--1--txt--menninger------3-7-6-5-3--------------0-1.

102. David Wallace-Wells, "The Uninhabitable Earth," *New York Magazine*, July 10, 2017.

103. Jeff Nesbit, "The Earth Breathes," *U.S. News and World Report*, January 15, 2013.

104. "Immediately Dangerous to Life or Health Concentrations: Carbon Dioxide," Centers For Disease Control and Prevention, accessed July 13, 2019, https://www.cdc.gov/niosh/idlh/124389.html.

105. Joe Romm, "Fossil Fuel Industry Spent Nearly $2 Billion to Kill U.S. Climate Action, New Study Finds," *Think Progress*, July 19, 2018, https://thinkprogress.org/fossil-fuel-industry-outspends-environment-groups-on-climate-new-study-231325b4a7e6/; "Attacks on Renewable Energy Policies in 2015," Energy and Policy Institute, July 27, 2015, https://www.energyandpolicy.org/renewable-energy-state-policy-attacks-report-2015/.

106. John Cook, Dana Nuccitelli, Sarah Green, Mark Richardson, Barbel Winkler, Rob Painting, Robert Way, Peter Jacobs, and Andrew Skuce, "Quantifying the Consensus on Anthropogenic Global Warming in the Scientific Literature," *Environmental Research Letters* 8, no. 2 (May 15, 2013).

107. Melissa Davey, "Humans Causing Climate to Change 170 Times Faster Than Natural Forces," *The Guardian*, February 12, 2017.

108. "Report: All Major Oil Companies Knew of Climate Change by 1970s," *Democracy Now!*, December 24, 2015, https://www.democracynow.org/2015/12/24/headlines/report_all_major_oil_

companies_knew_of_climate_change_by_1970s.

109. Justin Gillis and John Schwartz, "Deeper Ties to Corporate Cash for Doubtful Climate Researcher," *New York Times*, February 21, 2015.

110. Justin Gillis, "U.S. Climate Has Already Changed, Study Finds, Citing Heat and Floods," *New York Times*, May 6, 2014.

111. "Report: Climate Crisis Already Causing Unprecedented Damage to World Economy; Human Impact on Large-Scale," DARA, September 26, 2012, http://daraint.org/wp-content/uploads/2012/09/CVM_RELEASE_FINAL_ENGLISH.pdf.

112. Wallace-Wells, "The Uninhabitable Earth."

113. Kendra Pierre-Louis, "As Climate Warms, Plants Will Absorb Less CO2, Study Finds," *New York Times*, January 23, 2019.

114. Coral Davenport, "Major Climate Report Describes a Strong Risk of Crisis as Early as 2040," *New York Times*, October 7, 2018.

115. Christopher Flavelle, "Corporate America Is Getting Ready to Monetize Climate Change," *Bloomberg*, January 22, 2019.

116. Martin Luther King, Jr., *The Lost Massey Lectures: Recovered Classics from Five Great Thinkers* (Toronto: House of Anansi Press, 2008), 172.

117. Wallace-Wells, "The Uninhabitable Earth."

118. "Report: Climate Crisis," DARA.

119. Katie Silver, "Pollution Linked to One in Six Deaths," BBC, October 20, 2017.

120. Susan Brink, "Report: Pollution Kills 3 Times More Than AIDS, TB and Malaria Combined," NPR, October 19, 2017, http://www.npr.org/sections/goatsandsoda/2017/10/19/558821792/report-pollution-kills-3-times-more-than-aids-tb-and-malaria-combined.

121. Silver, "Report: Pollution Kills."

122. Wallace-Wells, "The Uninhabitable Earth."

123. Ibid.

124. Kim Eckart, "Air Pollution is Damaging Our Mental Health," World Economic Forum, November 8, 2017, https://www.weforum.org/agenda/2017/11/why-high-air-pollution-could-cause-poor-mental-health/.

125. Nick Van Mead, "Tipping Point: Revealing the Cities Where Exercise Does More Harm Than Good," *The Guardian*, February 13, 2017.

126. Pyarelal Nayyar, *Mahatma Gandhi, vol. 10, The Last Phase* (Ahmedabad: Navajivan, 1958), https://www.mkgandhi.org/ebks/mahatma-gandhi-volume-ten.pdf. See page 668.

5: POVERTY

1. London, *War of the Classes*. See the final chapter, "How I Became a

Socialist."

2. "Census Data: Half of U.S. Poor or Low Income," CBS, December 15, 2011.

3. Michelle Chen, "Almost Half of All American Workers Make Less Than $15 an Hour," *The Nation*, November 11, 2015; Maurie Backman, "This is the Average American's Salary. How Does Yours Compare? Some Tips For Improving It," *USA Today*, October 16, 2018.

4. Aimee Picchi, "The Surging Ranks of America's Ultrapoor," CBS, September 1, 2015.

5. Steve Reilly, "Watchdog Report: Workers with Disabilities Earn Pennies Per Hour," *Press Connects*, July 3, 2014, https://www.pressconnects.com/story/news/2014/06/28/watchdog-report-workers-with-disabilities-earn-pennies-per-hour/11629369/.

6. Carimah Townes, "'It's Just Dressed Up Slavery': America's Shadow Workforce Rises Up Against Prison Labor," *Think Progress*, September 9, 2016, https://thinkprogress.org/its-just-dressed-up-slavery-america-s-shadow-workforce-rises-up-against-prison-labor-e8ee1b5a8738/; David Love and Vijay Das, "Slavery in the US Prison System," *Al Jazeera*, September 9, 2017; Azadeh Shahshahani, "Why Are For-Profit US Prisons Subjecting Detainees to Forced Labor?," *The Guardian*, May 17, 2018.

7. John Schmitt and Janelle Jones, "Where Have All the Good Jobs Gone?," Center for Economic and Policy Research, July 2012, http://cepr.net/documents/publications/good-jobs-2012-07.pdf.

8. Michelle Jamrisko and Ilan Kolet, "Cost of College Degrees in U.S. Soars 12 Fold: Chart of the Day," *Bloomberg*, August 15, 2012.

9. Emmie Martin, "Here's How Much Housing Prices Have Skyrocketed over the Last 50 Years," CNBC, June 23, 2017; Emmie Martin, "Home Prices Have Risen 114% since 1960—Here's How Much More Expensive Life Is Today," CNBC, April 17, 2018.

10. "US Residential Rent and Rental Statistics," Department of Numbers, accessed July 21, 2019, http://www.deptofnumbers.com/rent/us/.

11. Lauren Debter, "The Cities Where Rent Is Rising the Fastest," *Forbes*, February 24, 2015.

12. Maggie McGrath, "63% of Americans Don't Have Enough Savings to Cover a $500 Emergency," *Forbes*, January 6, 2016.

13. Jessica Dickler, "Most Americans Live Paycheck to Paycheck," CNBC, August 24, 2017.

14. Matthew Boesler, "New York Fed Study Finds 15% of U.S. Households Have No Wealth," *Bloomberg*, August 1, 2016.

15. Daniel J.B. Mitchell, "Upton Sinclair Was a Socialist Candidate Who

Succeeded through Failure," *Smithsonian Magazine*, March 1, 2016.

16. Victor Hugo, "Victor Hugo's Letter to the Rich," *Gavroche*, accessed July 21, 2019, http://www.gavroche.org/vhugo/GlancesAtSocialism.shtml.

17. Sabrina Tavernise, "Disparity in Life Spans of the Rich and the Poor Is Growing," *New York Times*, February 12, 2016.

18. Jim Erickson, "Targeting Minority, Low-income Neighborhoods for Hazardous Waste Sites," University of Michigan, January 19, 2016, https://news.umich.edu/targeting-minority-low-income-neighborhoods-for-hazardous-waste-sites/.

19. Stephen Smith, "Tobacco Signs Still Target City's Poorer Areas," *Boston Globe*, August 30, 2010.

20. Kimberly Brown, "Shocking Need: American Kids Go Hungry," *ABC News*, August 24, 2011; "Ketchup Sandwiches and Other Things Stupid Poor People Eat," *Think Progress*, September 8, 2016, https://thinkprogress.org/ketchup-sandwiches-and-other-things-stupid-poor-people-eat-41617483b497/.

21. Orwell, *Road to Wigan Pier*, 203.

22. Stephen Pimpare, *A People's History of Poverty in America* (New York: The New Press, 2011).

23. Stephen Bezruchka, "The Deteriorating International Ranking of U.S. Health Status," *Annual Review of Public Health* 33 (April 2012): 157–73; John Daley, "Tooth Decay: A Silent Epidemic, Especially For Poor Kids in Colo.," *CPR*, March 12, 2015, https://www.cpr.org/2015/03/12/tooth-decay-a-silent-epidemic-especially-for-poor-kids-in-colo/.

24. Melanie Haiken, "More Than 10,000 Suicides Tied to Economic Crisis, Study Says," *Forbes*, June 12, 2014.

25. "How Many People Experience Homelessness?," National Coalition For the Homeless, July 2009, http://www.nationalhomeless.org/factsheets/How_Many.html; Bill Quigley, "10 Facts About Homelessness," *Huffington Post*, December 6, 2017, https://www.huffpost.com/entry/ten-facts-about-homelessn_b_5977946.

26. Ibid; "Discrimination and Economic Profiling among the Homeless of Washington, DC," National Coalition for the Homeless, April 2014, http://www.frontsteps.org/wp-content/uploads/2014/04/DiscriminationReport20141.pdf.

27. Robert Rosenberger, "How Cities Use Design to Drive Homeless People Away," *The Atlantic*, June 19, 2014.

28. Scott Keyes, "7 Homeless People Freeze to Death in Wealthiest Area of the Country," *AlterNet*, December 19, 2013, https://www.alternet.org/news-amp-politics/7-homeless-people-freeze-death-wealthiest-area-country.

29. Richard Florida, "Vacancy: America's Other Housing Crisis," *CityLab*, July 27, 2018, https://www.citylab.com/equity/2018/07/vacancy-americas-other-housing-crisis/565901/.

30. London, *War of the Classes*. See the chapter "Wanted: A New Law of Development."

31. "Policy Basics: The Supplemental Nutrition Assistance Program (SNAP)," Center on Budget and Policy Priorities, June 25, 2019, https://www.cbpp.org/research/food-assistance/policy-basics-the-supplemental-nutrition-assistance-program-snap.

32. Dorian Merina, "When Active Duty Service Members Struggle to Feed Their Families," *NPR*, April 19, 2017, https://www.npr.org/sections/thesalt/2017/04/19/524563155/when-active-duty-service-members-struggle-to-feed-their-families.

33. Pimpare, *Poverty in America*.

34. Derek Thompson, "Busting the Myth of 'Welfare Makes People Lazy,'" *The Atlantic*, March 8, 2018.

35. Charles Dickens, *Hard Times*, Project Gutenberg, accessed July 22, 2019, https://www.gutenberg.org/files/786/786-h/786-h.htm. See book 2, chapter 1, "Effects in the Bank."

36. Wilde, *Soul of Man*, 10.

37. Alyssa Davis, Will Kimball, and Elise Gould, "The Class of 2015: Despite an Improving Economy, Young Grads Still Face an Uphill Climb," Economic Policy Institute, May 27, 2015, http://www.epi.org/publication/the-class-of-2015/.

38. Alan Pyke, "Half a Million People With College Degrees Are Working For Minimum Wage," *Think Progress*, March 31, 2014, http://thinkprogress.org/economy/2014/03/31/3420987/college-degree-minimum-wage/.

39. Keith Speights, "Success Rate: What Percentage of Businesses Fail in Their Firth Year?," *USA Today*, May 21, 2017.

40. Ross Levine and Yona Rubinstein, "Smart and Illicit: Who Becomes an Entrepreneur and Do They Earn More?," National Bureau of Economic Research, August 2013, https://www.nber.org/papers/w19276.pdf?new_window=1.

41. Aimee Groth, "Entrepreneurs Don't Have a Special Gene For Risk—They Come from Families with Money," *Quartz*, July 17, 2015, https://qz.com/455109/entrepreneurs-dont-have-a-special-gene-for-risk-they-come-from-families-with-money/.

42. Martin Luther King, Jr., "Dr. Martin Luther King, Jr. Speaking at The New School," Amherst College, accessed July 22, 2019, https://www.amherst.edu/library/archives/holdings/mlk/transcript.

43. James Loewen, *Lies My Teacher Told Me* (New York: Simon & Schuster,

1996), 203–5; "Effects of Poverty, Hunger, and Homelessness on Children and Youth," American Psychological Association, accessed July 22, 2019, https://www.apa.org/pi/families/poverty.aspx?item=1.

44. Sarah E. Cusick and Michael K. Georgieff, "The Role of Nutrition in Brain Development: The Golden Opportunity of the 'First 1000 Days,'" *Journal of Pediatrics* 175 (August 2016): 16-21, https://www.ncbi.nlm.nih.gov/pmc/articles/PMC4981537/.

45. "Lead Poisoning and Health," World Health Organization, August 23, 2018, http://www.who.int/news-room/fact-sheets/detail/lead-poisoning-and-health; Katie Claflin, "Can Your Housing Situation Affect Your Mental Health? Studies Say Yes," Texas State Affordable Housing Corporation, August 12, 2016, https://www.tsahc.org/blog/post/can-your-housing-situation-affect-your-mental-health-studies-say-yes.

46. "Effects of Poverty," American Psychological Association.

47. Guy Boulton, "Growing Up in Severe Poverty Affects Brain Size, UW-Madison Study Shows," *Journal Sentinel*, August 29, 2015; Nicole L. Hair, Jamie Hanson, Barbara Wolfe, and Seth Pollak, "Association of Child Poverty, Brain Development, and Academic Achievement," *JAMA Pediatrics* 169, no. 9 (September 2015).

48. Emily Badger, "How Poverty Taxes the Brain," *CityLab*, August 29, 2013, http://www.citylab.com/work/2013/08/how-poverty-taxes-brain/6716/.

49. Jessica Lahey, "Poor Kids and the 'Word Gap,'" *The Atlantic*, October 16, 2014.

50. Heather Long, "By Age 3, Inequality Is Clear: Rich Kids Attend School. Poor Kids Stay with a Grandparent," *Washington Post*, September 26, 2017.

51. Jennifer L. Hochschild, "Social Class in Public Schools," *Journal of Social Issues* 59, no. 4 (December 2003): 821–40; Mayke Poesen-Vandeputte and Ides Nicaise, "Rich Schools, Poor Schools. Hidden Resource Inequalities Between Primary Schools," *Education Research* 57, no. 1 (December 2014); Bruce D. Baker, "How Money Matters For Schools," Learning Policy Institute, December 2017, https://learningpolicyinstitute.org/sites/default/files/product-files/How_Money_Matters_REPORT.pdf.

52. Corey Turner, "Why America's Schools Have a Money Problem," NPR, April 18, 2016, https://www.npr.org/2016/04/18/474256366/why-americas-schools-have-a-money-problem; Lauren Camera, "In Most States, Poorest School Districts Get Less Funding," *U.S. News & World Report*, February 27, 2018, ; Michael B. Sauter, Thomas C. Frohlich, Sam Stebbins, and Evan Comen. "America's Richest (and Poorest) School Districts," *USA Today*, October 3, 2015, ; "The ABCs of ESEA, ESSA and No Child Left Behind," *Education Post*, accessed July 23, 2019, https://educationpost.org/

the-abcs-of-esea-essa-and-no-child-left-behind/.

53. "Students of Color Still Receiving Unequal Education," Center for American Progress, August 22, 2012, http://www.americanprogress. org/issues/education/news/2012/08/22/32862/students-of-color-still-receiving-unequal-education/.

54. "Detroit Student: 'I Want to Be Able to Go to School without Worrying about Being Bitten by Mice,'" *Democracy Now!*, January 21, 2016, https://www. democracynow.org/2016/1/21/detroit_student_i_want_to_be.

55. Loewen, *Lies*, 203–5; Jonathon Kozol, *Ordinary Resurrections* (New York: Broadway Books, 2012). Indeed, read all of Kozol's works to get a sense of how poor children are viewed, and the effects.

56. Christie Blazer, "The Effect of Poverty on Student Achievement," Research Services, Miami-Dade County Public Schools, July 2009, https:// eric.ed.gov/?id=ED544709; Juan Battle and Michael Lewis, "The Increasing Significance of Class: The Relative Effects of Race and Socioeconomic Status on Academic Achievement," *Journal of Poverty* 6, no. 2 (November 5, 2008): 21–35; Selcuk R. Sirin, "Socioeconomic Status and Academic Achievement: A Meta-Analytic Review of Research," *Review of Educational Research* (September 1, 2005); Misty Lacour and Laura D. Tissington, "The Effects of Poverty on Academic Achievement," *Educational Research and Reviews* 6, no. 7 (July 2011): 522–27; Sauter, "America's Richest."

57. Motoko Rich, Amanda Cox, and Matthew Bloch. "Money, Race and Success: How Your School District Compares," *New York Times*, April 29, 2016.

58. Loewen, *Lies*, 203–05.

59. Meredith Broussard, "Why Poor Schools Can't Win at Standardized Testing," *The Atlantic*, July 15, 2014.

60. Josh Zumbrun, "SAT Scores and Income Inequality: How Wealthier Kids Rank Higher," *Wall Street Journal*, October 7, 2014.

61. Ben Cosman, "The High School Graduation Rate Is Great, Unless You're Poor," *The Atlantic*, April 28, 2014; Alanna Bjorklund-Young, "Family Income and the College Completion Gap," John Hopkins School of Education, March 10, 2016, http://edpolicy.education.jhu.edu/family-income-and-the-college-completion-gap/.

62. "If You're So Smart, Why Aren't You Rich? Turns Out It's Just Chance," *MIT Technology Review*, March 1, 2018, https://www. technologyreview.com/s/610395/if-youre-so-smart-why-arent-you-rich-turns-out-its-just-chance/.

63. Malcolm Gladwell, *Outliers* (New York: Back Bay Books, 2011), 111.

64. "Understanding Mobility in America," Center for American Progress, April 26, 2006, https://www.americanprogress.org/issues/economy/news/

2006/04/26/1917/understanding-mobility-in-america/.

65. Sean McElwee, "The Myth Destroying America: Why Social Mobility Is Beyond Ordinary People's Control," *Salon*, March 7, 2015, http://www.salon.com/2015/03/07/the_myth_destroying_america_why_social_mobility_is_beyond_ordinary_peoples_control/.

66. Julia B. Isaacs, "Economic Mobility of Families Across Generations," Brookings Institute, November 13, 2007, http://www.brookings.edu/research/papers/2007/11/generations-isaacs.

67. Bhashkar Mazumder, "Sibling Similarities, Differences and Economic Inequality," Federal Reserve Bank of Chicago, September 3, 2004, https://papers.ssrn.com/sol3/papers.cfm?abstract_id=586190; Nadarajan Chetty, Nathaniel Hendren, Patrick Kline, and Emmanuel Saez, "Where Is the Land of Opportunity? The Geography of Intergenerational Mobility in the United States," *The Quarterly Journal of Economics* 129, no. 4 (2014): 1553–1623.

68. David Leonhardt, "The American Dream, Quantified at Last," *New York Times*, December 8, 2016.

69. McElwee, "Myth Destroying America."

70. Sinclair, *The Jungle*, chap. 17.

71. John Steinbeck, *America and Americans and Selected Nonfiction* (London: Penguin, 2003).

6: CAPITALIST POLITICS

1. Grant Suneson, "The Net Worth of Every US President From George Washington to Donald Trump," *USA Today*, February 13, 2019; Andrew Katz, "Congress is Now Mostly a Millionaire's Club," *Time*, January 9, 2014.

2. "Money Wins Presidency and 9 of 10 Congressional Races in Priciest U.S. Election Ever," Center for Responsive Politics, November 5, 2008, http://www.opensecrets.org/news/2008/11/money-wins-white-house-and/; Philip Bump, "Does More Campaign Money Actually Buy More Votes: An Investigation," *The Atlantic*, November 11, 2013.

3. Dorothy Herrmann, *Helen Keller: A Life* (Chicago: University of Chicago Press, 1999), 227–28.

4. Fredreka Schouten and Christopher Schnaars, "Mega-influence: These 42 Dominate Super PAC Donations," *USA Today*, October 28, 2014.

5. "Election Overview," Center For Responsive Politics, accessed August 3, 2019, https://www.opensecrets.org/overview/; "2018 Outside Spending, by Super PAC," Center for Responsive Politics, accessed August 3, 2019, https://www.opensecrets.org/outsidespending/summ.php?cycle=2018&chrt=V&disp=O&type=S.

6. Smith, *Wealth of Nations*. See book 5, chapter 1, part 2.

7. London, *War of the Classes*. See the chapter entitled "The Question of the Maximum."

8. Zinn, *A People's History*, 548; Andrew Prokop, "Donald Trump Made One Shockingly Insightful Comment During the First GOP Debate," *Vox*, August 6, 2015, https://www.vox.com/2015/8/6/9114565/donald-trump-debate-money.

9. Spencer MacColl, "Democrats and Republicans Sharing Big-Dollar Donors, DCCC's Million-dollar Pay-off and More in Capital Eye Opener: November 10," Center for Responsive Politics, November 10, 2010, https://www.opensecrets.org/news/2010/11/democrats-and-republicans-sharing-b/.

10. Peter Olsen-Phillips, "'Fixed Fortunes' Companies Investing Heavily on Both Sides of the Aisle," Sunlight Foundation, February 23, 2015, https://sunlightfoundation.com/2015/02/23/fixed-fortunes-companies-investing-heavily-on-both-sides-of-the-aisle/; Jacob Pramuk, "Apple's Tim Cook Has Spread His Political Money to Both Sides of the Aisle," *CNBC*, August 24, 2016.

11. Eric W. Dolan, "'Oligarchic Tendencies': Study Finds Only the Wealthy Get Represented in the Senate," *RawStory*, August 19, 2013, http://www.rawstory.com/rs/2013/08/19/oligarchic-tendencies-study-finds-only-the-wealthy-get-represented-in-the-senate/.

12. Dylan Matthews, "Remember That Study Saying America Is an Oligarchy? 3 Rebuttals Say It's Wrong," *Vox*, May 9, 2016, https://www.vox.com/2016/5/9/11502464/gilens-page-oligarchy-study.

13. Russ Choma, "Republicans Say They've Got to Act on Tax Reform—or Donors Might Get Mad," *Mother Jones*, November 10, 2017, https://www.motherjones.com/politics/2017/11/republicans-say-theyve-got-to-act-on-tax-reform-or-donors-might-get-mad/.

14. Charles Austin, "What Proof That Corporate Money Influences Politicians? This New Study Has It," *In These Times*, September 22, 2017, http://inthesetimes.com/article/20543/corporate-money-citizens-united-corruption.

15. Douglas A. Luke and Melissa Krauss, "Where There's Smoke There's Money: Tobacco Industry Campaign Contributions and U.S. Congressional Voting," *American Journal of Preventive Medicine* 27, no. 5 (December 2004): 363–72.

16. Julia Conley, "Dems Not Backing Medicare for All Get Twice as Much Industry Cash as Co-sponsors," *Common Dreams*, September 14, 2017, https://www.commondreams.org/news/2017/09/14/dems-not-backing-medicare-all-get-twice-much-industry-cash-co-sponsors; Jacqueline Thomsen, "Charles Koch Donated $500K to Ryan Days After GOP Tax Plan Passed," *The Hill*,

January 21, 2018, https://thehill.com/homenews/campaign/370037-charles-koch-donated-500k-to-ryan-days-after-gop-tax-plan-passed.

17. Justin Grimmer and Eleanor Neff Powell, "Money in Exile: Campaign Contributions and Committee Access," *The Journal of Politics* 78, no. 4 (October 2016).

18. Elise Shanbacker, "Influence of Corporate Campaign Contributions in Government Contract Award Decisions," Harvard Kennedy School Shorenstein Center on Media, Politics and Public Policy, October 25, 2011, https://journalistsresource.org/studies/politics/finance-lobbying/corporate-campaign-contributions-contract-awards.

19. "Money in Politics: Empirical Evidence Database," The Brennan Center for Justice, April 4, 2017, https://www.brennancenter.org/analysis/money-politics-database#Public%20Pol. See the "Policy Outcomes and Representation" list of studies; Damon M. Cann, "Justice for Sale? Campaign Contributions and Judicial Decisionmaking," *State Politics & Policy Quarterly* 7, no. 3 (September 1, 2007): 281–97; Chris W. Bonneau and Damon M. Cann, "The Effect of Campaign Contributions on Judicial Decisionmaking," SSRN, February 4, 2009, https://papers.ssrn.com/sol3/papers.cfm?abstract_id=1337668; Filipe R. Campante, "Redistribution in a Model of Voting and Campaign Contributions," *Journal of Public Economics* 95, no 7–8 (August 2011): 646–56; Robert E. Baldwin and Christopher S. Magee, "Is Trade Policy For Sale? Congressional Voting on Recent Trade Bills," *Public Choice* 105, no. 1–2 (October 2000), 79–101, https://link.springer.com/article/10.1023/A:1005121716315.

20. Ralph Waldo Emerson, John H. Woods, and James Elliot Cabot, *The Works of Ralph Waldo Emerson: Miscellanies* (Ann Arbor: University of Michigan Library, 2006), 11:245. "Representative government is really misrepresentative."

21. Helen Keller, "To an English Woman-Suffragist," in *Helen Keller: Her Socialist Years*, ed. Philip S. Foner (New York: International Publishers NYC, 1967), 31, https://archive.org/stream/helenkellerherso00hele/helenkellerherso00hele_djvu.txt.

22. Upton Sinclair, *The Brass Check*, Archive, accessed August 3, 2019, 222, https://archive.org/stream/cu31924026364251?ref=ol#page/n225/mode/2up/search/cast+their+ballots+for.

23. Sinclair, *The Brass Check*, 153. "Politics, Journalism, and Big Business work hand in hand for the hoodwinking of the public and the plundering of labor."

24. Malcolm X, *Malcolm X Speaks*, ed. George Breitman (New York: Grove Press, 1994), 201.

25. "Who's Up, Who's Down? View Industries with the Greatest Increases and Decreases in Lobbying Spending by Quarter and by Year," Center for Responsive

Politics, accessed August 3, 2019, https://www.opensecrets.org/lobby/incdec. php; "Ranked Sectors," Center for Responsive Politics, accessed August 3, 2019, https://www.opensecrets.org/lobby/top.php?showYear=2017&indexType=c.

26. London, *Revolution*. See the chapter "Revolution."

27. Renae Merle, "Mulvaney Discloses ' Hierarchy' for Meeting Lobbyists, Saying Some Would Be Seen Only if They Paid," *Washington Post*, April 25, 2018.

28. David Gura, "How Lobbyists Get the Attention of the White House," *Marketplace*, May 3, 2013, https://www.marketplace.org/2013/05/03/ business/how-lobbyists-get-attention-white-house.

29. Joshua L. Kalla and David E. Broockman, "Campaign Contributions Facilitate Access to Congressional Officials: A Randomized Field Experiment," *American Journal of Political Science* 60, no. 3 (April 2015).

30. Nathan Grasse and Brianne Heidbreder, "The Influence of Lobbying Activity in State Legislatures: Evidence From Wisconsin," *Legislative Studies Quarterly* 36, no. 4 (October 26, 2011); Nauro F. Campos and Francesco Giovannoni, "Lobbying, Corruption and Political Influence," *Public Choice* 131, no. 1-2 (April 2007): 1–21; Stephen Weymouth, "Firm Lobbying and Influence in Developing Countries: A Multilevel Approach," *Business and Politics* 14, no. 4 (December 2012): 1–26; Simon F. Haeder and Susan Webb Yackee, "Influence and the Administrative Process: Lobbying the U.S. President's Office of Management and Budget," *American Political Science Review* 109, no. 3 (August 2015): 507–22; Susan Webb Yackee, "The Politics of *Ex Parte* Lobbying: Pre-proposal Agenda Building and Blocking During Agency Rulemaking," *Journal of Public Administration Research and Theory* 22, no. 2 (April 2012): 373–93; Joshua Ozymy, "Assessing the Impact of Legislative Lobbying Regulations on Interest Group Influence in U.S. State Legislatures," *State Politics & Policy Quarterly* (December 1, 2010).

31. Ralph Nader, *The Seventeen Solutions: Bold Ideas For Our American Future* (New York: HarperCollins, 2012); One organization built a program that compares model legislation and final bills word-for-word to judge lobbyist influence, a valuable tool. See "Legislative Influence Detector (LID)," University of Chicago, accessed August 6, 2019, https://dssg.uchicago.edu/lid/.

32. "Wall St. Lobbyists and Financial Regulation," *New York Times*, October 28, 2013; Erika Eichelberger, "House Passes Bill Written by Citigroup Lobbyists," *Mother Jones*, October 31, 2013, http://www.motherjones.com/ politics/2013/10/citigroup-bill-passes-house/.

33. Eric Lipton, "A Lobbyist Wrote the Bill. Will the Tobacco Industry Win Its E-Cigarette Fight?," *New York Times*, September 2, 2016.

34. Karen Olsson, "Ghostwriting the Law," *Mother Jones*, September/ October 2002, http://www.motherjones.com/politics/2002/09/

ghost-writing-law/; Molly Jackman, "ALEC's Influence Over Lawmaking in State Legislatures," Brookings Institute, December 6, 2013, https://www.brookings. edu/articles/alecs-influence-over-lawmaking-in-state-legislatures/.

35. Mike Spies, "The N.R.A. Lobbyist Behind Florida's Pro-Gun Policies," *New Yorker*, February 23, 2018.

36. Nell London, "It's Common for Lobbyists to Write Bills for Congress. Here's Why," Colorado Public Radio, May 10, 2016, https://web.archive.org/web/20190615122635/https://www.cpr.org/news/story/its-common-lobbyists-write-bills-congress-heres-why.

37. Avi Asher-Schapiro, "Trump Administration Fights Effort to Unionize Uber Drivers," *The Intercept*, March 26, 2018, https://theintercept.com/2018/03/26/uber-drivers-union-seattle/.

38. Emily Stewart, "The Trump Administration is Reportedly Following Industry 'Scripts' in Rolling Back Oil and Gas Drilling Restrictions," *Vox*, October 28, 2018, https://www.vox.com/policy-and-politics/2018/10/28/18034390/trump-oil-gas-drilling-fracking-ryan-zinke.

39. Toni Dixon, "Tax Lobbying Provides 22,000 Percent Return to Firms, KU Researchers Find," University of Kansas, April 9, 2009, http://archive.news.ku.edu/2009/april/9/taxlobbying.shtml.

40. Bill Allison and Sarah Harkins, "Fixed Fortunes: Biggest Corporate Political Interests Spend Billions, Get Trillions," Sunlight Foundation, November 17, 2014, https://sunlightfoundation.com/2014/11/17/fixed-fortunes-biggest-corporate-political-interests-spend-billions-get-trillions/.

41. Ibid.

42. David C. Kimball, Frank R. Baumgartner, Jeffrey M. Berry, Marie Hojnacki, Beth L. Leech, and Bryce Summary, "Who Cares About the Lobbying Agenda?," *Interest Groups and Advocacy* 1, no. 1 (May 2012): 5–25.

43. Sinclair, *The Jungle*, chap. 28.

44. "Thomas Jefferson to James Madison," University of Chicago, accessed August 3, 2019, http://press-pubs.uchicago.edu/founders/documents/v1ch15s32.html.

45. "Thomas Jefferson to George Logan, 12 November 1816," National Archives, accessed August 3, 2019, https://founders.archives.gov/documents/Jefferson/03-10-02-0390; "From Thomas Jefferson to William Branch Giles, 26 December 1825," National Archives, accessed August 3, 2019, https://founders.archives.gov/documents/Jefferson/98-01-02-5771.

46. Zinn, *A People's History*, 255.

47. Ibid., 577.

48. David Dayen, "Sen. Jeff Merkley Wants to Stop Congress Members from Insider Trading by Banning Them from Owning Stocks," *The Intercept*,

December 17, 2018, https://theintercept.com/2018/12/17/jeff-merkley-james-inhofe-ban-stock-trading/.

49. Sinclair, *The Jungle*, chap. 31.

50. Jonathan Weisman, "Trans-Pacific Partnership Seen as Door For Foreign Suits Against U.S.," *New York Times*, March 25, 2015.

51. Arthur Miller, *Timebends: A Life* (New York: Harper & Row, 1988), 184.

52. Harold Bloom, *Arthur Miller* (New York: Infobase Publishing, 2007), 157.

53. Nader, *Seventeen Solutions*.

54. Noam Chomsky, *The Common Good* (Berkeley: Odonian Press, 1998), 37.

55. Jeff Plungis, "Congress Budget Deal Suspends Trucker Rest Rule," Insurance Journal, December 10, 2014, https://www.insurancejournal.com/news/national/2014/12/10/349479.htm.

56. Bill Whitaker, "Ex-DEA Agent: Opioid Crisis Fueled by Drug Industry and Congress," *CBS*, October 15, 2017.

57. Malcolm X, *Malcolm X Speaks*, 132.

58. Eric Pianin, "15 Fortune 500 Companies Paid No Federal Income Taxes in 2014," *The Fiscal Times*, April 9, 2015, http://www.thefiscaltimes.com/2015/04/09/15-Fortune-500-Companies-Paid-No-Federal-Income-Taxes-2014.

59. Matt Krantz, "20 Big Profitable US Companies Paid No Taxes," CNBC, August 13, 2014.

60. Stephen Cohen, "Amazon Paid No US Income Taxes For 2017," *SFGate*, February 27, 2018, https://www.sfgate.com/business/tech/article/Amazon-paid-no-US-income-taxes-for-2017-12713961.php.

61. "The 35 Percent Corporate Tax Myth," Institute on Taxation and Economic Policy, March 9, 2017, https://itep.org/the-35-percent-corporate-tax-myth/; Alison Vekshin, "Tax Havens," SAGE, February 5, 2018, http://businessresearcher.sagepub.com/sbr-1946-105696-2879247/20180205/tax-havens.

62. Rob Davies, "US Corporations Have $1.4tn Hidden in Tax Havens, Claims Oxfam Report," *The Guardian*, April 14, 2016.

63. "Big U.S. Firms Hold $2.1 Trillion Overseas to Avoid Taxes: Study," *Reuters*, October 5, 2015.

64. Matthew Gardner, "Corporations Dodge $718 Billion in U.S. Taxes through Offshore Tax Havens," *The Hill*, October 7, 2016, https://thehill.com/blogs/congress-blog/economy-budget/299640-corporations-dodge-718-billion-in-us-taxes-through.

65. Thomas L. Hungerford, "Corporate Tax Rates and Economic Growth

Since 1947," Economic Policy Institute, June 4, 2013, https://www.epi.org/publication/ib364-corporate-tax-rates-and-economic-growth/.

66. Martin Luther King, Jr., *"All Labor Has Dignity,"* ed. Michael K. Honey (Boston: Beacon Press, 2012). See his "Local 1199" speech.

67. "Policy Basics: Where Do Federal Tax Revenues Come From?," Center on Budget and Policy Priorities, June 20, 2019, https://www.cbpp.org/research/federal-tax/policy-basics-where-do-federal-tax-revenues-come-from.

68. "Federal Spending: Where Does the Money Go," National Priorities Project, accessed August 3, 2019, https://www.nationalpriorities.org/budget-basics/federal-budget-101/spending/.

69. "What Are the Sources of Revenue for the Federal Government?," Tax Policy Center, accessed August 3, 2019, http://www.taxpolicycenter.org/briefing-book/background/numbers/revenue.cfm.

70. Joseph Stiglitz, "A Tax System Stacked Against the 99 Percent," *New York Times*, April 14, 2013; Thomas Piketty, *Capital in the Twenty-First Century* (Cambridge: Harvard University Press, 2014).

71. Alvin Chang, "How Marginal Tax Rates Actually Work, Explained With a Cartoon," *Vox*, January 7, 2019, https://www.vox.com/policy-and-politics/2019/1/7/18171975/tax-bracket-marginal-cartoon-ocasio-cortez-70-percent.

72. Sam Pizzigati, "For Top 400 U.S. Taxpayers, a Near-Record Year," *Too Much*, May 14, 2011, http://toomuchonline.org/for-top-400-taxpayers-a-near-record-year/.

73. Stiglitz, "A Tax System Stacked."

74. Christopher Ingraham, "As the Rich Become Super-rich, They Pay Lower Taxes. For Real," *Washington Post*, June 4, 2015.

75. Ibid.

76. Drew Desilver, "A Closer Look at Who Does (and Doesn't) Pay U.S. Income Tax," Pew Research Center, October 6, 2017, http://www.pewresearch.org/fact-tank/2017/10/06/a-closer-look-at-who-does-and-doesnt-pay-u-s-income-tax/.

77. "Who Pays? 6th Edition," Institute on Taxation and Economic Policy, October 2018, https://itep.org/whopays/?fbclid=IwAR3nJBaYrjCaldqp157VyccRVNOS-kr_8Es_dhKT1_vlmlb_sdaomOMrDX0.

78. Christopher Ingraham, "Thousands of Millionaires Don't Pay Federal Income Taxes," *Boston Globe*, October 3, 2016.

79. Pedro Nicolaci da Costa, "The Ultrawealthy Have 10% of Global GDP Stashed in Tax Havens—and It's Making Inequality Worse Than It Appears," *Business Insider*, https://www.businessinsider.com/wealthy-money-offshore-makes-inequality-look-even-worse?r=UK&IR=T.

80. Nader, *Seventeen Solutions*; Paul Kiel, Jesse Eisinger, and ProPublica, "The Golden Age of Rich People Not Paying Their Taxes," *The Atlantic*, December 11, 2018; Matthew Yglesias, "Tax Evasion is Shockingly Prevalent Among the Very Rich," *Vox*, June 7, 2017, https://www.vox.com/2017/6/7/15745978/tax-evasion-zucman.

81. Thomas Frank, *What's the Matter with Kansas?* (New York: Henry Holt & Company, 2005), 86-88.

82. Alana Semuels, "How Amazon Helped Kill a Seattle Tax on Business," *The Atlantic*, June 13, 2018.

83. J. David Goodman, "Amazon Pulls Out of Planned New York City Headquarters," *New York Times*, February 14, 2019.

84. Julio Wiziack and Maeli Prado, "Coca-Cola Threatens to Leave Brazil if Free Trade Zone's Subsidies Are Not Returned," *Folha de S.Paulo*, August 21, 2018, https://www1.folha.uol.com.br/internacional/en/business/2018/08/1979447-coca-cola-threatens-to-leave-brazil-if-free-trade-zones-subsidies-are-not-returned.shtml.

85. Marc Davis, "U.S. Government Financial Bailouts," Investopedia, April 30, 2019, https://www.investopedia.com/articles/economics/08/government-financial-bailout.asp; Chomsky, *The Common Good*, 73.

86. Mike Collins, "The Big Bank Bailout," *Forbes*, July 14, 2015.

87. Cate Reavis, "The Global Financial Crisis of 2008: The Role of Greed, Fear, and Oligarchs," MIT Sloan School of Management, March 16, 2012, https://mitsloan.mit.edu/LearningEdge/CaseDocs/09-093%20The%20Financial%20Crisis%20of%202008.Rev.pdf; Ben Chu, "Financial Crisis 2008: How Lehman Brothers Helped Cause 'The Worst Financial Crisis in History,'" *Independent*, September 12, 2018, https://www.independent.co.uk/news/business/analysis-and-features/financial-crisis-2008-why-lehman-brothers-what-happened-10-years-anniversary-a8531581.html; "Bailed Out Banks," CNN, accessed August 4, 2019, https://money.cnn.com/news/specials/storysupplement/bankbailout/.

88. Julie Creswell and Ben White, "The Guys from 'Government Sachs,'" *New York Times*, October 17, 2008; "The People from 'Government Sachs,'" *New York Times*, March 16, 2017.

89. Alan Maass, *The Case for Socialism* (Chicago: Haymarket Books, 2010), 93.

90. "$1.6B of Bank Bailout Went to Execs," *CBS*, December 21, 2008, https://www.cbsnews.com/news/16b-of-bank-bailout-went-to-execs/.

91. Zinn, *A People's History*, 575.

92. T.C. Sottek, "Comcast, Verizon, and AT&T Want Congress to Make a Net Neutrality Law Because They Will Write It," *The Verge*, July 12, 2017,

https://www.theverge.com/2017/7/12/15959932/comcast-verizon-att-net-neutrality-day-of-action; Kim Bindrim, "Donald Trump Is Picking People to Run Agencies They Hate," *Quartz*, December 13, 2016, https://qz.com/861897/fox-in-the-henhouse-trumps-cabinet-nominees-are-being-chosen-to-run-agencies-they-hate/; Michael Sebastian, "A Close Look at Donald Trump's Cabinet," *Marie Claire*, July 28, 2017, http://www.marieclaire.com/politics/a23922/donald-trump-cabinet-appointments/; Bob Herman, "Alex Azar Made Millions in the Drug Industry," *Axios*, November 20, 2017, https://www.axios.com/alex-azar-made-millions-in-the-drug-industry-1513307070-2fdf898e-f5a1-409e-a7bf-53d5535a5f1b.html.

93. John Dewey, *John Dewey: The Later Works, 1925–1953*, ed. Jo Ann Boydston (Carbondale: Southern Illinois University Press, 2008), 6:163.

94. Timothy M. LaPira and Herschel F. Thomas III, "Revolving Door Lobbyists and Interest Representation," *Interest Groups & Advocacy* 3, no. 1 (March 2014): 4–29; Simon Luechinger and Christoph Moser, "The Value of the Revolving Door: Political Appointees and the Stock Market," *Journal of Public Economics* 119 (November 2014): 93–107; Jordi Blanes i Vidal, Mirko Draca, and Christian Fons-Rosen, "Revolving Door Lobbyists," *American Economic Review* 102, no. 7 (December 2012): 3731–48; Sounman Hong and Jeehum Lim, "Capture and the Bureaucratic Mafia: Does the Revolving Door Erode Bureaucratic Integrity?," *Public Choice* 166, no. 1-2 (January 2016): 69–86.

95. "Revolving Door: Reverse Revolvers of the 112th Congress," Center for Responsive Politics, accessed August 4, 2019, https://www.opensecrets.org/revolving/reverse.php.

96. "Influence and Lobbying," Center for Responsive Politics, accessed August 4, 2019, http://www.opensecrets.org/influence/; Geoff West, "Revolving Door: Former Lobbyists in Trump Administration," Center for Responsive Politics, July 16, 2018, https://www.opensecrets.org/news/2018/07/revolving-door-update-trump-administration/.

97. Holly Yeager, "Lobbyists Find Mixed Reception Running for Office, but a Few Have Won Elections," *Washington Post*, May 18, 2014.

98. "Top Agencies," Center for Responsive Politics, accessed August 4, 2019, https://www.opensecrets.org/revolving/top.php?display=G.

99. Christopher Buckley, "A Confederacy of Lunches," *New York Times*, July 25, 2013.

100. Lee Fang, "When a Congressman Becomes a Lobbyist, He Gets a 1,452 Percent Raise (On Average)," *The Nation*, March 14, 2012, http://www.thenation.com/article/166809/when-congressman-becomes-lobbyist-he-gets-1452-percent-raise-average#.

101. Ibid.

102. Ralph Waldo Emerson, "Politics," Emerson Central, accessed August 4, 2019, https://emersoncentral.com/texts/essays-second-series/politics/.

7: WAR

1. Jen Wieczner, "Syria Airstrikes Instantly Added Nearly $5 Billion to Missile-maker's Stock Value," *Fortune*, April 7, 2017, http://fortune.com/2017/04/07/syria-airstrikes-tomahawk-missile-boeing-raytheon-stock/.

2. Jake Johnson, "'Peace is Bad For Business': War Profiteer Stocks Plummet After Diplomatic Progress with North Korea," *Common Dreams*, June 12, 2018, https://www.commondreams.org/news/2018/06/12/peace-bad-business-war-profiteer-stocks-plummet-after-diplomatic-progress-north.

3. Samuel Stebbins and Thomas C. Frohlich, "20 Companies Profiting the Most From War," MSN, May 31, 2017, https://www.msn.com/en-us/money/savingandinvesting/20-companies-profiting-the-most-from-war/ar-AAmTAzm#page=1; Hazel Sheffield, "Arms Trade: One Chart That Shows the Biggest Weapons Exporters of the Last Five Years," *Independent*, February 24, 2016.

4. Andrew Taylor, "F-35 Contractors a Big Winner in Federal Budget Bill," *Standard-Examiner*, December 16, 2014, https://web.archive.org/web/20170509215558/http://www.standard.net/Military/2014/12/16/Defense-tourism-among-winners-in-spending-bill-1.html.

5. Keller, "Menace."

6. Langston Hughes, "One More 'S' in the U.S.A.," Poetry Nook, accessed August 11, 2019, https://www.poetrynook.com/poem/one-more-s-usa.

7. Zinn, *A People's History*, 548; Julia Angwin, Charlie Savage, Jeff Larson, Henrik Moltke, Laura Poitras, and James Risen, "AT&T Helped U.S. Spy on Internet on a Vast Scale," *New York Times*, August 15, 2015.

8. Orwell, "Review: *The Road to Serfdom*"; Keller, "Menace." She said, "Capitalists want to develop new markets for their hideous traffic."

9. Upton Sinclair, *The Book of Life*, Project Gutenberg, accessed August 12, 2019, http://gutenberg.readingroo.ms/3/8/1/1/38117/38117.txt. See chap. 60.

10. Orwell, *Wigan Pier*, 191.

11. Langston Hughes, "Always the Same," *Poetry Nook*, accessed August 12, 2019, https://www.poetrynook.com/poem/always-same.

12. Zinn, *A People's History*, 299–301, 305–06, 310, 317.

13. London, *War of the Classes*. See "The Question of the Maximum" chapter.

14. Zinn, *A People's History*, 362.

15. This was in National Security Council (N.S.C.) 68, of April 14, 1950. See *Foreign Relations of the United States, 1950* (Washington: U.S. Government Printing Office, 1977), 1:234–92. Read online at "NSC 68: United States Objectives and Programs For National Security," Federation of American Scientists, accessed August 12, 2019, https://fas.org/irp/offdocs/nsc-hst/nsc-68-6.htm.

16. Zinn, *A People's History*, 550.

17. Kevin Young and Diana C. Sierra Becerra, "Hillary Clinton's Empowerment," *Jacobin*, March 9, 2015, https://www.jacobinmag.com/2015/03/hillary-clinton-womens-rights-feminism/.

18. Malcolm X, *Malcolm X Speaks*, 128.

19. Pranab Bardhan, "Does Globalization Help or Hurt the World's Poor?: Overview/Globalization and Poverty," *Scientific American*, March 26, 2006, https://www.scientificamerican.com/article/does-globalization-help-o-2006-04/.

20. Laura Carlsen, "Under Nafta, Mexico Suffered, and the United States Felt Its Pain," *New York Times*, November 24, 2013.

21. Goldwin, *Imagine*, 143.

22. Chomsky, *The Common Good*, 108.

23. Miller, *Timebends*, 81.

24. Zinn, *A People's History*, 409.

25. Ibid., 410–11.

26. Charles Higham, *Trading With The Enemy* (New York: Dell Publishing, 1984).

27. Orwell, *The Lion*, part 2, chapter 1.

28. George Orwell, *Homage to Catalonia*, Project Gutenberg, accessed August 12, 2019, http://gutenberg.net.au/ebooks02/0201111.txt.

29. James A. Paul, "Great Power Conflict Over Iraqi Oil: The World War I Era," *Global Policy Forum*, October 2002, https://www.globalpolicy.org/component/content/article/185/40479.html.

30. Keller, "Menace."

31. "Policy in the Middle East, CAE Shuckburgh to FO For Distribution," August 24, 1958, Public Records Office (PRO), FO371/132545, page 2. As cited in Roby Barrett, "Intervention in Iraq, 1958-1959," The Middle East Institute, April 2008, https://www.globalpolicy.org/images/pdfs/408intervention.pdf.

32. Zinn, *A People's History*, 471.

33. Ibid., 472.

34. Ibid., 475.

35. Ibid., 471, 550.

36. Joyce and Gabriel Kolko, "The Limits of Power," *Global Policy Forum*,

accessed August 12, 2019, https://www.globalpolicy.org/component/content/article/185/40457.html.

37. Zinn, *A People's History*, 413.

38. Noam Chomsky, *Who Rules the World?* (London: Picador, 2017), 44.

39. "Newly Declassified Documents Confirm U.S. Backed 1953 Coup in Iran Over Oil Contracts," *Democracy Now!*, July 24, 2017, https://www.democracynow.org/2017/7/24/newly_declassified_documents_confirm_us_backed.

40. Lizette Alvarez, "Britain Says US Planned to Seize Oil in '73 Crisis," *Global Policy Forum*, January 2, 2004, https://www.globalpolicy.org/component/content/article/169/36414.html.

41. Oliver Stone and Peter Kuznick, *The Concise Untold History of the United States* (New York: Gallery Books, 2014), 276–77.

42. Ibid., 290.

43. See sources in G.S. Griffin, "Lies and Oil: A Brief History of the U.S. in Iraq," GSGriffin.com, July 3, 2017, https://gsgriffin.com/2017/07/03/lies-and-oil-a-brief-history-of-the-u-s-in-iraq/.

44. Andrew Kramer, "US Companies Get Slice of Iraq's Oil Pie," *New York Times*, June 14, 2011.

45. Jillian Ambrose, "BP Returns to Northern Iraq's Recaptured Oil Fields," *The Telegraph*, January 18, 2018.

46. Charlie Savage, "Bush Asserts Authority to Bypass Defense Act," *Boston Globe*. In Bush's words, the bill couldn't stop his efforts to "establish any military installation or base for the purpose of providing for the permanent stationing of United States Armed Forces in Iraq" or "to exercise United States control of the oil resources of Iraq."

47. "How Much Petroleum Does the United States Import and Export?," U.S. Energy Information Administration, May 14, 2019, https://www.eia.gov/tools/faqs/faq.php?id=727&t=6; "U.S.-Saudi Arabia Relations," Council on Foreign Relations, December 7, 2018, https://www.cfr.org/backgrounder/us-saudi-arabia-relations.

48. Osama bin Laden, "Declaration of Jihad Against the Americans Occupying the Land of the Two Holiest Sites," United States Military Academy, accessed August 13, 2019, https://ctc.usma.edu/app/uploads/2013/10/Declaration-of-Jihad-against-the-Americans-Occupying-the-Land-of-the-Two-Holiest-Sites-Translation.pdf; "Full Text: Bin Laden's 'Letter to America,'" *The Guardian*, November 24, 2002.

49. Noam Chomsky and Gilbert Achcar, *Perilous Power* (London: Penguin Books, 2007); Vijay Prashad, *The Darker Nations* (New York: The New Press, 2008).

50. "'Good for Business': Trump Advisor Bolton Admits US Interest

in Venezuela's 'Oil Capabilities,'" *Russia Today*, January 28, 2019, https://www.rt.com/usa/449982-john-bolton-oil-venezuela/; Eli Rosenberg and Dan Lamothe, "'5,000 Troops': Photo of John Bolton's Notes Raises Questions About U.S. Military Role in Venezuela Crisis," *Washington Post*, January 1, 2019.

51. Noam Chomsky, "The Footnotes For *Understanding Power*," *Understanding Power*, http://understandingpower.com/files/AllChaps.pdf, 25–27.

52. Ibid; Chomsky, *Hopes and Prospects*, 173.

53. Chomsky, *Hopes and Prospects*, 24–25.

54. Chomsky, *Who Rules the World*, 73.

55. Chomsky, *Hopes and Prospects*, 174. The National Security Council aimed to "achieve a successful order elsewhere in the world."

56. Ibid., 24.

57. Ibid., 166.

58. Eric Foner, *Give Me Liberty!* (New York: W.W. Norton & Company, 2009), 1045.

59. Nafeez Ahmed, "Pentagon Study Declares American Empire is 'Collapsing,'" *Medium*, July 17, 2017, https://medium.com/insurge-intelligence/pentagon-study-declares-american-empire-is-collapsing-746754cdaebf.

60. Mark Landler and James Risen, "Trump Finds Reason for the U.S. to Remain in Afghanistan: Minerals," *New York Times*, July 25, 2017, https://www.nytimes.com/2017/07/25/world/asia/afghanistan-trump-mineral-deposits.html.

61. Keller, "Menace."

62. King, "Beyond Vietnam."

63. Mahatma Gandhi, *The Essential Gandhi: An Anthology of His Writings on His Life, Work, and Ideas* (New York: Vintage Books, 2002), 175.

64. Garance Franke-Ruta, "All the Previous Declarations of War," *The Atlantic*, August 31, 2013; Barbara Salazar Torreon and Sofia Plagakis, "Instances of Use of United States Armed Forces Abroad, 1798–2019," Congressional Research Service, July 17, 2019, https://fas.org/sgp/crs/natsec/R42738.pdf.

65. Keller, "Menace."

66. Jeff Desjardins, "U.S. Military Personnel Deployments by Country," Visual Capitalist, March 18, 2017, http://www.visualcapitalist.com/u-s-military-personnel-deployments-country/.

67. "Federal Spending," National Priorities Project; Ryan Browne, "Trump Administration to Propose $750 Billion Military Budget Next Week," CNN, March 10, 2019.

68. Gordon Lubold, "U.S. Spent $5.6 Trillion on Wars in Middle East and Asia: Study," *Wall Street Journal*, November 8, 2017.

69. Anne Frank, *The Diary of a Young Girl*, Archive, accessed August 13, 2019, https://archive.org/stream/AnneFrankTheDiaryOfAYoungGirl_201606/Anne-Frank-The-Diary-Of-A-Young-Girl_djvu.txt. See May 3, 1944 entry.

70. Dwight D. Eisenhower, "Chance for Peace Speech," Temple University, accessed August 13, 2019, https://astro.temple.edu/~rimmerma/chance_for_peace_speech.htm.

71. King, "Beyond Vietnam."

72. Sarah Lazare, "Body Count Report Reveals at Least 1.3 Million Lives Lost to US-led War on Terror," *Common Dreams*, March 26, 2015, http://www.commondreams.org/news/2015/03/26/body-count-report-reveals-least-13-million-lives-lost-us-led-war-terror.

73. Frank, *Diary*. See May 3, 1944 entry.

74. "The Drone Papers," *The Intercept*, accessed August 13, 2019, https://theintercept.com/drone-papers; See also news reports such as: Spencer Ackerman, "41 Men Targeted but 1,147 People Killed: US Drone Strikes—the Facts on the Ground," *The Guardian*, November 24, 2014.

75. London, *War of the Classes*. See the final chapter, "How I Became a Socialist."

76. Thomas Paine, "Agrarian Justice," University of Michigan, accessed August 13, 2019, https://quod.lib.umich.edu/e/ecco/004809374.0001.000/1:3?rgn=div1;view=fulltext; Nichols, *The "S" Word*, 33, 46, 53; Sean Monahan, "Reading Paine From the Left," *Jacobin*, March 6, 2015, https://www.jacobinmag.com/2015/03/thomas-paine-american-revolution-common-sense/.

77. Thomas Paine, *The Rights of Man*, University of Groningen, accessed August 13, 2019, http://www.let.rug.nl/usa/documents/1786-1800/thomas-paine-the-rights-of-man/text.php. See chapter 5.

78. Keller, "Menace." She said, "I look upon the whole world as my fatherland, and every war has to me a horror of a family feud. I look upon true patriotism as the brotherhood of man and the service of all to all."

79. Nick Spitzer, "The Story of Woody Guthrie's 'This Land is Your Land,'" NPR, February 15, 2012, https://www.npr.org/2000/07/03/1076186/this-land-is-your-land.

80. "For a World Government; Einstein Says This Is Only Way to Save Mankind," *New York Times*, September 15, 1945.

81. See sources in Griffin, "A History of Violence: Facing U.S. Wars of Aggression."

82. Ibid.

83. Zinn, *A People's History*, 316.

84. Alfred Blumrosen, *Slave Nation: How Slavery United the Colonies and Sparked the American Revolution* (Chicago: Sourcebooks, 2006).

85. King, "Beyond Vietnam."

8: WORKER OWNERSHIP

1. Mahatma Gandhi, *India of My Dreams* (Ahmedabad: Navajivan, 1947), https://www.mkgandhi.org/ebks/India-Dreams.pdf. See page 39. "We shall evolve a truer socialism and truer communism than the world has yet dreamed of."

2. Pablo Picasso, "Why I Became a Communist," in "Picasso, the FBI, and Why He Became a Communist," Columbia University, February 24, 2010, https://blogs.cul.columbia.edu/schapiro/2010/02/24/picasso-and-communism/.

3. John Harris, Paul Wood, Francis Frascina, and Charles Harrison, *Modernism in Dispute: Art Since the Forties* (New Haven: Yale University Press, 1993), 140.

4. Jesse Olsen and Bernd Reinhard, "Frida Kahlo Retrospective in Berlin," World Socialist Web Site, September 14, 2010, https://www.wsws.org/en/articles/2010/09/kahl-s14.html

5. Angela Davis, *An Autobiography* (New York: International Publishers, 1988), 214.

6. Wilde, "Soul of Man," 14.

7. H.G. Wells, *New Worlds for Old: A Plain Account of Modern Socialism*, Project Gutenberg, accessed August 17, 2019, https://www.gutenberg.org/files/30538/30538-h/30538-h.htm, 257.

8. Leo Tolstoy, *Pamphlets, Translated From the Russian*, Hathitrust Mobile Digital Library, accessed August 17, 2019, https://babel.hathitrust.org/cgi/pt?id=mdp.39015073373360&view=1up&seq=250. See the essay "On Anarchy" on page 250 (slider).

9. Peter Dunwoodie, "Albert Camus and the Anarchist Alternative," *Australian Journal of French Studies* 30, no. 1 (January 1993); "Albert Camus," *Stanford Encyclopedia of Philosophy*, April 10, 2017, https://plato.stanford.edu/entries/camus/#VioIneImp; Neil Foxlee, *Albert Camus's "The New Mediterranean Culture": A Text and Its Contexts* (Oxford: Peter Lang, 2010); David Porter, *Eyes to the South: French Anarchists and Algeria* (Oakland: AK Press, 2011).

10. Martin Luther King, Jr., *"In a Single Garment of Destiny": A Global Vision of Justice* (Boston: Beacon Press, 2014). See the essay "The Greatest Hope For World Peace"; Orwell, *Wigan Pier*, 178-179.

11. Jack London, *The Human Drift*, Sonoma State University, accessed August 17, 2019, http://london.sonoma.edu/Writings/HumanDrift/human.html

12. W.E.B. Du Bois, *The World of W.E.B. Du Bois: A Quotation Sourcebook* (Westport: Greenwood Publishing Group, 1992), 158.

224 • WHY AMERICA NEEDS SOCIALISM

13. Elizabeth Cady Stanton, "Elizabeth Cady Stanton on Socialism," University of Pittsburgh, accessed August 17, 2019, https://digital.library.pitt.edu/islandora/object/pitt%3A31735060481847/viewer#page/2/mode/2up.

14. Mill, *Principles*, 147.

15. Upton Sinclair, *Jimmie Higgins*, Project Gutenberg, accessed August 17, 2019, https://www.gutenberg.org/files/5677/5677-h/5677-h.htm. See chapter 21, section 4.

16. R.K. Prabhu and U.R. Rao, *The Mind of Mahatma Gandhi* (Ahmedabad: Navajivan, 1960), https://www.mkgandhi.org/momgandhi/chap53.htm.

17. Blackwell, "Christian Socialism."

18. Victor Hugo, *Les Misérables*, Project Gutenberg, accessed August 17, 2019, http://www.gutenberg.org/files/135/135-h/135-h.htm. See volume 4, chapter 4.

19. Orwell, *Wigan Pier*, 208.

20. George Orwell, "Arthur Koestler," Orwell Foundation, accessed August 18, 2019, https://www.orwellfoundation.com/the-orwell-foundation/orwell/essays-and-other-works/arthur-koestler/.

21. Hyung-sik Eum, "Cooperatives and Employment: Second Global Report," International Organisation of Industrial and Service Cooperatives (CICOPA), 2017, http://www.cicopa.coop/wp-content/uploads/2018/01/Cooperatives-and-Employment-Second-Global-Report-2017.pdf. See page 25, table 1. If we add in people who are self-employed but members of "producer cooperatives" that support them (farmers and fishermen, for instance, especially in Asia), 280 million people are involved in cooperative employment. Bringing these workers into the analysis would also swell the U.S. numbers mentioned earlier.

22. London, *War of the Classes*. See "Wanted: A New Law of Development."

23. Curl, *For All the People*.

24. "What is a Worker Cooperative?," Democracy at Work Institute, accessed August 18, 2019, http://institute.coop/what-worker-cooperative.

25. Marissa Lang, "Employee Ownership May Help Businesses Stay Open as Boomers Retire," *San Francisco Chronicle*, February 17, 2017.

26. King, "Beyond Vietnam"; Martin Luther King, Jr., "Where Do We Go from Here?" (speech, 11th Annual SCLC Convention, August 16, 1967), Stanford University, https://kinginstitute.stanford.edu/king-papers/documents/where-do-we-go-here-address-delivered-eleventh-annual-sclc-convention.

27. "US Worker Cooperatives: A State of the Sector," Democracy at Work Institute, accessed August 23, 2019, https://institute.coop/sites/default/files/resources/State_of_the_sector_0.pdf; Virginie Pérotin, "Worker Cooperatives: Good, Sustainable Jobs in the Community," *Journal of Entrepreneurial and*

Organizational Diversity 2, no. 2 (2013): 34–47; Gabriel Burdín and Andrés Dean, "Revisiting the Objectives of Worker-Managed Firms: An Empirical Assessment," *Economic Systems* 36, no. 1 (March 2012): 158–71; Virginie Pérotin, "What Do We Really Know About Workers' Cooperatives?," report prepared for ILO-ICA Research Conference on Cooperatives and the World of Work, November 2015, http://ccr.ica.coop/sites/ccr.ica.coop/files/attachments/5.3Virginie%20 Perotin%20What%20Do%20we%20Really%20Know%20ilo%20ica.pdf; "Worker-Owned Cooperatives Are Larger Than Conventional Firms," Boston Center for Community Ownership, November 14, 2016, http://bcco.coop/ worker-owned-cooperatives-are-larger-than-conventional-firms/.

   28. Shannon Rieger, "Reducing Economic Inequality through Democratic Worker-Ownership," The Century Foundation, August 10, 2016, https:// tcf.org/content/report/reducing-economic-inequality-democratic-worker-ownership/.

   29. Hughes, "One More 'S.'"; Corey Franklin, "Moral Clarity? Kate Smith's 'God Bless America' vs. Woody Guthrie's 'This Land is Your Land,'" *Chicago Tribune*, April 24, 2019.

   30. Laura Flanders, "How America's Largest Worker Owned Co-op Lifts People Out of Poverty," *Common Dreams*, August 15, 2014, http://www. commondreams.org/views/2014/08/15/how-americas-largest-worker-owned-co-op-lifts-people-out-poverty.

   31. Rieger, "Reducing Economic Inequality."

   32. Ralph Waldo Emerson, *The Conduct of Life*, Project Gutenberg, accessed August 18, 2019, https://www.gutenberg.org/files/39827/39827-h/39827-h. html. See the chapter called "Wealth."

   33. N.C. Beohar, *Wisdom of Mahatma Gandhi* (Chennai: Notion Press, 2018).

   34. Wilde, "Soul of Man," 16.

   35. Georgeanne M. Artz and Younjun Kim, "Business Ownership by Workers: Are Worker Cooperatives a Viable Option?," *Economics Working Papers* (2002–2016), November 9, 2011; Rieger, "Reducing Economic Inequality"; Fathi Fakhfakh, Virginie Pérotin, and Mónica Gago, "Productivity, Capital, and Labor in Labor-Managed and Conventional Firms: An Investigation on French Data," *ILR Review* 65, no. 4 (2012); Louis Putterman, "Labour-managed Firms," *The New Palgrave Dictionary of Economics*, accessed August 18, 2019, https://link. springer.com/referenceworkentry/10.1057%2F978-1-349-95121-5_2535-1; Derek C. Jones, "The Productive Efficiency of Italian Producer Cooperatives: Evidence from Conventional and Cooperative Firms," in *Cooperative Firms in Global Markets*, ed. S. Novkovic and V. Sena (Bingley: Emerald Group Publishing Limited, 2007); Pérotin, "What Do We Really Know?"; Marina

Albanese, Cecilia Navarra, Ermanno C. Tortia, "Employer Moral Hazard and Wage Rigidity. The Case of Worker Owned and Investor Owned Firms," *International Review of Law and Economics* 43 (August 2015): 227–37; Cecilia Navarra, "Employment Stabilization Inside Firms: An Empirical Investigation of Worker Cooperatives," *Annals of Public and Cooperative Economics* 87, no. 4 (January 2016); José Alberto Bayo-Moriones, Pedro Javier Galilea-Salvatierra, and Javier Merino-Díaz de Cerio, "Participation, Cooperatives and Performance: An Analysis of Spanish Manufacturing Firms," in *Advances in the Economic Analysis of Participatory & Labor-Managed Firms* (Bingley: Emerald Group Publishing Limited, 2003), https://www.emeraldinsight.com/doi/abs/10.1016/S0885-3339%2803%2907004-2; Stephen C. Smith and Jonathan Rothbaum, "Cooperatives in a Global Economy: Key Economic Issues, Recent Trends, and Potential For Development," *Institute for the Study of Labor* (IZA), September 2013, http://ftp.iza.org/pp68.pdf; Erik K. Olsen, "The Relative Survival of Worker Cooperatives and Barriers to Their Creation," in *Sharing Ownership, Profits, and Decision-making in the 21st Century* (Bingley: Emerald Group Publishing Limited, 2013), https://www.emeraldinsight.com/doi/abs/10.1108/S0885-3339%282013%290000014005; Rhokeun Park, Douglas Kruse, and James Sesil, "Does Employee Ownership Enhance Firm Survival?," in *Employee Participation, Firm Performance and Survival*, ed. V. Perotin and A. Robinson (Bingley: Emerald Group Publishing Limited, 2004), https://www.emeraldinsight.com/doi/abs/10.1016/S0885-3339%2804%2908001-9; Zuray Melgarejo, Katrin Simon, and F.J. Arcelus, "Differences in Financial Performance Amongst Spanish SMES According to Their Capital-Ownership Structure: A Descriptive Analysis," *Annals of Public and Cooperative Economics* 81, no. 1 (February 2010): 105–29.

36. Smith, "Global Economy"; Imanol Basterretxea and Ricardo Martínez, "Impact on Performance of Management and Innovation Capabilities: Are Cooperatives Different?," *Annals of Public and Cooperative Economics* 83, no. 3 (2012): 357–81; Robert Garrett, "Does Employee Ownership Increase Innovation?," *New England Journal of Entrepreneurship* 13, no. 2 (2010); Felix Hofmann, Andranik Tumasjan, and Isabell Melanie Welpe, "Employee Share Ownership and Innovative Work Behavior: Does Ownership Foster Innovative Behaviors?," *Academy of Management Proceedings 2018*, no. 1 (July 2018); Stephen C. Smith, "Innovation and Market Strategy in Italian Industrial Cooperatives: Econometric Evidence on Organizational Comparative Advantage," *Journal of Economic Behavior & Organization* 23, no. 3 (May 1994): 303–20.

37. Sonja Novkovic and Wendy Holm, "Co-operative Networks as a Source of Organizational Innovation," *International Journal of Co-Operative Management* 6, no 1.1 (October 2012): 51–60.

38. Johnston Birchall and Lou Hammond Ketilson, "Resilience of the Cooperative Business Model in Times of Crisis," *International Labour Organization*, 2009.

39. "Worker Cooperatives: Performance and Success Factors," *Co-Op Law*, accessed August 18, 2019, http://www.co-oplaw.org/special-topics/worker-co-operatives-performance-and-success-factors/; Gabriel Burdín, "Are Worker-managed Firms More Likely to Fail Than Conventional Enterprises? Evidence From Uruguay," *ILR Review* 67, no. 1 (January 2014): 202–38, "Are Worker-managed Firms Really More Likely to Fail?," *Institute for the Study of Labor* (IZA), May 2013, http://repec.iza.org/dp7412.pdf.

40. Ajowa Nzinga Ifateyo, "A Co-op State of Mind," *In These Times*, August 18, 2014, http://inthesetimes.com/article/17061/a_co_op_state_of_mind.

41. Michelle Chen, "Worker Cooperatives Are More Productive Than Normal Companies," *The Nation*, March 28, 2016, https://www.thenation.com/article/worker-cooperatives-are-more-productive-than-normal-companies/.

42. "Worker Cooperatives," *Co-Op Law*.

43. Ibid.

44. Rieger, "Reducing Economic Inequality."

45. Ibid.

46. Saioa Arando, Mónica Gago, Derek C. Jones, and Takao Kato, "Efficiency in Employee-owned Enterprises: An Econometric Case Study of Mondragon," *Institute for the Study of Labor* (IZA), May 23, 2011, https://papers.ssrn.com/sol3/papers.cfm?abstract_id=1849466.

47. Adam Hayes, "Stock," *Investopedia*, August 16, 2019, https://www.investopedia.com/university/stocks/stocks1.asp.

48. "President Ronald Reagan's Speech on Project Economic Justice," Center for Economic and Social Justice, accessed August 18, 2019, http://www.cesj.org/about-cesj-in-brief/history-accomplishments/pres-reagans-speech-on-project-economic-justice/; "Bipartisan Bill Boosts ESOPs," *National Association of Plan Advisors*, May 14, 2018, https://www.napa-net.org/news/technical-competence/legislation/bipartisan-bill-boosts-esops/.

49. Steven F. Freeman, "Effects of ESOP Adoption and Employee Ownership: Thirty Years of Research and Experience," *Organizational Dynamics*, 2007, https://repository.upenn.edu/cgi/viewcontent.cgi?referer=&httpsredir=1&article=1001&context=od_working_papers.

50. "Worker Cooperatives," Co-Op Law; "Academic Research on Employee Ownership," National Center for Employee Ownership, July 2019, https://www.nceo.org/articles/studies-employee-ownership-corporate-performance; Fibírová Jana and Petera Petr, "Profit-sharing: A Tool For Improving Productivity, Profitability and Competitiveness of Firms?," *Journal of Competitiveness* 5, no. 4

(December 2013): 3-25.

51. Ernest H. O'Boyle, Pankaj C. Patel, and Erik Gonzalez-Mulé, "Employee Ownership and Firm Performance: A Meta-analysis," *Human Resource Management Journal* 26, no. 4 (June 2016).

52. Artz, "Business Ownership."

53. John Pencavel, "Worker Cooperatives and Democratic Governance," in *Handbook of Economic Organization*, ed. Anna Grandori (Cheltenham: Edward Elgar Publishing, 2013), 462–76.

54. Chen, "Worker Cooperatives"; Jack Graham, "How Cleveland's Cooperatives Are Giving Ex-offenders a Fresh Start," *Apolitical*, September 19, 2017, https://apolitical.co/solution_article/clevelands-cooperatives-giving-ex-offenders-fresh-start/; Peter Moskowitz, "Meet the Radical Workers' Cooperative Growing in the Heart of the Deep South," *The Nation*, April 24, 2017, https://www.thenation.com/article/meet-the-radical-workers-cooperative-growing-in-the-heart-of-the-deep-south/.

55. Genna R. Miller, "Gender Equality in Worker Cooperatives," *Grassroots Economic Organizing*, 2011, http://www.geo.coop/node/615; Anca Voinea, "How Are Co-operatives Ensuring No One is Left Behind?," *Co-op News*, July 1, 2017, https://web.archive.org/web/20171211084214/https://www.thenews.coop/119294/sector/worker-coops/co-operatives-ensuring-no-one-left-behind/.

56. Rieger, "Reducing Economic Inequality."

57. Voinea, "Left Behind."

58. Artz, "Business Ownership."

59. Alan Sennett, *Revolutionary Marxism in Spain 1930–1937* (Chicago: Haymarket Books, 2015); Frank Mintz, *Anarchism and Workers' Self-management in Revolutionary Spain* (Oakland: AK Press, 2013).

60. Orwell, *Homage to Catalonia*.

61. Mary Hansen, "What's Next for the World's Largest Federation of Worker-owned Co-ops?," *Yes! Magazine*, June 12, 2015, http://www.yesmagazine.org/new-economy/world-s-largest-federation-of-worker-owned-co-operatives-mondragon-josu-ugarte.

62. Giles Tremlett, "Mondragon: Spain's Giant Co-operative Where Times Are Hard But Few Go Bust," *The Guardian*, March 7, 2013.

63. Hansen, "What's Next."

64. Mikal Khoso Hussain, "Mondragon: Economic Democracy in the Startup Age," *Northeastern University*, November 16, 2016, http://www.northeastern.edu/econpress/2016/11/16/mondragon-economic-democracy-in-the-startup-age/; Tremlett, "Mondragon."

65. Ibid.

66. Pérotin, "Good, Sustainable Jobs."

67. Orwell, *Homage to Catalonia*.

68. Sinclair, *The Jungle*, chap. 30.

69. Mark Twain, "The New Dynasty," in *Mark Twain: Collected Tales, Sketches, Speeches, and Essays, vol. 1, 1852–1890*, ed. Louis J. Budd (New York: Library of America, 1992).

70. "Glances at Socialism as Taught by Prominent Persons: Victor Hugo," *Gavroche*, accessed August 23, 2019, http://www.gavroche.org/vhugo/GlancesAtSocialism.shtml.

71. Tariq Ali, *Street Fighting Years* (London: Verso, 2005). Read an excerpt of the interview with Lennon at Tariq Ali and Robin Blackburn, "The Lost John Lennon Interview," *CounterPunch*, December 8, 2005, https://www.counter-punch.org/2005/12/08/the-lost-john-lennon-interview/.

9: SOCIALIST DEMOCRACY

1. Thomas F. Jackson, *From Civil Rights to Human Rights: Martin Luther King, Jr., and the Struggle For Economic Justice* (Philadelphia: University of Pennsylvania Press, 2009), 230.

2. Orwell, "James Burnham."

3. Jack London, "What Socialism Is," in *Jack London: The Socialist Writings*, ed. Thomas Alan Young (Tucson: Sabino Falls Publishing, 2015).

4. Brad Plumer, "Why More Than 80 Million Americans Won't Vote on Election Day," *Vox*, November 8, 2016, https://www.vox.com/policy-and-politics/2016/11/7/13536198/election-day-americans-vote; Elisa Shearer and Jeffery Gottfried, "Half of Those Who Aren't Learning About the Election Feel Their Vote Doesn't Matter," Pew Research Center, March 4, 2016, http://www.pewresearch.org/fact-tank/2016/03/04/half-of-those-who-arent-learning-about-the-election-feel-their-vote-doesnt-matter/.

5. Reiland Rabaka, *W.E.B. Du Bois and the Problems of the Twenty-First Century* (Lanham: Lexington Books, 2008), 114.

6. John Dewey, "Imperative Need: A New Radical Party," in *Robert B. Westbrook, John Dewey and American Democracy* (Ithaca: Cornell University Press, 1991), 442.

7. "Victor Hugo," *Gavroche*.

8. Fitzgerald wrote "I'm still a socialist" in a letter to his editor Maxwell Perkins in 1922. Cited on page 112 of Tim Randell, "Metafiction and the Ideology of Modernism in Fitzgerald's 'Winter Dreams,'" *The F. Scott Fitzgerald Review* 10 (2012): 108-29, http://www.jstor.org/stable/41693881.

9. F. Scott Fitzgerald, *This Side of Paradise*, Project Gutenberg, accessed August 28, 2019, https://www.gutenberg.org/files/805/805-h/805-h.htm. See

book 2, chapter 5.

10. See sources in G.S. Griffin, "How the Founding Fathers Protected Their Own Wealth and Power," GSGriffin.com, June 30, 2017, https://gsgriffin.com/2017/06/30/how-the-founding-fathers-protecting-their-riches-and-power/.

11. Miller, *Timebends*, 71.

12. "Statistics and Historical Comparison: Bills by Final Status," GovTrack, accessed August 28, 2019, https://www.govtrack.us/congress/bills/statistics.

13. Lee Drutman and Alexander Furnas, "Why Congress Might Be More Productive—and Less Partisan—Than You Think," Sunlight Foundation, January 16, 2014, https://sunlightfoundation.com/2014/01/16/congress-in-2013/#gplus.

14. Jordain Carney, "Dems Knock McConnell for Refusing Vote on Election Reform Bill," *The Hill*, March 7, 2019, https://thehill.com/homenews/senate/433050-dems-knock-mcconnell-for-refusing-vote-on-election-reform-bill.

15. The exact process of getting something on the ballot varies by state. See Missouri's process as an example: John R. Ashcroft, "Make Your Voice Heard: Missouri's Initiative Petition Process," Missouri Secretary of State's office, accessed August 28, 2019, https://www.sos.mo.gov/CMSImages/Elections/Petitions/MakeYourVoiceHeard2018Cycle.pdf.

16. "States with Initiative or Referendum," *Ballotpedia*, accessed August 28, 2019, https://ballotpedia.org/States_with_initiative_or_referendum.

17. David Crary, "Which Ballot Initiatives Passed? Marijuana, Minimum Wage, and More," PBS, November 9, 2016, https://www.pbs.org/newshour/politics/ballot-initiatives-passed-marijuana-minimum-wage.

18. Michael J. New, "Limiting Government Through Direct Democracy," CATO Institute policy analysis, December 13, 2001, http://pdemokracie.ecn.cz/cs/doc/PA420.PDF.

19. Virginia Beramendi, Andrew Ellis, Bruno Kaufman, Miriam Kornblith, Larry LeDuc, Paddy McGuire, Theo Schiller, Palle Svensson, *Direct Democracy* (Stockholm: International Institute For Democracy and Electoral Assistance, 2008), http://www.forskningsdatabasen.dk/en/catalog/2389308509.

20. Mark Cartwright, "Athenian Democracy," *Ancient History Encyclopedia*, April 3, 2018, https://www.ancient.eu/Athenian_Democracy/; Tod Newcombe, "America's Oldest Town Hall Meeting," *Governing*, December 2010, https://www.governing.com/topics/mgmt/267-year-old-community-tradition-Massachusetts.html.

21. Wright, *Envisioning Real Utopias*, 155–60.

22. "Participatory Budgeting," New York City Council, accessed

August 28, 2019, https://council.nyc.gov/pb/; "Research and Evaluation of Participatory Budgeting in the U.S. and Canada," *Public Agenda*, February 20, 2015, https://www.publicagenda.org/pages/research-and-evaluation-of-participatory-budgeting-in-the-us-and-canada; "Hope For Democracy: 25 Years of Participatory Budgeting Worldwide," Nelson Dias, April 2014, http://www.in-loco.pt/upload_folder/edicoes/1279dd27-d1b1-40c9-ac77-c75f31f82ba2.pdf.

23. Micol Lucchi, "This Is How Switzerland's Direct Democracy Works," *World Economic Forum*, July 31, 2017, https://www.weforum.org/agenda/2017/07/switzerland-direct-democracy-explained/.

24. Brian Daigle, "Switzerland: The Ultimate Democracy?," *The National Interest*, September 7, 2014, http://nationalinterest.org/feature/switzerland-the-ultimate-democracy-11219?page=2; Ian Vásquez and Tanja Porčnik, "The Human Freedom Index 2017," CATO Institute, 2017, https://object.cato.org/sites/cato.org/files/human-freedom-index-files/2017-human-freedom-index-2.pdf.

25. Geissbühler, "Direct Democracy"; "Fragility in the World 2019," *The Fund For Peace*, accessed August 28, 2019, https://fragilestatesindex.org; Mrinalini Krishna, "The Richest and Poorest Countries Per Capita in 2018," *Investopedia*, June 29, 2019, https://www.investopedia.com/articles/managing-wealth/112916/richest-and-poorest-countries-capita-2016.asp.

26. Beramendi, *Direct Democracy*; "Initiative," *Wikipedia*.

27. Frey, "Direct Democracy"; Lupia, "Direct Democracy"; Maduz, "Direct Democracy"; Geissbühler, "Direct Democracy."

28. Kim Taehee, "The Effect of Direct Democracy on Political Efficacy: The Evidence from Panel Data Analysis," *Japanese Journal of Political Science* 16, no. 1 (2015): 52–67, "Direct Democracy"; Maduz, "Direct Democracy"; Benjamin A. Olken, "Direct Democracy and Local Public Goods: Evidence From a Field Experiment in Indonesia," *American Political Science Review* 104, no. 2 (May 2010): 243–67; Caroline J. Tolbert, Daniel C. Bowden, and Todd Donovan, "Initiative Campaigns: Direct Democracy and Voter Mobilization," *American Politics Research* 37, no. 1 (January 1, 2009): 155–92.

29. Lupia, "Direct Democracy"; Maduz, "Direct Democracy"; Geissbühler, "Direct Democracy."

30. Ibid; Kevin Arceneaux, "Direct Democracy and the Link Between Public Opinion and State Abortion Policy," *State Politics & Policy Quarterly* 2, no. 4 (December 1, 2002): 372–87.

31. Lupia, "Direct Democracy"; Maduz, "Direct Democracy"; Lars P. Feld and Marcel R. Savioz, "Direct Democracy Matters For Economic Performance: An Empirical Investigation," *Kyklos International Review For*

Social Sciences 50, no. 4 (June 28, 2008): https://onlinelibrary.wiley.com/doi/pdf/10.1111/1467-6435.00028.

32. Zareh Asatryan and Kristof De Witte, "Direct Democracy and Local Government Efficiency," *European Journal of Political Economy* 39 (September 2015): 58–66; Michael Seebauer, "Does Direct Democracy Foster Efficient Policies? An Experimental Investigation of Costly Initiatives," Friedrich-Alexander University Erlangen-Nuremberg, Institute for Economics, January 2015, https://ideas.repec.org/p/zbw/iwqwdp/012015.html.

33. Klaus W. Zimmermann and Tobias Just, "Interest Groups, Referenda, and the Political Process: On the Efficiency of Direct Democracy," *Constitutional Political Economy* 11, no. 2 (June 2000): 147–63.

34. Patricia Funk and Christina Gathmann, "Direct Democracy as a Safeguard to Limit Public Spending," *Vox*, CEPR Policy Portal, February 10, 2012, https://voxeu.org/article/direct-democracy-way-limit-public-spending-evidence-switzerland.

35. Lupia, "Direct Democracy."

36. John G. Matsusaka, "Direct Democracy and Fiscal Gridlock: Have Voter Initiatives Paralyzed the California Budget?," *State Politics & Policy Quarterly* 5, no. 3 (September 1, 2005): 248–64.

37. Melody Gutierrez, "California Has 'Extraordinary' Budget Surplus, Analysts Say," *San Francisco Chronicle*, November 14, 2018.

38. H.G. Wells, *In the Days of the Comet*, Project Gutenberg, accessed August 28, 2019, http://gutenberg.net.au/ebooks13/1303041h.html. See book 1, chapter 4.

39. Lupia, "Direct Democracy"; Geissbühler, "Direct Democracy."

40. Norman Solomon, "The Twain That Most Americans Never Meet," *Fairness & Accuracy in Reporting*, November 4, 1999, https://fair.org/media-beat-column/the-twain-that-most-americans-never-meet/.

41. "Unicameral and Bicameral Legislatures," *Encyclopedia Britannica*, accessed August 28, 2019, https://www.britannica.com/topic/constitutional-law/Unicameral-and-bicameral-legislatures#ref384652.

42. Vann R. Newkirk II, "American Voters Are Turning to Direct Democracy," *The Atlantic*, April 18, 2018; Richard Wike, Katie Simmons, Bruce Stokes, and Janell Fetterolf, "Globally, Broad Support for Representative and Direct Democracy," Pew Research Center, October 16, 2017, https://www.pewresearch.org/global/2017/10/16/globally-broad-support-for-representative-and-direct-democracy/. Click on "Complete Report PDF" and see page 22.

43. Ralph Waldo Emerson, "A Historical Discourse, Delivered Before the Citizens of Concord, 12th September, 1835," Archive, accessed September 1,

2019, https://archive.org/details/historicaldiscou1835emer/page/n33. See pages 34–38 (slider).

44. "Recall of State Officials," National Conference of State Legislatures, July 8, 2019, http://www.ncsl.org/research/elections-and-campaigns/recall-of-state-officials.aspx.

10: THE SOCIALIST LIFE

1. Wilde, "Soul of Man," 3. We should "try and reconstruct society on such a basis that poverty will be impossible"; Miller, *Timebends*, 86.

2. London, *War of the Classes*. See the chapter "Wanted: A New Law of Development."

3. King, "Where Do We Go From Here?"

4. Paine, "Agrarian Justice."

5. Brian Merchant, "The Only State Where Everyone Gets Free Money," *Vice*, September 4, 2015, https://motherboard.vice.com/en_us/article/jp5wdb/only-state-free-money-alaska.

6. Dylan Matthews, "Hawaii Is Considering Creating a Universal Basic Income," *Vox*, June 15, 2017, https://www.vox.com/policy-and-politics/2017/6/15/15806870/hawaii-universal-basic-income.

7. John D. Sutter, "The Argument For a Basic Income," *CNN*, March 10, 2015.

8. Chris Weller, "Iran Introduced a Basic Income Scheme, and Something Strange Happened," *World Economic Forum*, May 31, 2017, https://www.weforum.org/agenda/2017/05/iran-introduced-a-basic-income-scheme-and-something-strange-happened.

9. Jesse McLean, "Life in Kuwait Too Good a Deal For Revolt," *The Toronto Star*, February 16, 2011.

10. Furui Cheng, "Wealth Partaking Scheme: Macau's Small UBI," *Basic Income Earth Network*, July 27, 2017, http://basicincome.org/news/2017/07/wealth-partaking-scheme-macaus-small-ubi/.

11. Kate McFarland, "Overview of Current Basic Income Related Experiments," *Basic Income Earth Network*, October 19, 2017, http://basicincome.org/news/2017/10/overview-of-current-basic-income-related-experiments-october-2017/; Alix Langone, "This U.S. City Will Give Its Poorest People $500 a Month—No Strings Attached," *Time*, January 24, 2018.

12. Milton Friedman and Rose Friedman, *Free to Choose* (Boston: Mariner Books, 1990).

13. Charles Murray, "A Plan to Replace the Welfare State," *The Wall Street Journal*, March 22, 2006.

14. Benjamin Fernandez, "Rupees in Your Pocket," *Le Monde Diplomatique*,

May 2013, https://mondediplo.com/2013/05/04income.

15. David Calnitsky, "Debating Basic Income," *Catalyst* 1, no. 3 (Fall 2017), https://catalyst-journal.com/vol1/no3/debating-basic-income.

16. Joshua Copeland, "Universal Basic Income: More Empirical Studies," Seven Pillars Institute, May 16, 2018, https://sevenpillarsinstitute.org/universal-basic-income-more-empirical-studies/; Sutter, "Basic Income"; Ioana Marinescu, "No Strings Attached: The Behavioral Effects of U.S. Unconditional Cash Transfer Programs," *National Bureau of Economic Research*, February 2018, https://www.nber.org/papers/w24337.

17. Dan Kopf, "Definitive Data on What Poor People Buy When They're Just Given Cash," *Quartz*, December 7, 2016, https://qz.com/853651/definitive-data-on-what-poor-people-buy-when-theyre-just-given-cash/; David K. Evans and Anna Popova, "Cash Transfers and Temptation Goods: A Review of the Global Evidence," *The World Bank*, May 2014, http://documents.worldbank.org/curated/en/617631468001808739/pdf/WPS6886.pdf.

18. J.S. Mill, *Principles of Political Economy*, Project Gutenberg, accessed September 17, 2019, https://www.gutenberg.org/files/30107/30107-pdf.pdf. See page 195.

19. King, "Where Do We Go From Here?"

20. Ibid. King: "The problem indicates that our emphasis must be twofold: We must create full employment, or we must create incomes. People must be made consumers by one method or the other"; Michalis Nikiforos, Marshall Steinbaum, and Gennaro Zezza, "Modeling the Macroeconomic Effects of a Universal Basic Income," Roosevelt Institute, August 2017, http://rooseveltinstitute.org/wp-content/uploads/2017/08/Modeling-the-Macroeconomic-Effects-of-a-Universal-Basic-Income.pdf.

21. Chris Weller, "A Basic Income Could Boost the US Economy by $2.5 Trillion," *World Economic Forum*, September 14, 2017, https://www.weforum.org/agenda/2017/09/a-basic-income-could-boost-the-us-economy-by-2-5-trillion/.

22. Dylan Matthews, "Study: A Universal Basic Income Would Grow the Economy," *Vox*, August 30, 2017, https://www.vox.com/policy-and-politics/2017/8/30/16220134/universal-basic-income-roosevelt-institute-economic-growth; Copeland, "Universal Basic Income"; Marinescu, "No Strings Attached"; Guy Standing, "How Cash Transfers Promote the Case For Basic Income," *Basic Income Studies* 3, no. 1 (July 2008): https://www.degruyter.com/view/j/bis.2008.3.1/bis.2008.3.1.1106/bis.2008.3.1.1106.xml.

23. Ben Leubsdorf, "Giving Alaskans Free Money Didn't Stop Them From Working," *The Wall Street Journal*, February 20, 2018.

24. Antoine Terracol, "Guaranteed Minimum Income and Unemployment

Duration in France," *Labour Economics* 16, no. 2 (April 2009): 171–82.

25. Weller, "Iran."

26. Guy Standing, "India's Experiment in Basic Income Grants," *Global Dialogue* 3, no. 5 (October 2013); "Piloting Basic Income Transfers in Madhya Pradesh, India," *SEWA Bharat and Unicef,* January 2014, http://www.unicef.in/Uploads/Publications/Resources/pub_doc83.pdf; Scott Santens, "Evidence and More Evidence of the Effect on Inflation of Free Money," *Medium,* November 21, 2014, https://medium.com/basic-income/evidence-and-more-evidence-of-the-effect-on-inflation-of-free-money-a3dcc2a9ea9e.

27. Claudia Haarmann, Dirk Haarmann, Herbert Jauch, Hilma Shindondola-Mote, Nicoli Nattrass, Ingrid van Niekerk, and Michael Samson, "Making the Difference: The BIG in Namibia," *Basic Income Grant Coalition,* April 2009, http://bignam.org/Publications/BIG_Assessment_report_08b.pdf.

28. Philip Harvey, "Funding a Job Guarantee," *International Journal of Environment, Workplace and Employment* 2, no. 1 (2006): 114–32; L. Randall Wray, Flavia Dantas, Scott Fullwiler, Pavlina R. Tcherneva, and Stephanie A. Kelton, "Public Service Employment: A Path to Full Employment," *Levy Economics Institute,* April 2018, http://www.levyinstitute.org/pubs/rpr_4_18.pdf.

29. Paine, *Rights of Man.* See chapter 5.

30. Robert Milder, "The Radical Emerson?," *The Cambridge Companion to Ralph Waldo Emerson,* ed. Joel Porte and Saundra Morris (Cambridge: University of Cambridge Press, 1999), 70; London, "What Socialism Is."

31. Mandela, *Long Walk to Freedom,* chap. 13.

32. Jeff Spross, "You're Hired!," *Democracy Journal,* no. 44 (Spring 2017): https://democracyjournal.org/magazine/44/youre-hired/; Wray, "Public Service Employment"; Pavlina R. Tcherneva, "The Jobs Guarantee: Design, Jobs, and Implementation," *Levy Economics Institute,* April 2018, http://www.levyinstitute.org/pubs/wp_902.pdf; Karthik Muralidharan, Paul Niehaus, and Sandip Sukhtankar, "General Equilibrium Effects of (Improving) Public Employment Programs: Experimental Evidence From India," *National Bureau of Economic Research,* January 2018, https://www.nber.org/papers/w23838.

33. Helen Keller, "Brutal Treatment of the Unemployed in Sacramento," in *Helen Keller: Her Socialist Years,* ed. Philip S. Foner (New York: International Publishers NYC, 1967), 57, https://archive.org/stream/helenkellerherso-00hele/helenkellerherso00hele_djvu.txt.

34. Jules Verne, *Paris in the Twentieth Century* (New York: Random House, 1996), 90; for sources on Verne's socialism: John Lichfield, "Jules Verne: Mythmaker of the Machine Age," *Independent,* March 2005; Walter A.

McDougall, "Journey to the Center of Jules Verne . . . and Us," *Foreign Policy Research Institute*, September 1, 2001, https://www.fpri.org/article/2001/09/journey-to-the-center-of-jules-verne-and-us; Edward Adams Cantrell, *Socialism and the World's Intellectuals* (Los Angeles: The Citizen Press, 1911), 47.

35. H.G. Wells, *The New World Order* (New York: Orkos Press, 2014), 43. The New Deal was "an attempt to achieve a working socialism."

36. "Civilian Conservation Corps," *History*, October 17, 2018, https://www.history.com/topics/great-depression/civilian-conservation-corps; "Works Progress Administration," *History*, June 10, 2019, http://www.history.com/topics/works-progress-administration; "The Great Depression," *Encyclopedia Britannica*, accessed September 13, 2019, https://www.britannica.com/place/United-States/The-Great-Depression#ref613079.

37. Dylan Matthews, "Job Guarantees, Explained," *Vox*, April 24, 2018, https://www.vox.com/policy-and-politics/2017/9/6/16036942/job-guarantee-explained.

38. Grace Guarnieri, "Homeless People Are Being Paid to Clean up the Streets in this Texas City," *Newsweek*, January 21, 2018, http://www.newsweek.com/homeless-paid-clean-streets-texas-786311; Jerod MacDonald-Evoy, "Tempe Will Offer Temporary Jobs to Homeless to Fight 'Crisis,'" *AZ Central*, October 16, 2017, https://www.azcentral.com/story/news/local/tempe/2017/10/16/tempe-hire-homeless-temporary-jobs-fight-mill-avenue/754199001/; Claire Hogan and Christopher Dawson, "The Homeless in San Diego Are Getting Jobs—Thanks to a 16-Year-Old Boy," CNN, June 21, 2018; Anh Gray, "Reno's Beautification Program Provides Jobs to Homeless People," *KUNR*, October 21, 2015, https://www.kunr.org/post/renos-beautification-program-provides-jobs-homeless-people#stream/0.

39. Terrence P. Jeffrey, "21,995,000 to 12,329,000: Government Employees Outnumber Manufacturing Employees 1.8 to 1," *CNS News*, September 8, 2015; Elizabeth McNichol, "Some Basic Facts on State and Local Government Workers," Center on Budget and Policy Priorities, June 15, 2012, https://www.cbpp.org/research/some-basic-facts-on-state-and-local-government-workers; Robert Reich, "America's Biggest Jobs Program: The US Military," *Christian Science Monitor*, August 13, 2010.

40. Rhonda Breitkreuz, Carley-Jane Stanton, Nurmaiya Brady, John Pattison-Williams, E.D. King, Chudhury Mishra, and Brent Swallow, "The Mahatma Gandhi National Rural Employment Guarantee Scheme: A Policy Solution to Rural Poverty in India?," *Development Policy Review* 35, no. 3 (March 2017).

41. Shobhit Mathur and Nomesh Bolia, "Why 2015-'16 Was the Worst Year Ever For MGNREGA," *IndiaSpend*, May 2, 2016, https://scroll.in/

article/807379/why-2015-16-was-the-worst-year-ever-for-mgnrega; Atul Dev, "The Need For Guaranteed Employment," *Huffington Post*, February 8, 2015, https://www.huffingtonpost.com/atul-dev/the-need-for-guaranteed-e_b_6295050.html.

42. Stefan Klonner and Christian Oldiges, "Safety Net For India's Poor or Waste of Public Funds? Poverty and Welfare in the Wake of the World's Largest Job Guarantee Program," Alfred Weber Institute of Economics, Heidelberg University, 2014, https://www.econstor.eu/handle/10419/127381.

43. Pavlina Tcherneva and L. Randall Wray, "Employer of Last Resort Program: A Case Study of Argentina's Jefes de Hogar Program," Center for Full Employment and Price Stability, April 2005, http://www.cfeps.org/pubs/wp-pdf/WP41-Tcherneva-Wray-all.pdf; Daniel Kostzer, "Argentina: A Case Study on the Plan Jefes y Jefas de Hogar Desocupadoes, or the Employment Road to Economic Recovery," *Levy Economics Institute*, May 2008, http://www.levyinstitute.org/pubs/wp_534.pdf.

44. "Public Works & Infrastructure," Expanded Public Works Programme, accessed September 14, 2019, http://www.epwp.gov.za/; "Expanded Public Works Programme," Western Cape Government, accessed September 14, 2019, https://www.westerncape.gov.za/general-publication/expanded-public-works-programme-epwp-0; T.W. Nxesi, "2016 Expanded Public Works Programme (EPWP) Summit: Closing Remarks," Public Works Department, Republic of South Africa, November 17, 2016, http://www.publicworks.gov.za/PDFs/Speeches/Minister/2016/Minister_EPWP_2016_Summit_closing_remarks_17112016.pdf.

45. Fadhel Kaboub, "Honoring Dr. King's Call For a Job Guarantee Program," *New Economic Perspectives*, August 28, 2013, http://www.neweconomicperspectives.org/2013/08/honoring-dr-kings-call-for-a-job-guarantee-program.html.

46. William Mitchell, "The Job Guarantee and Inflation Control," *Centre of Full Employment and Equity*, January 2000, http://citeseerx.ist.psu.edu/viewdoc/download?doi=10.1.1.526.7530&rep=rep1&type=pdf; Matthew C. Klein, "Debunking the NAIRU Myth," *Financial Times*, January 19, 2017, https://ftalphaville.ft.com/2017/01/19/2182705/debunking-the-nairu-myth/; Allison Schrager, "The Strange Thing About America's Historically Low Unemployment Rate," *Quartz*, May 10, 2018, https://qz.com/1272656/nairu-and-the-phillips-curve-the-strange-thing-about-the-low-us-unemployment-rate/; Jon D. Wisman, "The Moral Imperative and Social Responsibility of Government-Guaranteed Employment and Reskilling," *Review of Social Economy* 68, no. 1 (March 2010): 35–67.

47. "The Phillips Curve May Be Broken for Good," *The Economist*, November

1, 2017, https://www.economist.com/blogs/graphicdetail/2017/11/daily-chart; Mitchell Thompson, "The Phillips Curve Is Broken—Here's Why That Is Keeping Economists Up at Night," *Financial Post*, August 21, 2017, https://business.financialpost.com/news/economy/the-phillips-curve-is-broken-heres-why-that-is-keeping-economists-up-at-night; Matthew Boesler, "Phillips Curve Doesn't Help Forecast Inflation, Fed Study Finds," *Bloomberg*, August 24, 2017; Mike Konczal, "How Low Can Unemployment Go? Economists Keep Getting the Answer Wrong," *Vox*, May 5, 2018, https://www.vox.com/the-big-idea/2018/5/4/17320188/jobs-report-natural-rate-unemployment-inflation-economics-april.

48. See sources in G.S. Griffin, "The Last Article on the Minimum Wage You Will Ever Need to Read," GSGriffin.com, December 8, 2016, https://gsgriffin.com/2016/12/08/the-last-article-on-the-minimum-wage-you-will-ever-need-to-read/.

49. Mario Seccareccia, "What Type of Full Employment? A Critical Evaluation of 'Government as the Employer of Last Resort' Policy Proposal," *Investigación Económica* 63, no. 247 (January-March 2004): 15–43; Mitchell, "The Job Guarantee"; Harvey, "Funding a Job Guarantee"; L. Randall Wray, "The Employer of Last Resort Approach to Full Employment," Center for Full Employment and Price Stability, July 2000, http://www.cfeps.org/pubs/wp-pdf/WP9-Wray.pdf.

50. Scott T. Fullwiler, "The Job Guarantee and Economic Stability," in *Creating a Culture of Full Employment*, ed. Graham Wrightson (Callaghan: University of Newcastle, Centre of Full Employment and Equity, 2005): 1–23, https://search.informit.com.au/documentSummary;dn=138455330442715;res=IELBUS; Tom Ramsay, "The Jobs Guarantee: A Post Keynesian Analysis," *Journal of Post Keynesian Economics* 25, no. 2 (2002): 273–91; Tcherneva, "The Jobs Guarantee"; L. Randall Wray, "Government as Employer of Last Resort: Full Employment Without Inflation," *Levy Economics Institute*, April 1998, https://papers.ssrn.com/sol3/papers.cfm?abstract_id=74942; L. Randall Wray, "Minsky's Approach to Employment Policy and Poverty: Employer of Last Resort and the War on Poverty," Levy Economics Institute, 2007, https://www.econstor.eu/bitstream/10419/31634/1/571704611.pdf.

51. L. Randall Wray, "Government as Employer."

52. Tejvan Pettinger, "Methods to Control Inflation," *Economics Help*, May 1, 2019, https://www.economicshelp.org/blog/2269/economics/ways-to-reduce-inflation/.

53. Gayatri Nayak, "MGNREGA Has Not Contributed to Food Inflation: Report," *The Economic Times*, October 22, 2014, https://economictimes.indiatimes.com/news/economy/indicators/mgnrega-has-not-contributed-

to-food-inflation-report/articleshow/44903564.cms.

54. Kaboub, "Employer of Last Resort Schemes"; Peter Hurford and Fadhel Kaboub, "The Employer of Last Resort: A Policy to Ensure Full Employment and Greater Price Stability," *Denison University*, 2012, http://peterhurford.com/stats/elr.pdf.

55. "Inflation in Argentina," Focus Economics, accessed September 14, 2019, https://www.focus-economics.com/country-indicator/argentina/inflation; Tcherneva, "Employer of Last Resort Program."

56. "South Africa Inflation Rate," *Trading Economics*, accessed September 14, 2019, https://tradingeconomics.com/south-africa/inflation-cpi; "Public Works & Infrastructure," Expanded Public Works Programme.

57. Santens, "Evidence and More Evidence"; "Evidence Cash-Transfers & Basic Income Don't Cause Inflation," *Universal Basic Income*, accessed September 14, 2019, http://ubi.earth/inflation/. Click each headline on the list for PDFs of the research; Dylan Matthews, "A New Study Debunks One of the Biggest Arguments Against Basic Income," *Vox*, September 20, 2017, https://www.vox.com/policy-and-politics/2017/9/20/16256240/mexico-cash-transfer-inflation-basic-income.

58. Calnitsky, "Debating Basic Income."

59. Tyler Prochazka, "Interview: Basic Income Can 'Mend the Net,'" *Basic Income Earth Network*, December 14, 2016, https://basicincome.org/news/2016/12/interview-basic-income-can-mend-net/.

60. Jeanne Theoharis, *A More Beautiful and Terrible History* (Boston: Beacon Press, 2018), 161; Martin Luther King, Jr. to Coretta Scott, July 18, 1952, Stanford University, https://kinginstitute.stanford.edu/king-papers/documents/coretta-scott.

61. "In Full: Mandela's Poverty Speech," *BBC News*, February 3, 2005, http://news.bbc.co.uk/2/hi/uk_news/politics/4232603.stm.

62. Kurt Vonnegut, *A Man Without a Country* (New York: Random House, 2007), 97.

63. H.G. Wells, *Tono-Bungay*, Project Gutenberg, accessed September 14, 2019, http://www.gutenberg.org/files/718/718-h/718-h.htm. See book 3, chapter 1.

64. Jomo Kwame Sundaram, "The World Produces Enough Food to Feed Everyone. So Why Do People Go Hungry?," *World Economic Forum*, July 11, 2016, https://www.weforum.org/agenda/2016/07/the-world-produces-enough-food-to-feed-everyone-so-why-do-people-go-hungry; Tanuka Loha, "Housing: It's a Wonderful Right," *Amnesty International*, December 21, 2011, https://blog.amnestyusa.org/us/housing-its-a-wonderful-right/; "Housing Inventory Estimate: Vacant Housing Units For the United States," Federal

Reserve Bank of St. Louis, accessed September 14, 2019, https://fred.stlouisfed. org/series/EVACANTUSQ176N. Note that units are in thousands.

65. Dana Gunders, "Wasted: How America is Losing Up to 40 Percent of Its Food From Farm to Fork to Landfill," *Natural Resources Defense Council*, August 2012, https://www.nrdc.org/sites/default/files/wasted-food-IP.pdf.

66. Wells, *New Worlds*, 58.

67. Ralph Waldo Emerson, *Journals of Ralph Waldo Emerson, 1845–1848*, ed. Edward Waldo Emerson and Waldo Emerson Forbes (New York: Houghton Mifflin, 1912), 7:428, https://archive.org/stream/journalswithann07emeruoft/ journalswithann07emeruoft_djvu.txt.

68. "Health Care Systems—Four Basic Models," Physicians For a National Health Program, accessed September 14, 2019, http://www.pnhp.org/single_ payer_resources/health_care_systems_four_basic_models.php.

69. Tim Worstall, "It's Surprising How Few Countries Have National, Single Payer Health Care Systems," *Forbes*, March 26, 2017.

70. Richard Knox, "History of Tinkering Helps German System Endure," NPR, July 3, 2008, http://www.npr.org/templates/story/story. php?storyId=92189596.

71. Elias Mossialos, Ana Djordjevic, Robin Osborn, and Dana Sarnak, "International Profiles of Health Care Systems," *The Commonwealth Fund*, May 2017, https://www.commonwealthfund.org/sites/default/files/docu- ments/___media_files_publications_fund_report_2017_may_mossialos_ intl_profiles_v5.pdf.

72. Ibid.

73. Irene Papanicolas, Liana R. Woskie, and Ashish K. Jha, "Health Care Spending in the United States and Other High-Income Countries," *Journal of the American Medical Association* 319, no. 10 (2018): 1024–39.

74. Ibid.

75. Olga Khazan, "U.S. Healthcare: Most Expensive and Worst Performing," *The Atlantic*, June 16, 2014; Eric C. Schneider, Dana O. Sarnak, David Squires, Arnav Shah, and Michelle M. Doty, "Mirror, Mirror 2017: International Comparison Reflects Flaws and Opportunities For Better U.S. Health Care," *The Commonwealth Fund*, 2017, https://interactives.commonwealthfund. org/2017/july/mirror-mirror/; Joseph Shapiro, "Health Care Lessons From France," NPR, July 11, 2008, http://www.npr.org/templates/story/story. php?storyId=92419273; Ajay Tandon, Christopher J.L. Murray, Jeremy A. Lauer, and David B. Evans, "Measuring Overall Health System Performance For 191 Countries," *World Health Organization*, January 2000, https://www. who.int/healthinfo/paper30.pdf; Cathy Schoen and Michelle M. Doty, "Inequities in Access to Medical Care in Five Countries: Findings From the 2001

Commonwealth Fund International Health Policy Survey," *Health Policy* 67, no. 3 (March 2004): 309–22, https://www.sciencedirect.com/science/article/pii/S016885100300174X.

76. Tandon, "Health System Performance"; Will Martin, "The 19 Countries with the World's Best Healthcare Systems," *Business Insider*, February 14, 2018, https://www.businessinsider.com/the-healthiest-countries-in-the-world-according-to-legatum-2018-2; Schneider, "Mirror, Mirror."

77. Elisabeth Rosenthal, "The Growing Popularity of Having Surgery Overseas," *New York Times*, August 6, 2013.

78. Renae Reints, "Sen. Rand Paul is Having Surgery in Canada, Where Healthcare is Publicly Funded," *Fortune*, January 14, 2019, http://fortune.com/2019/01/14/rand-paul-surgery-canada/; Ibid.

79. Wright, *Envisioning Real Utopias*, 62.

80. Papanicolas, "Health Care Spending"; David U. Himmelstein, Miraya Jun, Reinhard Busse, Karine Chevreul, Alexander Geissler, Patrick Jeurissen, Sarah Thomson, Marie-Amelie Vinet, and Steffie Woolhandler, "A Comparison of Hospital Administrative Costs in Eight Nations: US Costs Exceed All Others by Far," *Health Affairs* 33, no. 9 (September 2014).

81. Robert H. Frank, "Why Single-Payer Health Care Saves Money," *New York Times*, July 7, 2017.

82. Ibid; Louis Jacobson, "How Expensive Would a Single-Payer System Be?," *Politifact*, July 21, 2017, http://www.politifact.com/truth-o-meter/article/2017/jul/21/how-expensive-would-single-payer-system-be/.

83. Anupam B. Jena, "US Drug Prices Higher Than in the Rest of the World, Here's Why," *The Hill*, January 19, 2018, https://thehill.com/opinion/healthcare/369727-us-drug-prices-higher-than-in-the-rest-of-the-world-heres-why.

84. "Nobel Prize For Physiology or Medicine Per Capita," *Areppim*, November 8, 2018, http://stats.areppim.com/stats/stats_nobelxmedxcapita.htm.

85. "List of Countries by Nobel Laureates Per Capita," Project Gutenberg, accessed September 15, 2019, https://web.archive.org/web/20170805053445/http://www.gutenberg.us/articles/list_of_countries_by_nobel_laureates_per_capita; Claudius Gros, "An Empirical Study of the Per Capita Yield of Science Nobel Prizes: Is the US Era Coming to an End?," *Royal Society Open Science* 5, no. 5 (May 2018): https://www.ncbi.nlm.nih.gov/pmc/articles/PMC5990748/.

86. Salomeh Keyhani, Steven Wang, Paul Hebert, Daniel Carpenter, and Gerard Anderson, "US Pharmaceutical Innovation in an International Context," *American Journal of Public Health* 100, no. 6 (June 2010): 1075–80.

87. "Invention: United States and Comparative Global Trends," in *Science and Engineering Indicators* 2018 (Alexandria: National Science Foundation, 2018), chap. 8, https://www.nsf.gov/statistics/2018/nsb20181/report/sections/invention-knowledge-transfer-and-innovation/invention-united-states-and-comparative-global-trends.

88. "U.S. Extends Lead in International Patent and Trademark Filings," *World Intellectual Property Organization*, March 16, 2016, https://www.wipo.int/pressroom/en/articles/2016/article_0002.html.

89. "Patents by Technology," Organisation For Economic Co-operation and Development, accessed September 15, 2019, https://stats.oecd.org/Index.aspx?DataSetCode=PATS_IPC. Set the first tab to "Patent applications filed under the PCT," an international patent filing; set the last tab to "Medical Technology."

90. Ibid.

91. Ibid.

92. Ibid.

93. Alex Gray, "These Are the 10 Most Innovative Countries in the World," *World Economic Forum*, October 11, 2017, https://www.weforum.org/agenda/2017/10/these-are-the-10-most-innovative-countries-in-the-world/; John McKenna, "South Korea and Sweden Are the Most Innovative Countries in the World," *World Economic Forum*, February 6, 2018, https://www.weforum.org/agenda/2018/02/south-korea-and-sweden-are-the-most-innovative-countries-in-the-world/.

94. Schneider, "Mirror, Mirror"; Mossialos, "International Profiles"; Bradley Sawyer and Daniel McDermott, "How Does the Quality of the U.S. Healthcare System Compare to Other Countries?," *Peterson Center on Healthcare and the Kaiser Family Foundation*, March 28, 2019, https://www.healthsystemtracker.org/chart-collection/quality-u-s-healthcare-system-compare-countries/#item-adults-comparable-countries-quicker-access-doctor-nurse-need-care.

95. Bob Doherty, "Which Countries Have the Longest Waits For Medical Care?," American College of Physicians, January 27, 2010, http://advocacy-blog.acponline.org/2010/01/which-countries-have-longest-waits-for.html; Mossialos, "International Profiles"; Sawyer, "Quality."

96. Mossialos, "International Profiles."

97. Ibid.

98. "Waiting Times For Elective Surgery," in *Health at a Glance 2017* (Paris: Organisation For Economic Co-operation and Development Publishing, 2017), 96–97, https://www.oecd-ilibrary.org/social-issues-migration-health/health-at-a-glance-2017/waiting-times-for-elective-surgery_health_glance-2017-28-en; Sharon Willcox, Mary Seddon, Stephen Dunn, Rhiannon Tudor Edwards, Jim Pearse, and Jack V. Tu, "Measuring and Reducing Waiting Times: A

Cross-National Comparison of Strategies," *Health Affairs* 26, no. 4 (July/August 2007): https://www.healthaffairs.org/doi/abs/10.1377/hlthaff.26.4.1078.

99. Karl Bilimoria, Clifford Ko, James Tomlinson, Andrew Stewart, Mark Talamonti, Denise Hynes, David Winchester, and David Bentrem, "Wait Times For Cancer Surgery in the United States: Trends and Predictors of Delays," *Annals of Surgery* 253, no. 4 (April 2011): 779–85.

100. Olena Mazurenko, Casey Balio, Rajender Agarwal, Aaron E. Carroll, and Nir Menachemi, "The Effects of Medicaid Expansion Under the ACA: A Systematic Review," *Health Affairs* 37, no. 6 (June 2018): https://www.healthaffairs.org/doi/10.1377/hlthaff.2017.1491; Renuka Tipirneni, Karin Rhodes, Rodney Hayward, Richard Lichtenstein, HwaJung Choi, Elyse Reamer, and Matthew Davis, "Primary Care Appointment Availability and Nonphysician Providers One Year After Medicaid Expansion," *American Journal of Managed Care* 22, no. 6 (2016): 427–31; Les Masterson, "Medicaid Expansion Doesn't Impede Care Access or Cause Longer Wait Times, Study Finds," *Health Care Dive*, October 18, 2018, https://www.healthcaredive.com/news/medicaid-expansion-doesnt-impede-care-access-or-cause-longer-wait-times-s/539944/.

101. "Assessment B (Health Care Capabilities)" report for U.S. Department of Veterans Affairs, RAND Corporation, September 1, 2015, https://www.va.gov/opa/choiceact/documents/assessments/assessment_b_health_care_capabilities.pdf; Richard Sisk, "VA Wait Times as Good or Better than Private Sector: Report," *Military*, 2019, https://www.military.com/daily-news/2017/09/20/va-wait-times-good-better-private-sector-report.html.

102. Daniel Pincus, Bheeshma Ravi, David Wasserstein, Anjie Huang, J. Michael Paterson, Avery Nathens, Hans Kreder, Richard Jenkinson, and Walter Wodchis, "Association Between Wait Time and 30-Day Mortality in Adults Undergoing Hip Fracture Surgery," *Journal of the American Medical Association* 318, no. 20 (2017): 1994–2003; Richard F. Davies, "Waiting Lists For Health Care: A Necessary Evil?," *Canadian Medical Association Journal* 160, no. 10 (May 1999): 1469–70.

103. Ryan Whitacker, "How Much Universal Healthcare Would Cost in the US," *Decision Data*, November 11, 2015, http://decisiondata.org/news/how-much-single-payer-uhc-would-cost-usa/; Jacobson, "How Expensive"; "National Health Expenditures 2017 Highlights," *Centers For Medicare & Medicaid Services*, 2017, https://www.cms.gov/Research-Statistics-Data-and-Systems/Statistics-Trends-and-Reports/NationalHealthExpendData/downloads/highlights.pdf.

104. See an example of the math breakdown at Whitacker, "Universal Healthcare"; Alison Galvani, David Durham, Sten Vermund, and Meagan Fitzpatrick, "California Universal Health Care: An Economic Stimulus and Life-saving Proposal," *Lancet* 390, no. 10106 (October 2017): 2012–14.

105. Matt Bruenig, "Even Libertarians Admit Medicare for All Would Save Trillions," *Jacobin*, July 20, 2018, https://jacobinmag.com/2018/07/medicare-for-all-mercatus-center-report; see full report at Charles Blahous, "The Costs of a National Single-payer Healthcare System," *Mercatus Center*, 2018, https://www.mercatus.org/system/files/blahous-costs-medicare-mercatus-working-paper-v1_1.pdf. Note the "2022 currently projected national health expenditures (NHE)" versus "2022 federal share of NHE under M4A" on the table on page 4. Savings ("4 percent") regarding "total health expenditures" are reiterated on page 18.

106. Jake Johnson, "'Easy to Pay For Something That Costs Less': New Study Shows Medicare For All Would Save US $5.1 Trillion Over 10 Years," *Common Dreams*, November 30, 2018, https://www.commondreams.org/news/2018/11/30/easy-pay-something-costs-less-new-study-shows-medicare-all-would-save-us-51-trillion; Gerald Friedman, "Funding HR 676: The Expanded and Improved Medicare For All Act," *Physicians For a National Health Program*, July 31, 2013, http://www.pnhp.org/sites/default/files/Funding%20HR%20676_Friedman_7.31.13_proofed.pdf; "Shorter Waits and Higher Efficiency: The Truth About Medicare For All," Public Citizen, February 4, 2019, https://www.citizen.org/media/press-releases/shorter-waits-and-higher-efficiency-truth-about-medicare-all; Steffie Woolhandler and David Himmelstein, "Single-payer Reform—'Medicare For All,'" *Journal of the American Medical Association* 321, no. 24 (May 2019): 2399–2400.

107. Robert Pollin, James Heintz, Peter Arno, and Jeannette Wicks-Lim, "Economic Analysis of the Healthy California Single-payer Health Care Proposal (SB-562)," *Political Economy Research Institute*, May 31, 2017; Jodi Liu, Chapin White, Sarah Nowak, Asa Wilks, Jamie Ryan, and Christine Eibner, "An Assessment of the New York Health Act," RAND Corporation, 2018, https://www.rand.org/pubs/research_reports/RR2424.html; Dane Smith, "Single-payer Health Care System Would Cut Costs For Minnesotans," *Star Tribune*, October 23, 2018; "Listing of Single Payer Studies," Healthcare Now.

108. Benjamin Fearnow, "NYC Mayor De Blasio Guarantees Health Care For All Residents, Including 300k Undocumented Immigrants," *Newsweek*, January 8, 2019, https://www.newsweek.com/nyc-mayor-bill-deblasio-health-care-immigrants-comprehensive-coverage-1283504.

109. "Health Care as a Human Right: Medicare For All," Bernie Sanders campaign website, accessed September 15, 2019, https://berniesanders.com/issues/medicare-for-all/. See full act at "Medicare For All Act of 2017," Bernie Sanders Senate webpage, accessed September 15, 2019, https://www.sanders.senate.gov/download/medicare-for-all-act?id=

6CA2351C-6EAE-4A11-BBE4-CE07984813C8&download=1&inline=file.

110. Ben Carter, "Which Country Has the Highest Tax Rate?," *BBC News*, February 25, 2014, https://www.bbc.com/news/magazine-26327114.

111. Derek Thompson, "How Low Are U.S. Taxes Compared to Other Countries?," *The Atlantic*, January 14, 2013.

112. Kathleen Elkins, "12 Countries That Pay Less in Taxes Than the US," *CNBC*, March 2, 2018.

113. Kyle Pomerleau, "Corporate Income Tax Rates Around the World, 2016," Tax Foundation, August 18, 2016, https://taxfoundation.org/corporate-income-tax-rates-around-world-2016/.

114. Jeff Desjardins, "Here's How Much Debt Your Country Is In Right Now," *World Economic Forum*, January 14, 2019, https://www.weforum.org/agenda/2019/01/visualizing-the-snowball-of-government-debt/.

115. "How Do US Taxes Compare Internationally?," *Tax Policy Center*, accessed September 15, 2019, https://www.taxpolicycenter.org/briefing-book/how-do-us-taxes-compare-internationally.

116. "John Lennon Interview: *Playboy* 1980," *Beatles Interviews*, accessed September 15, 2019, http://www.beatlesinterviews.org/dbjypb.int2.html.

117. "Average Community College Tuition Costs," *Community College Review*, accessed September 16, 2019, https://www.communitycollegereview.com/avg-tuition-stats/national-data. It's about $5,000 a year; Farran Powell and Emma Kerr, "See the Average College Tuition in 2019–2020," *U.S. News & World Report*, September 9, 2019. It's about $10,000 per year.

118. "Early Childhood Education," *National Education Association*, accessed September 16, 2019, http://www.nea.org/home/18163.htm; Vicki Palmer, "The 13 Key Benefits of Early Childhood Education," *Huffington Post*, August 5, 2016, https://www.huffingtonpost.com/vicki-palmer/the-13-key-benefits-of-ea_b_7943348.html; Lynn A. Karoly, M. Rebecca Kilburn, and Jill S. Cannon, "Proven Benefits of Early Childhood Interventions," RAND Corporation, 2005, https://www.rand.org/pubs/research_briefs/RB9145.html; Eduardo Porter, "Investments in Education May Be Misdirected," *New York Times*, April 2, 2013; Claudio Sanchez, "Pre-k: Decades Worth of Studies, One Strong Message," *NPR*, May 3, 2017, https://www.npr.org/sections/ed/2017/05/03/524907739/pre-k-decades-worth-of-studies-one-strong-message.

119. Emmie Martin, "Here's How Much It Costs to Go to College in 25 Countries Around the World," CNBC, October 13, 2017.

120. Rick Noack, "Why Danish Students Are Paid to Go to College," *Washington Post*, February 4, 2015.

121. Katie Lobosco, "Americans Are Moving to Europe for Free College

Degrees," CNN, February 23, 2016, https://money.cnn.com/2016/02/23/pf/college/free-college-europe/index.html.

122. "Adult Education Level," Organisation For Economic Co-operation and Development, accessed September 21, 2019, https://data.oecd.org/eduatt/adult-education-level.htm#indicator-chart; Abigail Hess, "The 10 Most Educated Countries in the World," CNBC, February 7, 2018; Liz Weston, "OECD: The US Has Fallen Behind Other Countries in College Education," *Business Insider*, September 9, 2014, https://www.businessinsider.com/r-us-falls-behind-in-college-competition-oecd-2014-9.

123. Katie Lobosco, "Tuition-free College Is Getting Bigger. Here's Where It's Offered," CNN, August 4, 2017; Chuck Collins, "A Serious Push For Free College in California," *The Nation*, February 6, 2018, https://www.thenation.com/article/a-serious-push-for-free-college-in-california/; Bobby Allyn, "New Mexico Unveils Plan to Give Students Free College Tuition Regardless of Income," NPR, September 18, 2019, https://www.npr.org/2019/09/18/762071931/new-mexico-unveils-plan-to-give-students-free-college-tuition-regardless-of-inco.

124. Anya Kamenetz, "Clinton's Free-tuition Promise: What Would It Cost? How Would It Work?," NPR, July 28, 2016, https://www.npr.org/sections/ed/2016/07/28/487794394/hillary-s-free-tuition-promise-what-would-it-cost-how-would-it-work; Jordan Weissmann, "Here's Exactly How Much the Government Would Have to Spend to Make Public College Tuition-free," *The Atlantic*, January 3, 2014; Lauren Carroll, "Bernie Sanders Says Wall Street Would Pay For His Free Tuition Plan," *Politifact*, April 4, 2016, https://www.politifact.com/truth-o-meter/statements/2016/apr/04/bernie-sanders/bernie-sanders-says-wall-street-tax-would-pay-his-/.

125. Jillian Berman, "Canceling $1.4 Trillion in Student Debt Could Have Major Benefits For the Economy," *MarketWatch*, February 8, 2018, https://www.marketwatch.com/story/canceling-14-trillion-in-student-debt-could-have-major-benefits-for-the-economy-2018-02-07; Scott Fullwiler, Stephanie Kelton, Catherine Ruetschlin, and Marshall Steinbaum, "The Macroeconomic Effects of Student Debt Cancellation," *Levy Economics Institute*, February 2018, http://www.levyinstitute.org/publications/the-macroeconomic-effects-of-student-debt-cancellation; Eric Levitz, "We Must Cancel Everyone's Student Debt, For the Economy's Sake," *New York Magazine*, February 9, 2018.

126. Ralph Waldo Emerson, "The Young American," *Emerson Central*, accessed September 16, 2019, https://emersoncentral.com/texts/nature-addresses-lectures/lectures/the-young-american/.

127. Allie Bidwell, "A School Without Principals? Yes, Really," *U.S. News & World Report*, September 19, 2014.

128. Drew DeSilver, "U.S. Students' Academic Achievement Still Lags That of Their Peers in Many Other Countries," Pew Research Center, February 15, 2017, http://www.pewresearch.org/fact-tank/2017/02/15/u-s-students-internationally-math-science/.

129. Anu Partanen, "What Americans Keep Ignoring About Finland's School Success," *The Atlantic*, December 29, 2011.

130. "Private Schools: Who Benefits?," *Organisation For Economic Co-operation and Development*, August 2011, https://www.oecd.org/pisa/pisaproducts/pisainfocus/48482894.pdf.

131. Ibid.

132. Sarah Lubienski and Christopher Lubienski, *The Public School Advantage: Why Public Schools Outperform Private Schools* (Chicago: University of Chicago Press, 2013); Sarah Lubienski and Christopher Lubienski, "A New Look and Public and Private Schools: Student Background and Mathematics Achievement," *Phi Delta Kappan* 86, no. 9 (May 2005): 696, "School Sector and Academic Achievement: A Multilevel Analysis of NAEP Mathematics Data," *American Educational Research Journal* 43, no. 4 (Winter 2006): 651–98; Harold Wenglinsky, "Are Private High Schools Better Academically Than Public High Schools?," Center on Education Policy, October 10, 2007, https://www.cep-dc.org/displayDocument.cfm?DocumentID=121; Tom Loveless, "Charter School Study: Much Ado About Tiny Differences," Brookings Institute, July 3, 2013, https://www.brookings.edu/research/charter-school-study-much-ado-about-tiny-differences/; John Cloud, "Are Private Schools Really Better?," *Time*, October 10, 2007; Diana Jean Schemo, "Public Schools Perform Near Private Ones in Study," *New York Times*, July 15, 2006.

133. Nelson Mandela, *Prison Letters of Nelson Mandela* (New York: Liveright Publishing, 2018). See his letter "To the Liquidator, Department of Justice" from October 23, 1967.

134. Stanton, "Stanton on Socialism."

135. John Dewey, "Education vs. Trade-Training—Dr. Dewey's Reply," *The New Republic*, vol. 3, ed. Herbert David Croly (New York: Republic Publishing Company, 1915), 42–43.

136. Gandhi, *India of My Dreams*, 30; Narayan, *Selected Works*.

11: REVOLUTION

1. Oscar Wilde, "Review of *Chants of Labour: A Song-Book of the People*," cited in David Goodway, *Anarchist Seeds Beneath the Snow* (Liverpool: Liverpool University Press, 2006), 69, https://libcom.org/files/1846310253.pdf.

2. Niall McCarthy, "These Countries Have the Biggest Military Budgets as a Percentage of GDP," *World Economic Forum*, May 2, 2019, https://

www.weforum.org/agenda/2019/05/the-biggest-military-budgets-as-a-percentage-of-gdp/.

3. "National Health Expenditure Fact Sheet," Centers For Medicare & Medicaid Services, accessed September 23, 2019, https://www.cms.gov/research-statistics-data-and-systems/statistics-trends-and-reports/nationalhealthexpenddata/nhe-fact-sheet.html. 45.2 percent of $3.5 trillion in national healthcare expenditures come from federal, state, and local governments.

4. Alvin Chang, "Build Your Own Wealth Tax: Try Your Hand at Taxing the Superrich," *Vox*, February 12, 2019, https://www.vox.com/policy-and-politics/2019/2/12/18211833/wealth-tax-calculator-warren-sanders. Assumes a tax avoidance rate of 7 percent.

5. Wilde, "Soul of Man," 9.

6. Ian Vásquez and Tanja Porčnik, "The Human Freedom Index 2017," CATO Institute, 2017, https://object.cato.org/sites/cato.org/files/human-freedom-index-files/2017-human-freedom-index-2.pdf; "2019 Index of Economic Freedom: Country Rankings," Heritage Foundation, accessed September 27, 2019, https://www.heritage.org/index/ranking; Briony Harris, "These Are the Happiest Countries in the World," *World Economic Forum*, March 16, 2018, https://www.weforum.org/agenda/2018/03/these-are-the-happiest-countries-in-the-world/; Jeffrey D. Sachs, "America's Health Crisis and the Easterlin Paradox," in John F. Helliwell, Richard Layard, and Jeffrey D. Sachs, *World Happiness Report 2018* (New York: Sustainable Development Solutions Network, 2018), https://s3.amazonaws.com/happiness-report/2018/CH7-WHR-lr.pdf; "Fragile States Index Heat Map," The Fund For Peace, accessed September 27, 2019, https://fragilestatesindex.org/analytics/fsi-heat-map/; "Democracy Index 2018," *The Economist Intelligence Unit*, 2018, https://www.eiu.com/topic/democracy-index; Josephine Moulds, "These Are the World's Least—And Most—Corrupt Countries," *World Economic Forum*, February 5, 2019, https://www.weforum.org/agenda/2019/02/least-corrupt-countries-transparency-international-2018/.

7. George Orwell, "Why I Write," Orwell Foundation, accessed September 27, 2019, https://www.orwellfoundation.com/the-orwell-foundation/orwell/essays-and-other-works/why-i-write/.

8. Mandela, *Long Walk to Freedom*, chap. 76.

9. Langston Hughes, "Good Morning Revolution," *Poetry Nook*, accessed September 23, 2019, https://www.poetrynook.com/poem/good-morning-revolution.

10. John Nichols, "Socialism is on a Winning Streak," *The Nation*, May 18, 2018, https://*www.the*nation.com/article/socialism-is-on-a-winning-streak/; Nichols, The "S" Word; Alan Greenblatt, "Socialism Goes Local: DSA

Candidates Are Winning in Big Cities," *Governing*, July 24, 2019, https://www.governing.com/topics/politics/gov-socialist-cities-elected.html.

11. Wells, *New Worlds*, 222–23.

12. George Orwell, "Why I Joined the Independent Labour Party," *The Collected Essays, Journalism and Letters of George Orwell: An Age Like This, 1920–1940*, ed. Sonia Orwell and Ian Angus (Boston: Godine, 2000), 1:336.

13. Ralph Waldo Emerson, "Spiritual Laws," Virginia Commonwealth University, accessed September 23, 2019, https://archive.vcu.edu/english/engweb/transcendentalism/authors/emerson/essays/spirituallaws.html.

14. Guthrie, *Pastures*, 200–01.

15. "Historic 32nd Congress of Pakistani Section of IMT—First Day," *International Marxist Tendency*, March 10, 2013, http://www.marxist.com/historic-32nd-congress-of-pakistani-imt-1.htm.

16. Shermer, *The Moral Arc*, 87–89; Max Fisher, "Peaceful Protest Is Much More Effective than Violence for Toppling Dictators," *Washington Post*, November 5, 2013.

17. Prabhu, *Mind of Mahatma Gandhi*, https://www.mkgandhi.org/momgandhi/chap50.htm.

18. Ibid; Gandhi, *India of My Dreams*, 31.

19. Bose, *Selections From Gandhi*, https://www.mkgandhi.org/sfgbook/seventh.htm. "There would be no exploitation if people refuse to obey the exploiter. But self comes in and we hug the chains that bind us. This must cease."

20. Keller, "Strike Against War."

21. Helen Keller, "What is the IWW?," in *Helen Keller: Her Socialist Years*, ed. Philip S. Foner (New York: International Publishers NYC, 1967), 91, https://archive.org/stream/helenkellerherso00hele/helenkellerherso00hele_djvu.txt.

22. Wilde, "Soul of Man," 9–10.

23. "King's Home Bombed," Stanford University, accessed September 23, 2019, https://kinginstitute.stanford.edu/encyclopedia/kings-home-bombed.

24. "Report: 338 Killed During Tunisia Revolution," *Fox News*, November 20, 2014, https://www.foxnews.com/world/report-338-killed-during-tunisia-revolution.

25. "Fight For $15: Four Years, $62 Billion," *National Employment Law Project*, December 2016, https://www.nelp.org/wp-content/uploads/Fight-for-15-Four-Years-62-Billion-in-Raises.pdf.

26. Noam Scheiber, "Verizon Strike to End as Both Sides Claim Victories on Key Points," *New York Times*, May 30, 2016.

27. Doug Criss, "Every Public School in West Virginia is Closed," CNN, February 27, 2018; "West Virginia Raises Teachers' Pay to End Statewide Strike,"

New York Times, March 6, 2018; Dana Goldstein, "West Virginia Teachers Walk Out (Again) and Score a Win in Hours," *New York Times*, February 19, 2019.

28. Madison Park and Dave Alsup, "Arizona Governor Offers Teachers 20% Pay Raise, But Educators Have Questions," CNN, April 13, 2018; Bill Hutchinson, "As Oklahoma Teachers Declare Victory, Colorado Educators Walk Out of Class," *ABC News*, April 16, 2018.

29. Alexia Fernández Campbell, "Marriott Workers Just Ended the Largest Hotel Strike in US History," *Vox*, December 4, 2018, https://www.vox.com/policy-and-politics/2018/12/4/18125505/marriott-workers-end-strike-wage-raise.

30. Jennifer Medina and Dana Goldstein, "Los Angeles Teachers' Strike to End as Deal is Reached," *New York Times*, January 22, 2019.

31. Alexia Fernández Campbell, "The Denver Teachers Strike Is Over. They Won," *Vox*, February 14, 2019, https://www.vox.com/2019/2/14/18224848/denver-teachers-strike-over-deal.

32. Mandela, "Good Communist."

33. Langston Hughes, *The Collected Poems of Langston Hughes* (New York: Vintage Books, 1995), 533–34.

34. Mark Twain, *Autobiography of Mark Twain*, ed. Harriet Smith, Benjamin Griffin, Victor Fischer, Michael Frank, Amanda Gagel, Sharon Goetz, Leslie Myrick, and Christopher Ohge (Oakland: University of California Press, 2015), 3:451.

35. Mark Twain, "The New Dynasty," in *Mark Twain, Mark Twain: Collected Tales, Sketches, Speeches, & Essays, 1852–1890*, ed. Louis Budd (Library of America, 1992), 883–90.

36. Steinbeck, *Grapes of Wrath*, 206.

37. Abby Vesoulis, "This Presidential Candidate Wants to Give Every Adult $1,000 a Month," *Time*, February 13, 2019; Danielle Kurtzleben, "Likely 2020 Democratic Candidates Want to Guarantee a Job to Every American," NPR, May 8, 2018, https://www.npr.org/2018/05/08/609091985/likely-2020-democratic-candidates-want-to-guarantee-a-job-to-every-american.

38. Dylan Matthews, "Universal Child Care, a Basic Income, and 4 Other Radical Policies That Almost Became Law," *Vox*, July 1, 2015, https://www.vox.com/2014/8/13/5990657/basic-income-jobs-guarantee-child-care-flag-burning-btu-tax-balanced-budget; Frank Stockman, "Recalling the Nixon-Kennedy Health Plan," *Boston Globe*, June 23, 2012.

39. Wright, *Envisioning Real Utopias*, 223.

40. London, *War of the Classes*. See "Wanted: A New Law of Development."

41. Abraham Lincoln, *Collected Works of Abraham Lincoln*, (Ann Arbor: University of Michigan Digital Library Production Services, 2001), 1:412, https://

quod.lib.umich.edu/l/lincoln/lincoln1/1:423.1?rgn=div2;view=fulltext.

42. Simon Robb, "Largest Strike in Human History Is Taking Place in India," *Metro UK*; Kunal Chattopadhyay and Soma Marik, "India on Strike," *Jacobin*, October 4, 2016, https://www.jacobinmag.com/2016/10/indian-workers-general-strike; Vijay Prashad, "Here's What a Real Strike Looks Like: 150 Million Say No to Despotism in India," *Common Dreams*, January 8, 2019, https://www.commondreams.org/views/2019/01/08/heres-what-real-strike-looks-150-million-say-no-despotism-india; Charlie Campbell, "Huge Numbers Demand the Ouster of South Korea's President in a Fifth Week of Protests," *Time*, November 28, 2016; "South Korea's Presidential Scandal," BBC, April 6, 2018.

43. Hugo, "Letter to the Rich."

44. Grace Hauck, "Friday's Global Strike Was Likely the Largest Climate Rally Ever," *USA Today*, September 21, 2019.

45. Mahatma Gandhi, *The Collected Works of Mahatma Gandhi*, vol. 76, Archive, accessed September 24, 2019, https://archive.org/stream/HindSwaraj-CWMG-076/CWMG-v076-LXXVI-MC-BETA_djvu.txt. See page 381.

46. Shriman Narayan, *The Selected Works of Mahatma Gandhi, vol. 5, The Voice of Truth* (Ahmedabad: Navajivan, 1968), https://www.mkgandhi.org/voiceoftruth/worldfederation.htm.

47. Bose, *Selections From Gandhi*, https://www.mkgandhi.org/sfgbook/seventh.htm.

48. Albert Einstein, "Towards a World Government," in *Out of My Later Years: The Scientist, Philosopher, and Man Portrayed through His Own Words* (New York: Wings Books, 1956); "Einstein Urges World Government for Atomic Control to Avoid War," *New York Times*, October 27, 1945.

49. Orwell, *Lion and the Unicorn*. See "Part II: Shopkeepers at War," chapter 1.

50. H.G. Wells, *The Outline of History: Being a Plain History of Life and Mankind*, Project Gutenberg, accessed September 24, 2019, http://www.gutenberg.org/files/45368/45368-h/45368-h.htm. See page 588 of volume 2. We'd have "a federation of all humanity, together with a sufficient means of social justice to ensure health, education, and a rough equality of opportunity, would mean such a release and increase of human energy as to open a new phase in human history"; Wells, *New World Order*, chap. 7. "World Socialism" would mean "contemporary governments may vanish . . ."

51. Du Bois, *The World of W.E.B. Du Bois*, 197. "With such Socialist states and the education which they promote, the peace which is their goal and the morality toward which economic justice opens the way, a world state would gradually be realized"; Albert Camus, *Neither Victims Nor Executioners* (Eugene:

Wipf and Stock, 2008), 45. We must "create a world parliament through elections in which all peoples will participate, which will enact legislation which will exercise authority over national governments."

52. Cantrell, *World's Intellectuals*, 46; *Scribner's Magazine*, ed. Edward Livermore Burlingame, Robert Bridges, Alfred Sheppard Dashiell, Harlan Logan (New York: Charles Scriber's Sons, 1892), 12:574. Available at Cornell University Library.

53. King, *Single Garment*. See his essay "The Greatest Hope For World Peace."

54. David Fricke, "'Imagine': The Anthem of 2001," *Rolling Stone*, December 27, 2001, https://www.rollingstone.com/music/music-news/imagine-the-anthem-of-2001-83559/; John Blaney, *Lennon and McCartney: Together Alone* (London: Jawbone Press, 2007), 52.

55. Keller, "New Vision," 56.